JOE LONGTHORNE MBE

THE OFFICIAL AUTOBIOGRAPHY

with Chris Berry

To My Mam & Dad -

*I was the luckiest person in the world
to have you as my parents*

Great Northern Books
PO Box 213, Ilkley, LS29 9WS
www.greatnorthernbooks.co.uk

First published in hardback, 2010
This first paperback edition, 2012

Every effort has been made to acknowledge correctly and contact the copyright holders of material in this book. Great Northern Books apologises for any unintentional errors or omissions, which should be notified to the publisher.

For both legal and personal reasons some of the names of people referred to in this book have been changed.

ISBN: 978-1905080-82-3

Design and layout: David Burrill

Front cover photograph: Paul Fairclough

Printed and bound by CPI Group (UK) Ltd, Croydon, CR0 4YY

CIP Data
A catalogue for this book is available from the British Library

CONTENTS

FOREWORD

by
Ricky Tomlinson

It is difficult to know where to start when writing about Joe. His group of fanatical fans would describe him one way, fellow artistes would describe him another way and, of course, his band of faithful entourage would describe him their way.

I think the best way to describe Joe Longthorne is to use an old-fashioned expression used by my mother when describing something which was far more than it looked, and that saying was, 'there's good stuff in little parcels'.

I think this sums Joe up perfectly.

Offstage, talking to him or sharing a joke, he is Joe, the guy next door. Put him on a stage, under the bright lights and fronting his eight piece band, you are watching a 'megastar'.

I use that expression because his live show is simply breathtaking.

This man, who is probably 5′ 6″ or less, fills the stage with his amazing presence, wit and genuine love of his fans. He does, in my opinion, rank amongst the greatest performers we have ever produced in this country and, to this day, I cannot understand why he is not topping the bill in Las Vegas or New York. I've just come back from Vegas where I saw one of the biggest names in the world, a major US star, and the artiste (who I won't mention) was just not up to the standard that Joe reaches every time I have ever seen him.

His impressions are second to none, and his little schoolboy jokes are told exactly like a naughty school boy with a cheeky little grin at the tag line.

I have seen Joe perform many times and indeed have appeared on the same live show with him and his backstage demeanor is Mr. Cool. This makes such a change from some of the prima donnas I have worked with over the years.

He appeared at Liverpool one time for a charity show on behalf of a famous Liverpudlian, Herbert the Hairdresser. Joe was on the same bill as The Real Thing and Claire Sweeney, but he stole the show, as he always does.

I recently appeared on the Alan Titchmarsh Show and Joe was at the same studio getting ready to give yet another sparkling performance on the same show. When he knew I was in the dressing room he stopped rehearsals and came to see me.

'Joe,' I said, 'get back and finish your rehearsal.' Joe replied, 'friends are more important than rehearsals.' We sat in the dressing room and laughed as we swapped jokes and stories.

A short time ago I had a four-way heart by-pass and thought this would be the end of my performing career. Then I remembered the night Joe invited me to the Midland Hotel in Manchester. The Variety Club of Great Britain had arranged a Gala Benefit Night in honour of Joe who had recently undergone a bone-marrow transplant.

I remembered the illness he had been through and how he had always bounced back. I said to myself that compared to what Joe has been through my operation was only like having a tooth out.

On that night, I was struck by all of the other show business artistes who turned up to wish Joe well and show how much they loved and respected him. Needless to say, as frail as he was at the time as he was just recovering, Joe sang and made a lovely, moving little speech in which he said the star of the evening was not him or any of the very many well-known faces from the world of entertainment in the hall (which also included a Lord). The star was, in fact, his surgeon and Joe thanked him publicly.

There is a saying about the phoenix rising from the ashes; I think this applies to Joe Longthorne in more ways than one. He has been up and down many times but never out. He, like many of us, has had money troubles; and he has let himself down on occasions by being led astray.

However, Joe always takes responsibility for his mistakes and never blames anybody else - and more importantly, he always comes good.

The last time I saw Joe perform live was at the Floral Pavilion Theatre in New Brighton. My friend and I turned up on the night to see the 'House Full' sign in the foyer. The manager of the theatre knew us and he sat us in an area reserved for wheelchair users (it was not being used at the time) and he got us two deckchairs to sit on.

The lights dimmed, music played and on walked a slight figure in an all white suit – the audience erupted and he performed. It was electrifying. Joe sang, joked, played the piano and it was the finest performance I had ever seen.

The story of Joe's life is the stuff that novelists couldn't make up. I am so pleased that he has got round to writing it with his good friend and fellow singer, as well as excellent writer, Chris Berry.

This book tells his amazing life story, which has had more highs and lows than anyone I know. It is the best autobiography I have ever read!

Joe fully deserves his title of 'The Greatest British Entertainer' – as I said, there's good stuff in little parcels.

FOREWORD

by
Garry Bushell

MY eldest kids were teenagers when I first took them to see Joe Longthorne. They weren't happy about it. My daughter loved Shane Richie. My son was into Blink 182. They moaned all the way to the Blackpool Opera House, and they carried on moaning right up until the moment Joe started to sing...

They left the show that night absolute converts to the Longthorne cause, just as I knew they would.

Pretty much everyone who sees him is blown away by his range of impressions – critics don't call Joe the 'Human Juke Box' for nothing. But they're also touched by his humour, his vulnerability, and his unique relationship with his adoring audience.

Man of the people Joe Longthorne is more than just a class act. He is, as I once wrote, the spirit of showbusiness decanted into a suit. Pure variety.

Religious ecstasy is the closet parallel to the joyous intensity of a Longthorne live show. His powers of mimicry are uncanny. Close your eyes and he is Shirley Bassey or Tom Jones or pretty much whoever he chooses to be.

Bassey says, 'Joe does me better than I do myself.'

Last year, as an experiment, I sneaked his David Bowie impression onto the indie rock-orientated Total Rock Radio. The musicians in the studio were amazed. 'Who was this hot new talent?' they demanded to know. It was hot old Joe. A brand new albeit small audience were won over.

That is why it's a constant source of irritation to me that British television treats this incredible entertainer with such disdain. I'm not alone. The likes of Chris Evans, Peter Kay and Noel Edmonds have all sung his praises vocally over the years. And yet still TV bosses cock a deaf 'un.

Instead of wining and dining each other at the Groucho Club or foisting the likes of Jedward on the viewing public, they might consider going see Joe Longthorne live. Then they'd understand what a phenomenon the man is.

Inter-Flora should give him shares for the amount of business his fans put their way. They leave his stage decked out like the Chelsea Flower Show.

You never know what to expect with Joe. The first time I interviewed him at home, his cart horse casually sauntered into the house and was left there until he fancied wandering out again.

Other journalists have been known to moan about Joe's laissez-faire attitudes, or his penchant for the odd medicinal 'Jamaican woodbine'. I find it all endearing. How can a man this easy-going and seemingly disorganised off-stage be transformed into such a consummate pro when his band strike up?

The last time I saw Joe Longthorne in concert he was headlining at Blackpool North Pier. Joe promised my wife and I the royal box, which surprised me as I didn't think the North Pier had one. It hasn't. We were led up and over the roof of the venue to a very different box – the lighting box – where the scatty star had thoughtfully left us a bottle of champagne on ice...

Everything in Joe's life is touched with humour. Even the tragedy - and he has had his fair share of that. As you'll read in these pages, Joe Longthorne has had priests read him the last rites more times than Tiger Woods has had hot girlfriends.

The last time it happened Joe was ready to go.

'I'd been on the slab for six hours,' he told me. 'I was in agony and it was so cold I contracted pneumonia. My body had been weakened by eleven years of chemotherapy. I had food poisoning and my organs started shutting down.

'I heard one doctor say, "I wouldn't touch him with a barge pole."'

'I had reached the point where I was thinking, "Please God, just let me go – I've had enough pain."'

'And that's when it happened. Jesus came to me. I didn't see him, but I felt his presence and I heard a voice say, "Not just yet."'

Joe is not 'born again' and he hadn't gone mad either. But he assured me, 'In that hospital something came to me and my life has been different ever since.'

It's true. Last April, Joe performed at a Variety Club night in honour of Engelbert Humperdinck in Manchester – at the Hump's personal insistence. He was sensational, morphing from Tony Bennett to Willie Nelson via Barry Manilow and winning three standing ovations.

Afterwards Joe was approached by heavyweight US showbiz agents who wanted to make him a headline star in Las Vegas…and now it appears to be happening. He starts later this year, opening for the legendary comedian Don Rickles, who in his day had opened for the even more legendary Frank Sinatra.

Has Lady Luck finally dealt Romany Joe a decent hand? In 2009, his fortieth anniversary year as a performer, the troubled star's fortunes seemed to change dramatically. He beat the leukaemia that has dogged him for years making him so ill that his next of kin were informed that he had just hours to live on four separate occasions. He was also reunited with his long-lost son.

Could he crack Vegas, the showbiz capital of the world, as well?

You wouldn't bet against it. Joe is excited by the prospects but he isn't banking on it.

'I got offered Las Vegas seven years ago and ended up in the desert,' he says. 'Seriously, it was a cowboy joint eight miles from the strip on New Year's Eve and the audience were all truckers who only wanted to hear Willie Nelson…it wasn't what I'd expected at all.

'But these guys are proper and they're serious and it could be fantastic. We'll see.'

Conquering Vegas would be the ultimate twist in Longthorne's extraordinary career. Since finding fame in the 1980s, Joe, 54, has made and lost millions. He's battled serious illnesses for more than two decades and has spoken openly about his bisexuality.

His TV career came and went, like his Bentleys, his swimming pool and his six-bedroom Berkshire mansion. The only things that have stayed constant are Joe's incredible talent and his army of fans.

'People are so kind,' Joe says. 'I get bundles of letters every day. The fans are what matter to me. Cars, houses, money…I do not give a s*** about all that. They're nice to have, but material things don't matter so much. What matters is when I'm on stage – that's when I LIVE.'

Now free of bankruptcy, he lives in Blackpool and ploughs all of his earnings into his stage show.

A bone marrow transplant operation in 2005 seems to have fixed his health problems.

'If you last five years after the transplant you're doing well,' he smiles, his blue eyes twinkling. 'So fingers crossed.'

'I'm feeling much healthier in myself. I walk the dog every day, or he walks me…'

Hull-born Joe is 55 on May 31, 2010. His mum's family were Irish tinkers. Dad's side ran travelling fairs. 'I learned to speak in Romany before I did English,' he says.

Comic Billy Pearce's mother Jean discovered his talent and put him on TV's Junior Showtime. But stardom came later. Joe spent his teenage years helping his dad as a rag and bone man.

After ten long years in the clubs, Joe got through to the final of ITV's Search For A Star – the Britain's Got Talent of its day - in 1981.

Regular appearances on the Les Dennis Laughter Show were trumped by his own ITV series, The Joe Longthorne Show which ran between 1987 and 1991.

Back then the star was dogged with scandal: cocaine, violence, family problems and various sexual indiscretions. Now it looks like things are turning round for him.

'The last few months have been wonderful,' says Joe cautiously. 'But it seems strange that it's all happening at the same time. And now Vegas, we'll see...'

We will. But we can also be sure that whatever happens, Joe Longthorne's barmy army of UK fans will back him all the way.

PREFACE

by
Chris Berry

I met Joe for the first time in March 2009.

We share the same birthplace, the wonderful but often maligned city of Hull, or Kingston upon Hull if we're being exact. When I worked on the *Hull Daily Mail* in the late 70s and early-to-mid 80s the name Joe Longthorne was known by everyone in the city.

Brian Winchester, a legendary Hull entertainer, who worked in the advertising department at 'The Mail', told me stories of Joe's exploits. It never dawned on me that one day I would be writing his autobiography with him.

I had not seen Joe perform live until April 2009 – a sad indictment I know – but I had possessed one of his 'live' albums for a number of years, which I have constantly kept putting on in my car– in between spells of Frank Sinatra, Slade, Elvis Costello, Roy Wood, Oasis, The Beatles, Rolling Stones, Elvis (Presley), Elton John, Michael Buble, Ozark Mountain Daredevils, The Eagles, Chicago, America, Eurythmics, Led Zeppelin, Van Morrison and Whitesnake. It's a crowded musical market place to get played in my car!

I watched Joe's TV programmes too, but aside from the natural pride most Hull-born folk have in 'claiming' our city's sons and daughters as our own, I cannot claim to have been up there amongst his greatest fans.

That doesn't mean I didn't like or admire his singing, it's just that I'd probably never realised just how great a performer this man is and what a voice he possesses. One book later and having witnessed over a dozen of his performances last year, there is no doubt in my mind that Joe is one of the greatest vocal talents this country has ever seen.

I defy anyone not to be in awe of his renditions of *If I Never Sing Another Song* – surely the most poignant lyric he has ever sung, packed full of what he has gone through; or *Let Me Try Again*. He truly makes these songs his own.

The reason why we met was that I had put forward a story idea to the *Yorkshire Post*, about Joe's life and his celebration of 40 years in show business.

I visited Joe at his seaside resort home of Blackpool and my initial reaction was that he was a little shorter than I had expected. I think I'd anticipated someone about six-foot. He shuffled into the room rather than taking strides.

We sat facing each other in armchairs, with a roaring fire belting out heat in between us and soon found that we had common threads – Hull, music (I perform too), faith.

Part way through the interview Joe turned to his good friend Chris (the Greek) and said, 'He could write the f***ing book', meaning me. The die was cast.

I waited until the *Yorkshire Post* story had been published before pursuing matters further.

Writing Joe's autobiography sounded fabulous but by now I knew that Joe's life has rarely worked out as simply as all that. I have constantly referred to his life, with everyone I have talked with about Joe, as the ultimate rollercoaster. It's perhaps appropriate that he lives not too far from the Pleasure Beach and its massive up-and-down rides.

I went along to one of his first shows that year, at the start of his now annual UK Spring Tour, at Darlington Civic Theatre. I was met with open arms. All of Joe's closest friends and family who saw me said Joe had thought the story was great.

I took my seat to watch Joe in action. It was now April 2009, and having only ever seen him on TV, only ever having owned one recording and having written a five-page story all about him, I was to see him perform live for the first time.

The difference from the man I had seen at home in Blackpool, to the man I saw at the Civic Theatre, playing to an audience of nearly 1,000, was mesmeric. His performance was at once beautiful, powerful, heart-rending and majestic – and, uncannily, he looked taller, closer to what I had expected at that first meeting.

His voice was captivating. The voice of a man whose songs and stage presence is deserving of not just his army of loyal supporters all around the country, but a whole new audience that has been reawakened to 'proper' singing via the likes of Michael Buble, Harry Conick Jr and Michael Ball.

When Joe sang *September in the Rain*, *You & Me*, and *If* he showed his true class as a singer of great composure and magnificent delivery. When he sang *Say It With Flowers* and *If You Love Me* you could feel hearts melting towards him.

Joe's 'calling card' throughout his career has been his impressions. There are millions who are in awe of his Shirley Bassey, Tom Jones, Barry Manilow, Barry White, John Lennon, Englebert Humperdinck, Frank Sinatra, Tony Bennett, Judy Garland, Dean Martin, Sammy Davis Jr., Matt Monro, Ken Dodd and literally hundreds of others.

Yes, he's brilliant at those. He is perhaps the world's leading singing impressionist and they are still a great part of his show, his own 'special guests', but Joe is so much more than a man who can turn his art to others' voices.

20 years ago his impressions may well have been his calling card but I would now urge anyone to go and see one of Joe's shows for the songs he sings as himself. His album, *You & Me,* which was released in 2008, is testament to that.

There are those who continue to call out for him to 'Do Shirley' or 'Do Tom', but his voice and stage craft should really see him playing as himself to six-month-long sell-out shows in London's West End and on Broadway. His voice should be used to sing the big numbers for blockbuster movies. Sadly, life doesn't work out that way – or at least it hasn't so far.

Joe has been cast into the TV wilderness for far too long.

When you consider some of the utter dross that is served up on our screens in the name of entertainment and yet there is such a talented performer as Joe in our midst it is hard to fathom the minds of TV producers and executives.

'An Audience with Joe Longthorne' would be an ideal programme to show off Joe's unique and world-class talent. It is such a shame that it seems the only way previous TV favourites can get back on television regularly today is through a host of nebulous 'reality' shows.

Joe doesn't need any of those. He's been through enough 'jungles' in his life without looking for spurious fame elsewhere.

But, I hear you cry, what about the real man? What about the man behind that performance? What about Joe himself? What did I learn in those hours talking with him either in his travelling home after his concerts, with his friends in the bars and hotels, at home in Blackpool or back with his family in Hull?

Well, firstly, I learned that Joe really does see himself as 'Just Joe'. By that I mean he doesn't consider himself a superstar. Don't get me wrong, he has had a star's lifestyle, he has had the world at his feet, he does enjoy the applause, the adulation, but sometimes you just get the feeling that he's really not bothered about the stardom thing at all. Sure he likes the spotlight, but he earns that spotlight every single night.

Singing is his passion. He was never bothered about the money; it's just what came (and went) with the territory because of his talent. He simply lives to perform.

When Joe is not on stage, for any length of time, you can see in his eyes the need to be back. He freely admits that he drinks and smokes more when he's not working. It is as though he has little purpose otherwise. What he gives on the stage is his life!

He cares very much about the people around him, both those at home in Blackpool and his extensive family over in Hull. He is surrounded by friends who adore him for the man he is and he has an uncanny perception for what is happening in other people's lives, even if he has only just met with them.

Helping others has always been close to his heart and he is constantly raising funds for various charities. Earlier this year he was awarded the MBE in the Queen's Jubilee Honours. His fans have campaigned for his recognition over many years and there was no denying Joe's pride, as well as humility, when the announcement came.

When you have been through as much as Joe has in his life – cancer, bankruptcy, nervous breakdown, near-to-death experiences – it requires a strong will and spirit to come through. Joe will tell you that fortitude comes through his own faith in God. He doesn't attempt to explain it, he just feels it.

Joe never learned to read or write particularly well during his school days, so undertaking an autobiography was always going to be a challenge for him. When we met for the first time it was to be the catalyst for what you now hold in your hands.

Watching Joe reacting to every word, every line and paragraph in this book was sometimes not easy. In many ways, as I read out to him what I had written using his own words from the countless hours of interviews, it was like watching him re-live those nightmares. At times he was in tears himself as it brought everything back in sharp focus. At times he was in hysterics over the replaying of some of the funniest incidents and at times he simply couldn't believe I had found out what I had – even though he had told me himself!

I do hope you find that this book is everything you hoped it to be. It is Joe's life. These are his words. There are parts of it where, for obvious reasons, others have had to fill a few gaps, but this is all Joe!

It has been not only an honour to write this book on Joe's behalf, it has also been a very real privilege.

CHRIS BERRY is a writer and performer. His other books include: *Les Battersby & Me: The Bruce Jones Story*; *Boxster's Story: The Truth Behind The Bull*; and *The John Ireland Story*. He writes for the *Yorkshire Post* every Saturday. He is also a singer/songwriter and lead singer with his own band. www.chrisberry.tv

CHAPTER ONE

LAST ORDERS

You and me, we wanted it all, we wanted it all.
Passion without pain, sunshine without rainy days.
We wanted it always.
You and me, we reached for the sky, the limit was high,
never giving in, certain we could win that prize....

Joe Longthorne *You & Me* released 2008

'He's going at six o'clock we can't do any more for him.' I'm laid there and I'm fighting, but they can't see that. They're talking about me as though I'm not here any longer.

'He's dead, he's dead, he's gone.' I know they're trying to bring me back. I can hear them talking around me, so I know my brain is still alive. I'm saying to myself 'Jesus, sweet Jesus, if you've any decency about you take me now. I'm now not even thinking about how, if I go first, it would kill my mother. What's that all about?

I'm going through too much pain. I'm dying. Jesus, dear sweet Jesus, this is six hours I've been here in the theatre. There are seven people around me, either pumping blood or moving drips or, it seems to me, just jumping up and down. They are good people and they're all trying to help but I can't take any more. I just want him to take my body over, I can't take the pain any longer. I've fought all I can. I've nothing left. I've had enough.

There's a phone call. I'm sure I hear something like 'I wouldn't touch him with a barge pole'. Dear Lord, I cry from inside my body, help me now. I don't see his face - Jesus. People say they do. I don't. For me it's a feeling, he's there. I think again about my dear mother, my queen duchess, and about my sisters and brother, and how if any of us siblings are to pass away before my mother what it will do to her. She worries about me all the time, always has, and here I am, first on the agenda.

I know I said that I was leaving,
but I just couldn't say goodbye...
... you learn from every lonely day,
I have learned – and I've come back to stay...

That was 2005. I was not just at death's door, I had opened it and had at least one foot already through it. The medical staff thought I'd shut it behind me! When I went in for the bone marrow transplant, which I needed desperately, I had been told that the survival rate was something like one in 50. I've gambled on various things in my life, but not generally with such long odds. I wish I'd put a bet on now.

So much has happened since I came through those months of agony and those years of not knowing whether I would be here each following year, so many good things. I'm now busier than I have ever been, doing what I have always done and all that I ever wanted to do - and that's to sing and entertain.

But I know that for all the thousands of fans who come to see me there are still millions of people who used to watch my TV shows who maybe haven't seen me recently who may think I'm still suffering. Some days I do, some days I don't – that's the constant problem for people in my situation, but I've always lived for today and I'm not looking for sympathy either. There are enough in worse positions than me.

I like to put everyone at ease in my concerts when I talk about what's happened to me - cancer, leukaemia, it's called CLL (chronic lymphocytic lymphoma), the coming and going of the disease, the life-saving bone marrow transplant, which so very nearly saw me off, and the double pneumonia that nearly got me once I'd come through the transplant.

Hearts, brains, lungs, we've all got something wrong with us sometime and we all do get weary, so when I sing *The Impossible Dream* it's a sentiment that goes all through my show. I sing, and speak, to every single person in the theatre.

To dream the impossible dream,
to fight the unbeatable foe,
to try when your own heart is weary...

Joe Longthorne *The Impossible Dream* released 2007

I was given 'last orders' three times. That always gets a laugh at the concerts when I talk about it that way. Most of those fans, those loyal and wonderful people who come to my concerts know what I've been through and they have always been a great comfort to me, but I like to show them the funny side of it all. Everyone has had some sort of pain, whether they have suffered themselves or through someone dear to them, and we all need a bit of a laugh along the way to help us feel some relief.

Anyway, back to the theatre – the one in the hospital, not the one where I tread the boards and perform. If you're wondering where we are at the moment, it's Manchester Royal Infirmary by the way.

Last orders! I had three of them delivered to me by three different priests – Father John, Father Dennis and Father Geoff. All of them are wise and good men, they all gave up their time to come and see me, and I'm not saying they got it wrong but if I could have told them at the time I would have said they had no right coming to say to me this is the end. Strangely enough, when I saw them it just convinced me that I wasn't dying.

Come and lay down by my side
Til the early morning light
All I'm asking is your time
So help me make it through the night

Joe Longthorne *Help Me Make It Through The Night* released 2008

I was in hospital for nearly four months before, during and following the bone marrow transplant procedure, but there's always comedy to be found in everything you know. I'm laid there in intensive care one day and all I can hear is what sounds like organs playing 'Happy Birthday To You'. It wasn't, I was told it was just all the machines bleeping, but to me it sounded just like the song. Maybe the drugs I was taking at the time were making me think that way. Then I found out the guy in the next bed had been given my rosary beads. It was all just a mix-up because we had shared a bedside cabinet, but at the time I just thought, is nothing sacred! The wonderful Pat Mancini, who you will hear of later, got them back for me. The other patient survived too, so maybe those beads helped us both.

I was alive and the gifted people of Manchester Royal Infirmary are the reason why I am now able to write my story. Are you ready? If you think that first bit was dramatic enough then prepare yourselves for the rollercoaster ride that has been my life so far.

Sugar in the Morning

In my heyday, young girls wrote to me
Everybody seemed to have time to devote to me...

Joe Longthorne *If I Never Sing Another Song* released 2006

I'm not a me-me-me type of person really, so it's a bit funny coming up with your own life story, but I guess most people will know me from the TV shows, my theatre shows right across the UK, the States, Australia and the Royal Variety Performances. Back in 1988 through to 1991 the ratings for my shows recorded that we were pulling in over 12 million viewers on a Saturday night. It was a fabulous time for me, but just at the height of my TV career I was diagnosed as having the killer disease CLL, lymphoma, cancer.

I've been declared bankrupt. I've had a nervous breakdown. I've been to court on charges of affray. I've been in love many times. I was involved in a horrific car crash in between the publication of the original hardback version and this paperback. But the headlines don't even tell the half of it.

Looking back I have had one or two people around who just may have taken advantage of me. You see I'm not very good with cash, so I guess you could say that anything that happened on the money side has been my own fault, but I've always worked my way back from it.

I suppose it seems a bit odd saying that bankruptcies, nervous breakdowns and cancer have never really bothered me that much, but they truly haven't affected me and who I am. I'm still just Joe, the same person I have always been. I'm still a lad from Hull who has always loved his family very much. I've very few regrets and I don't dwell on things. As long as I've had a few bob, a shilling or two, that's all that I have needed. Just give me a proper song to sing and I'm a happy man.

It's all in here, the loves of my life, the funny things that have happened along the way, the tragedies, the highs, the lows. I didn't want to miss anything out. With me what you see is what you get. I'm a performer and I love life. Dear Lord, I've clung on desperately at times, but I'm still here and feeling stronger now than I have in many years. I'm about to tour Australia for the first time in over a decade and I now have a promoter who is organising dates in America. I am an entertainer, always have been, and if I wasn't on stage I wouldn't have anywhere else to go.

We'll come back to the life-saving bone-marrow transplant and the near-death experience in hospital in greater detail later on, but for now I want to tell you just where this is all leading. You see this book is in no way signalling an end to my career. In fact it seems as though it is all starting to happen for me once again. You know, we might even finish this story back in Vegas.

I'm really very excited at the moment, probably the most excited I've ever been. I've always been optimistic, sometimes maybe too much, but such a lot has happened in the last couple of years that I am extremely grateful for, and it feels like this really is a whole new chapter of my life which has only just begun.

This is my first ever book and it is what I have hoped to write for many years. Strictly it's now my second with you holding this copy because there was a hardback copy out two years ago and we've added a lot more now. Putting it together has brought back many happy memories and has also brought back every one of those immensely personal times when I was seriously down. I think people know that it's bound to contain enough highs and lows to last not just my lifetime but many others. You might need the odd Kleenex or two along the way though, if you haven't used them up already in chapter one. I certainly did!

What really prompted me to get on with the book was when I celebrated 40 years in the entertainment world having started out on TV in my early teens.

I am back playing nearly 100 concerts a year, just as I was doing back in the 80s and through the 90s. I've always said my last name should be Tour, not Longthorne, because that's what I do. So there you go. I'm now officially Joseph Patrick Tour.

Las Vegas. For my profession it's the Mecca, where I have always wanted to play, following those amazing talents of Frank Sinatra, Tony Bennett, Sammy Davis Jr, Dean Martin and many other worldwide million sellers. Maybe I'll headline there one day. It certainly looks a lot closer to happening just at the moment.

One bright and guiding light,
that taught me wrong from right
I found, in my mother's eyes
Those fairy tales that she told
Of streets all paved with gold...

Joe Longthorne *My Mother's Eyes* released 2006

I appeared in television for the first time when I was really small, even before the time when I first appeared properly on a Yorkshire Television show called *Junior Showtime* when I was 14.

At home we used to have this old TV set that didn't have a screen any more because it had been kicked through and I used to practise my act to my mam by singing from behind it.

We always had plenty of television sets. Some of the local TV companies used to offer one week's free trial in those days. We had 52 TV sets one year! My grannies used to smash the slot box off the back for bingo.

My mother's called Teresa. My dad was called Frederick, we lost him just two years ago. I've looked in every pub I could to try and find him, so we presume he's gone. Seriously, yes, he did pass away. Dad did everything for me in my early days in show business. He negotiated the deals, he took me to the working men's clubs where I would always go down well, and he made sure that they treated me right. He didn't leave anything to chance.

How lucky was I with my parents? My mam and dad were the best. I feel that to have been born by them makes me the luckiest person in the world. My family has always been the most important thing to me and it still is today. I love all of them dearly and anyone who hurts any member of my family hurts me, that's my way.

We're from a travelling, Romany background. Both mam and dad came from different forms of travellers. My dad comes from the tinkers side and fairground people. They can fix anything and make anything. My mam's side come from Irish stock. My grandfather had a boxing tent in travelling fairs and I seem to have been around boxers all my life.

The Longthornes have had their roots in Yorkshire for a long time. I have recently been researching my family history, with my great friend Chris (Bartholemiou) and we found out that my great great grandfather, Joseph Jack, was born in Skipton. He was later to move to Kingston upon Hull and help set up many a scrap dealer.

My mam's mother, Annie Sheridan, was born under a tarpaulin in Walmgate in York. She and my other grandmother Grannie Lizzie were both the same age and were very close, like sisters. They went to school together, were in the Land Army together, they drank together. I think they probably got on so well because of their shared experiences and travelling backgrounds.

Welcome to my world, won't you come on in,
Miracles, I guess, still happen now and then
Step into my heart, leave your cares behind...

Joe Longthorne *Welcome To My World* released 2008

Joseph Patrick Daniel Longthorne is my full name and I weighed in at seven and three-quarter pounds on 31 May 1955 at around 2 o'clock in the morning at Hedon Road Maternity Hospital in Hull. I was baptised at St Patrick's Catholic Church, Spring Street in Hull. My mam had nine children all together, but only four of us Anne, John, Lizzie and I made it through childhood. Even now if my mother hears 'Happy Birthday To You' it kills her.

We lived at No. 15 Rifle Terrace, just off Walker Street, near the famous Hessle Road in Hull. From what I can gather we (travellers families) were all moved there, from our trailers, so the terrace was packed full of people I knew. It's no longer there now. Actually it's been turned into a community centre, which I think is a nice touch because it was very much the centre of our community when I lived there. It was a great terrace. It was always full of hustle and bustle, with horses and carts everywhere, and I was comfortably cocooned there in my own world. There were great characters and our terrace was alive with activity all the time.

Singing is the thing that makes me want to live and for me that started at a very early age. I can remember listening to my mam singing; and then singing myself before learning to walk. It's just in me, in my genes. Music is what comes out of me. As far as I was concerned my mam was the best singer I'd ever heard. She calls herself a Vera Lynn singer. I always thought my dad could play the piano better than Russ Conway. He played both stride and vamp style.

We've some great singers in the family but for me singing has always been about entertaining an audience, hearing them applaud and seeing people smile, or even cry, when I sing.

I attended a nursery school called Villa Place and when we children were supposed to have half an hour's kip in the afternoon I would sing to them all. Miss Tibbs, I think her name was, got me to sing to everyone whilst she sat in her rocking chair. I would sing songs like *Paper Roses* (a big hit for the Kaye Sisters at the time and later Marie Osmond).

So that's where I gather my singing in front of people really started. Very soon, even at that tender age, I was appearing in front of much bigger audiences in the parks around Hull.

One of the first songs I can remember singing was 'Sugar in the Morning' (*Sugartime*, made famous by Alma Cogan).

> *'Sugar in the morning,*
> *sugar in the evening,*
> *sugar at supper-time!'*

Joe Longthorne Sugartime *never recorded or released!*

I just learned it straight-off and sang it dressed up in braces and a little boiler suit with a safety hat on and a pair of Dealer boots, like a proper little 'troweller' (builder) in a Kingston upon Hull Parks Department talent contest.

I was only about four years old, but to me it was the most natural thing in the world. If I'd done it like that today I would probably have been called Bob the Builder.

I won my first competition and got a big red plastic toy racing car and a quid. My sister Anne and I went off and bought fish and chips with it. From then on I was singing wherever I went, but it was mam who taught me how to go out and be a success. She also told me what would make me different from the rest. Her advice, even at such an early age, was what has stood me in good stead throughout my career.

Mam told me, I remember it clearly to this day, 'We have a lot of singers in the family Joe, like your Uncle Mick (Sherdan) and your Aunt Violet (Foley) from Leeds, and your singing's more than alright. I know you can sing better than lots of people but you need something else, something to make you stand out. There are a lot of singers going around Joe, so you need to do more than just sing.'

That's how the impressions came along. My first singing impression was Al Jolson – Asa Joelson, to use his real name, but before that I started out with Steptoe from *Steptoe & Son*. The TV programme was really popular at the time and I found that I could do both characters - Harold and Steptoe himself. I got myself a hat and a muffler from my granny's second hand shop and that's how my act was born. It was a bit like the children's TV programme *Mr Benn*, with me getting dressed up as different characters. There are still many people today who seem to regard me purely as an impressionist. I still do them and over the years I have added hundreds of 'star guests' to my shows.

Mam was right to advise me to start doing impressions as well as sing as myself. I have stuck by them, although many of my fans have been telling me in recent times that they now just want me to be me. That's a nice compliment and one I treasure, but I don't think I will ever be able to go on stage without someone shouting for me to 'Do Shirley!' or 'Do Tom!'.

When I was about eight or nine years old I would be singing at funerals – even stood on top of coffins - or performing in some of Hull's great pubs, or both inside and outside fish and chip shops, in front of senior citizens', anywhere just to get an audience and a few bob.

My mam tells a story about me going to get our tea from a local fish and chip shop, and that I would go in and sing to earn enough to pay for them. The lady would then put them on the top of the pan to keep them warm whilst somebody would say, 'Give us another one, Joe.' Then I'd say something like, 'I don't know, I'll have to hurry up', and if their hands didn't go into their pockets I'd be off home. Singing was already starting to become business, even then.

I learned all of the songs in my early repertoire from my mam and dad. She sang to me all the time and had the most beautiful, wonderful voice. Her complete and absolutely natural technique is where I took my lessons. She never had a proper singing lesson in her life.

I do find sometimes that I have difficulty in learning songs, especially those where I need to read the lines rather than learn them straight from hearing, because I'm dyslexic. I really have to learn things parrot-fashion. Being dyslexic has caused me one or two problems along the way, but it doesn't seem to have held me back from performing. When I was little the words just seemed to go straight into my head and mam would help me with them if I appeared to be struggling.

Mam's favourite song at that time was a Bing Crosby number *In the Cool, Cool, Cool of the Evening* which went 'Someone waits for me, if only my eyes could see her. Oh how happy I would be'. I remember that her eyes used to start filling up with tears as she sang it. She also liked my sister Anne singing *Put Another Nickel In*.

Sometimes she would send me down to the pub to get my dad to come home. I was only very young but in those days there wasn't the concern there is now over sending young ones out late at night – and I really was young. She'd say 'go and get your dad out of the Peever', that's Romany speak for the pub.

He was a bit of a lad, my dad, and I was the baby of the family, but I was the only one who could get him out. Once I'd get there – somewhere like the Fisherman's Arms - I'd get on one of the tables and sing. He would just say 'there's my boy, gnash on charver ('get on boy' in Romany) let's have *Danny Boy*, Joe'. So I did and I still get asked to sing it now, although I don't get on the tables anymore – or on any coffins!

It did me no harm. Then Dad would come home with me. The atmosphere in the pubs around Hessle Road and where we lived was something that I have always loved and it's why I still love going back. I'm still a Hull lad at heart and I always will be. But you're probably, by now, wondering what I was like when I was little, other than when I was singing. Well I was a blond haired lad and I liked smiling.

I suppose you could have called me a bit accident-prone too. I broke my arm falling down the stairs when I was only 18 months old and another time I got a bead stuck up my nose! It was a pearly bead and my sister Anne had to take me over to Park Street Children's Infirmary in Hull. I remember her saying, 'just don't ****ing sniff!' Do you know, you can't breathe very well with a bead stuck up your nose? Funny that.

Apart from the accidents, my early childhood was very happy. One of my grans, Granny Lizzie, had this second-hand clothes shop at the corner of our street and I used to love going in and getting dressed up. I'd wear everything – hats, shirts, skirts, trousers, shoes and wigs. There was just so much stuff to play with, to try on and to try out new characters. It was like having my own private props department store. My granny always used to save the best of the clothing for me.

I learned to play the piano when I was young too. My dad taught me. We always had a piano. Dad played and my mam sang. When they played together everyone in the pub would shut up and listen. They'd then shout at the end 'Go on Teresa!' They used to love her singing. She was compared to both Ella Fitzgerald and Patsy Cline quite a lot. She sang all around Hull and up as far as Bridlington on the East Coast.

My mam used to work so hard. She would go out to work at the fish house from eight til five and come home covered in scales. That meant I was looked after by my sisters. There was a time when, for years afterwards, because of this that I felt as though I was being sent away, but I wasn't. I only found that out for definite in writing this, so I've learned something too and it has set my mind at rest about something that had always troubled me.

It turns out that all that was really happening was that I was getting picked up by what had once been an old ambulance to take me to nursery. In my mind, over the years, I had felt that I had been sent to a nunnery.

It's funny how time can play tricks with you, isn't it? What Lizzie says is that she and Anne used to take it in turns to pick me up on an afternoon, or see me off from Rifle Terrace every morning. I was always immaculately dressed apparently. Lizzie tells me I can thank my grandma's shop for that.

Lizzie also tells me that my mam had always seen me as a star from the day I was born. She believes that because our mam had lost children and then had me, her life became wrapped around me. I was the youngest as well and mam put every bit of effort she could into helping me on my way. When she heard me singing at a very young age, and saw some of herself in me, she always said I had the talent born in me.

But my life wasn't all about singing. I worked hard and I used to go out with my dad on a horse and cart, tatting. We would go round calling and collecting all types of scrap metal. Later I had a little hand cart that my dad made for me and as I got a bit older I would go off and do a bit of tatting all around the area, collecting up bits of copper and brass. I would go out, come back, unload and off I'd go again. It was our way of life, what we did, and to me it was just a natural thing to do. No wonder doing Steptoe came naturally to me.

Most of my childhood was very happy, but there were two occasions when my happiness was interrupted. One of those was when my sister Anne was taken away from us for four years; and the other when we moved out from the Hessle Road area, although we moved back pretty quickly.

Anne had been sent to Rampton, the secure psychiatric hospital in Nottingham. She had been involved in violent behaviour. I wasn't told why she had been taken away from me. That's probably because I was only about five years old at the time, but I remember wondering where she had gone.

She was gone for a long while and although I was still quite young I remember thinking, 'Where has my Anne gone'. I was so glad when Anne came back that, being young and excited, I actually peed up her back when we were in bed together.

Anne has always been a tremendous sister to me, in fact all four of us – Lizzie, John, Anne and me – are all very close, as well as being brothers and sisters.

The move from Rifle Terrace, where I had spent the early years of my childhood was the worst thing ever for me. I can't put an exact date on when it happened but it was a terrible time. I was just so upset. My world had caved in. We moved out one summer so that redevelopment could take place. All of the travellers' families were shifted out of the terrace. It was like my world was falling apart and all my extended family was crumbling away. I couldn't even eat because it bothered me so much.

We went to what for us looked like a posh place called Elgar Grove, opposite the Costello playing fields in the Boothferry Road area of Hull. I'm sure it is a fabulous place to live for many people, but it just didn't suit me. Elgar may well have been a great composer, but the place didn't fill me with sweet music, and he certainly didn't know how to build houses. It just wasn't where I had come from and where I wanted to be. There were also so many things that, all of a sudden, you were not allowed to do as well.

You couldn't have a budgie or a dog, but we did! I wasn't allowed to play the piano because the walls through to next door were as thin as you find in Spain when you're on holiday in one of those newly built hotels. Coming from the great hubbub of horses, carts and great characters this was definitely not for me. Honestly, it really did make me ill and still does thinking about it now. But in the end our move away from the Hessle Road area only lasted three months, thank heavens for that.

I don't mean any disrespect to anyone who lived there then or who lives there now, but it was just such a big culture shock for me.

What put the tin lid on it was when tragedy struck. One of my friends, called Stephen, was drowned. It did my head in. That, on top of everything else, was enough. Dad said, 'That's it. We're getting out of here.'

That's when my mam pulled off her biggest and best deal ever. At that time she worked with a man called Harry Kavanagh who was the manager at the fish filleting factory. I think he suffered with gout. He knew she wanted to come back to Hessle Road and he fancied living where we had moved. He liked it better there. It was an ideal arrangement. He told my mam, 'Teresa, I've a nice house and yard for you', and we swapped.

So we ended up with all of the 'tatters' again at Number 39, Woodcock Street, just off Hessle Road. It changed my life. I was alive again! It was a beautiful house and had six garages, a gym and stables as well two bathrooms. There was even a Morgan car that had been left in one of the garages. I went back to the rag and bone, and back to the fish and chip shop singing. I was back where I knew I was from. Hessle Road's always been alright for me.

CHAPTER THREE

Junior Showtime

Grab your coat and get your hat
Leave your worries on the doorstep
Direct your feet
To the sunny side of the street

Joe Longthorne *On The Sunny Side Of The Street* released 1999

I was in and out of so many schools in Hull – Boulevard, St Wilfrid's, Westburn Street, Sir Thomas More, Eastfield – and I ended up at Sydney Smith. I wouldn't say I was disruptive at all, but I did get chucked out of a few. I was kicked out for scrapping from a couple of them, but I never got a report about me saying I was disruptive.

So why did I fight? Well, I was very erratic and had a temper on me. I'd like to say I'm a lot calmer now, but I'm not really. It wasn't that I was being bullied and I was never in a bullying gang, we didn't do that kind of thing. All I did was what a lot of kids do at that age.

I was bored with lessons. To be honest I don't know why I went to school at all and there were quite a few times when I wasn't there anyway.

I couldn't read or write properly even when I left school, but it was only once I'd left that I found out I was dyslexic. I can read and write now but I don't really write too much, apart from songs and autographs, but I do read, particularly biographies.

They put me in what they called the 'slow class' or sometimes the 'special class'. I really don't like the name 'slow' because of what it implies and because it's unfair to those to be labelled in that way, but that's what it was called. The 'difficulty in learning' class would be a better title for it. Anyway, I didn't mind being in it. In fact it's surprising just how many of those who were in 'slow classes' have ended up doing really well in life after school.

My own education, where I gave myself my own personal geography lessons was more to do with travel. Just over the River Humber, years before the Humber Bridge was built, there was a whole new land for me to visit, particularly during the days when I should have been at school.

Back in the 1960s the River Humber had ferries crossing 'on the hour' from Hull to New Holland in Lincolnshire. Mam took me across on the ferry the first time I ever went, but then I would play truant from school, what we used to call 'twagging' in Hull, and hop on to one called the Tattersall Castle.

I always went on my own. I wouldn't recommend it to any children today, but in those days everything seemed alright. There was never any talk of young children getting abducted or mistreated by strangers. It seems as though there was a lot more trust in those days.

First I'd go to school, get my mark, then I'd walk back out and go straight off to Hull Pier. I thought that I was going to another country, but I was just going across to Lincolnshire. When we landed at New Holland I'd get on the train and go to Barton-on-Humber. That was it, I loved it. I'd go and have beans on toast in a café and walk to Thornton Abbey, such a lovely place. So I was getting a bit of history as well.

What did I do it for? Well, like I said, I was bored, but maybe it was also because I thought that things like school were a bit too crowded for me. I just wanted to get away, be on my own. I still like doing that kind of thing today, although I don't do it as often as I really should.

Ravenscar, just above Scarborough on the North Yorkshire coast is my favourite place in the whole world. I found this, my perfect place, as a result of 'twagging' as well. For someone who lives most of his professional life on a stage and in the spotlight I really enjoy the isolation of Ravenscar. We'll come back to Ravenscar later on.

Anyway, back to the ferry across the Humber for the time being.

The Tattersall Castle had an upper and lower deck and the first time I ever 'twagged' I went on it. I had this ice cream. Unfortunately it fell from my cornet onto someone's head below. I laid low on the top deck for a while that day and made sure I wasn't caught with an empty cornet in my hand!

I used to get back to New Holland just in time to catch the last ferry back across to Hull. It was always great being on the ferry, especially if it was a beautiful summer's day. When I came back my dad used to ask just where I had been, because by then he knew I hadn't been at school.

Some days I'd just go and get my mark and then go off for a walk around the docks in Hull, then when it was kicking out time from school I'd get back to mingle with the others as they were leaving, especially if my dad was picking me up.

Anyhow, one day I was well and truly found out.

I've just got back from a wonderful day off and dad's there in his Bedford truck waiting for me. It's five to four. The bell goes and I'm second out. 'Hi Dad.' Who comes out after me? You've got it. It was my teacher Mr Gray and my headmaster Mr Billingham, in his Singer Vogue car. They ask me how I'm feeling, because I'd not been in all day, and the game's up. Dad had a right go at me on the way home!

It wasn't as though I hated school though – and I did have one or two really good teachers. I loved Miss Westaby. She was my favourite and she taught maths. She supported me because I think she knew I was a singer and that my mind was more on that than anything else. I couldn't do maths at all, but we had a real connection.

The others I admired most were Mr Stott, who taught Maths at Sydney Smith School, as well as Mr Woodcock and Mr Underwood, my headmaster at Sydney Smith.

Where I was incredibly fortunate was that at Sydney Smith School we had the greatest jazz pianist in the whole of Hull and to my mind the whole of the world alive at the time, Mr Graham Gordon. Lord, he could play jazz. I had more time for him than anyone else and he always had time for me. He was the one teacher who really helped my singing career whilst I was at school and I will always be grateful to him for that.

I didn't come out of school with any qualifications as such, no 'O' Levels or anything like that, but I did get an A for one piece of work I did in humanities and another in art. I painted a picture of a nun that we had framed at home.

My best mate at school was Kevin Rimmer. I never really took to football but he was one of the greatest footballers Hull City could have ever had. Kev was a great pal and I remember him coming along with me to a works' children's Christmas party at Armstrong Patents in Beverley, where my mother had moved to from the fish factory.

As for me, I'd start off playing a game with everyone but as soon as the ball went over a fence then they would never see me again. I'd go with it, I just wasn't bothered about that kind of sport. I like boxing, darts and motor racing, but I've never run around after a ball very much.

Kev didn't have the people around him to back him. He should have played for England. I remember his dad wasn't exactly the happiest soul in the world. The two sides of the street were like different worlds. We lived on one side with this big house with two bathrooms, stables and six garages – and Kev lived on the other. We weren't trying to be flash, that was just the way it was.

My dad would pop a fiver through Kev's letterbox for New Year's Eve as a present for him and then say 'Happy New Year!' the next day, but Kev's dad would just mumble something back in return. Dad made sure he took notice. I'll say no more.

My first love was Pauline Jubb and we were really good friends. She was a blonde and also very talented young lady. We spent a lot of time together. She was a singer too, and could have been one of the greatest comediennes. I remember we both loved dressing up and once went to my mam's with me dressed in drag. We were like Bonnie and Clyde when we were together.

Pauline was a great girl and we enjoyed each other's company immensely. Our first song we ever sang together was *Michael Row The Boat Ashore*. We once set up a little hairdressing business in her dad's shed. We were always up to something – and I'm not talking just cut and blow-drys.

I was always trying to make money. As well as the hairdressing I would also go out tatting, collecting clothes as well as scrap on my cart. I'd then sort the rubbish stuff from the good stuff, wash the clothes I was keeping, dry them out and get them ready for sale the next day. In the winter I ran my own snow team, clearing snow from driveways and the streets, with lads shovelling snow and throwing salt all over. I had three businesses on the go at one time. It's always been in me to try and earn a living.

My father was on the HMS Espiegle during WWII. It was a mine sweeper and operated in the Mediterranean between Malta and the North African coast. It's often said that you're ****ed if you get put on a mine sweeper, but my dad came through and was decorated for his war effort. He wasn't a big fellah but he was one of the fittest blokes on the sea. He was always up for a laugh as well.

As much as mam set me on my way, by suggesting what to do with my act, so too did dad. He would take me to all the pubs and clubs particularly when I was between the ages of 10 to 13. He was my agent, my minder, everything, but most of all a wonderful father.

When I first started out I would do just five songs. I used to come on and sing *I Believe*, followed by *Danny Boy*, then two others and finish off with *My Way*.

I loved singers like Hull's own David Whitfield of course. Songs like *Cara Mia*, *Answer Me* and *My September Love*. He was a great singer. Years later I played three nights at the Crystal Rooms in Hereford and the sign outside said, 'TONIGHT JOE LONGTHORNE with Special Guest Star David Whitfield'. I'd been given top billing. I asked them to change it around. I told them, 'Look, we both come from Hull and this man is a big star. The billing needs to be the other way around.'

I first met David at the Northwood Country Club in Cottingham, near Hull. He was still a big star. He'd had his own TV show and two Number One hit records. I believe he still holds the record for the most consecutive nights at the London Palladium as a solo artiste. He topped the bill and there was another fantastic Hull-born act who went on to become nationally famous, Norman Collier.

This was one of the first professional engagements I had after I left the TV show *Junior Showtime* and the first thing that struck me about David was his humility. I went on to work with him at least six or seven more times and enjoyed every one.

Hull has produced some great singers and bands over the years. Roland Gift (Fine Young Cannibals), The Housemartins, The Beautiful South, Ronnie Hilton – and some great actors too, John Alderton, Barrie Rutter, Brian Rix, Ian Carmichael, Tom Courtenay and Maureen Lipman. To my mind you can't get a better actress than Maureen. Tom's parents used to live not far from us. I'd love to spend just five minutes with him over a cup of tea talking about how he made it in acting. He puts so much into every part he plays. He must study his characters well.

These days I study what I sing all the time and try my best to interpret every lyric with what I feel is the right emotion. To be totally truthful, in the early days and indeed for many years I just 'went for it' without really thinking too much about what I was singing.

I've three advantages now. I'm older, I'm wiser (I hope) and my voice has, very fortunately, stayed with me throughout. No matter what has happened to me along the way my voice is still there, so I'm really very lucky, despite how unlucky some people might feel I have been. That's why I never ask my fans to feel sad for me. I've had a fantastic career so far. Of course I hope that it can take off even further again with all that is to come, but I would never want anyone to be sad for me over the lymphoma and other things that have happened along the way. I've had a brilliant life and some tremendous highs. Sure, the lows have been pretty damned low though.

In those early years of performing, dad was always there for me, like I said, and he had his own way of sorting things out when he faced up to people who were messing us about. It was the way things were done at that time.

I remember at one club in Hull, we went along and the club secretary told my dad, 'He does three spots'. My dad said, 'He does two spots, he just goes on twice. That's it.' The guy gets a bit clever. Dad continues arguing with him at one side while I'm now on stage. So dad followed him to his office and that's when I went with him. My dad had quite a good vocabulary, as well as being able to handle himself, and tried to explain to the club secretary again.

'If the performer is under the age of 14 you can't put him on three times. It's not on his licence.' The guy continued arguing with my dad who had by now had enough of him – so my dad hit him spark out. Dad's got my wages and I'm back on stage ready to do *When You're Smiling* when out comes the guy with claret all over him. The regulars in the club all start attacking my travellers' family and there's fists and furniture flying everywhere. It's mayhem, like something out of a western movie.

I saw 'Our Cathy' another of our many family members, a very strong lady I might add, built like a mountain, pick up a committee member by one arm and she's using his head like it's a bouncing ball. Everything's going mad and we're getting back in this Commer van trying to get the doors shut. My uncle - Sgt Billy Foley, ex-army - is making sure they can't get to us.

It was all self defence let me tell you, not violence, and none of it would have happened if the guy had just listened to what my dad was telling him in the first place.

It might seem funny now, like the Clampetts from the *Beverley Hillbillies*, but it was scary at the time. But that wasn't the end of things going on at my gigs, not by a long way!

I was still off tatting or knocking all the time, as well as singing on an evening. I had to be back in at half past five to get ready for a club gig if it was local. Lizzie and mam and dad would be shouting for me in the street to get in because I'd have to be at the gig for half past six backstage to see the drummer and the other musicians, usually a guitarist and maybe a keyboard player. I'd then come on at about 8 o'clock when everybody had settled. In those days, the clubs were packed by 7 o'clock. These were the days when the whole clubland scene throughout the north of England was really buzzing – and in Hull it was a great time to be a performer. There were hundreds of clubs but if you wanted a seat in any of them you had to get there early.

Dad used to say to my sisters Anne and Lizzie, 'When Joe starts up with *Is This The Way To Amarillo,* get up and dance.' That way everybody else got up as well. It always worked. My dad knew exactly what he was doing. I would get around £12-£16 for the night, but if I did an extra couple of songs dad would do a bit of negotiating to get a bit extra for me.

That sometimes led to a bit more than simply arguing my case as well. All of a sudden, whilst I'm still on stage, the curtains would go flying, arms and legs would be flailing - and the drums would come crashing down. It was dad having a fight with another club secretary. At least that way the local music stores were always kept busy with instrument repairs!

McLeod-Holden was one of the big theatrical and entertainment agents in the country at the time. Dad told me that Don Holden had asked him to stop doing deals because that was their job. My dad just told him that I was 13 years old and that if he had to negotiate for me he would. Dad always had a business brain and made sure I got what I was due.

Right from being four years old and winning that toy car I had always taken part in talent competitions either in clubs, pubs or parks. In the early days my sisters would always get me ready and make sure I looked good on stage, and it was one of the talent competitions that led to me getting my first big break when I was 14.

The big talent competitions in Hull were run by the Kingston upon Hull Parks Department. They were very forward thinking, bringing on the talent and giving Hull people a great opportunity to make their mark in show business. Hull had a fantastic live entertainment scene at the time with its masses of clubland activity. You had to get through one round and then on to another. It was held in the City Hall and although these days I prefer the acoustics in the New Theatre I thought it was absolutely amazing.

Whenever a talent show came up I was always put into it. Anne and Lizzie were always busying themselves looking after me.

The City Hall final was the biggest I'd been in yet. In the final there was a country singer, called Ian Attrell, who I think was blind if I remember correctly. He was very popular. Muriel Nifton was on the organ, but I found her a bit of a 'beng' ('strict' in Romany). I only wanted her to play *When You're Smiling* but she was just too bossy for me.

I remember my microphone fell to the floor in the final so I picked it up. Then I started playing the spoons as accompaniment. I wasn't going to be directed by some fat organist. No disrespect Muriel, if you are still around, it's just the way I felt as a young lad.

Everyone from my family was there, as well as all of the rest of the travellers' families. Both grannies were there too. The talent on the show was really of a very high standard, including a lady singer who Lizzie thought was going to win. There were all kinds of acts – jugglers, drummers, dancers, comedians – and I won it.

During the rehearsals there had been a lot of photographs taken but I seemed to get ignored. Maybe the photographers liked the idea of taking pictures of the girls in their nice outfits – who could blame them? Some of them looked gorgeous. Hull girls have always looked fantastic.

So when it turned out that I'd won, the local paper, the *Hull Daily Mail* didn't have a picture of me. Dad told them that since they didn't want to know me earlier on they'd have to come around to do a photo shoot the next day.

They did just that and I gave my prize money to my first girlfriend, Pauline. I also bought her a black and white plastic Beatles dress and plastic wig.

One of my fans, or as I call them my friends, Fiona Burt, kept a press cutting of the report from 3 October 1969, which read: *'Little Joe Has a Big Future – There's a twinkle in his eyes, a song in his heart and a cheery word for everyone he meets. At 14 years old Joseph Longthorne – 'Little Joe' – is a Hull lad we can all be proud of writes Pru Clark. In a few years time he might be one of the big names in show business. For 'Little Joe' he is 4ft 10in tall, has the determination to get to the top. After winning last month's Hull*

Parks Department talent competition he appears to have the ability too. 'Little Joe' of 39, Woodcock Street, found the world his stage at the age of 5. 'He used to sing in the street and people took notice of him,' said his father, Mr F Longthorne. For several years he has been the favourite of the fish and chip shops and the wonder of the working men's clubs. 'He's a natural born entertainer. Send him out for fish and chips and he sings to the waiting queue,' said Mr Longthorne. A local police officer entered Joe in a Withernsea talent contest when he was 10 and he came second out of 20 contestants. 'Since then he's played in clubs and done charity acts at hospitals,' said his father. 'He has never had a music teacher,' said Mr Longthorne. 'He once went to a dancing class and left because he was the only boy. But he will spend about 20 to 30 minutes getting a song right.' At the talent contest final last month Joe won £25, which he said he would spend on clothes for his set. For all he's a little lad Joe looks set for a pretty big future.'

So it would appear that what I tell you is all true, as verified in the Hull Daily Mail back in the day! The City Hall final of the talent competition wasn't about the money though. It's never been about the money for me. What it led to was the landing of my first ever TV appearance. Dad wrote to *Junior Showtime*, which was a big children's show on Yorkshire Television at the time. It was a variety show and appropriately enough it was filmed at the City Varieties Theatre in Leeds, where the *Good Old Days* used to be filmed. Variety was all the rage back in the 60s and 70s.

This was also the time when I first realised that I wasn't just attracted to girls and that I might be bisexual, although that term wasn't really used at the time. I'm very comfortable with my bisexuality. Some people who have been around me, but are not family or close friends, have thought that they have been telling the papers something new when they have tried to make money out of me by saying I'm gay, but they have found that very little has come to fruition.

Whilst we're on the subject, my preference sexually has never been other than with a woman, and I've loved, respected and still love all of the ladies I have ever been with, no matter what might have been printed and said elsewhere. Yes, I am bisexual and let me tell you, I still really would know how to love a woman intimately.

James Moran has been my partner for the past 12 years and I love him dearly. He has been alongside me through some of the most difficult and trying times, but I very much love the ladies too. The best way I can put it is that I sometimes help the ladies out when they're busy!

And I have a son too, Ricky, who I also love dearly, and I have three grandchildren.

More of Ricky, his family and my grandchildren later, I just needed to introduce all of this now because you were probably wondering when I would and this is the time when it starts fitting in with my story, although there's a lot more to come before Ricky's birth. So far I'm just 'Little Joe' and I'm not yet at the City Varieties.

It's like a big jigsaw this, isn't it, trying to put all of your life down on paper. I hope I don't leave anyone out! I've certainly tried to make sure I haven't.

No matter how well I have performed on stage, whether in clubs or theatres, I have never really been that good at auditions. When I went to an audition in Grimsby for Yorkshire Television's *Junior Showtime* I was to meet Jean Pearce, comedian Billy Pearce's mother and on this occasion all went well. Jean was responsible for all the choreography on the show.

I was just 13 at the time and I went with my own piano player, David Carter. He was a bit posh, but he was a good lad for me. I played the spoons again and sang *I Believe* and Jean seemed to be impressed, but I wanted to make sure. I just said, 'wait a minute, I can play the spoons as well.' I was desperate for this. I wanted it so much. So I dashed to the kitchen of this church where the auditions were being held.

Jean put on her notes that Jess (Yates), the producer, 'must use this boy'. Jess was known as 'The Bishop' and he had a formidable reputation.

I warned Jean that whilst I could sing I couldn't read or write, but she stuck by me and told the Bishop that she'd got this kid with a good voice, 'a bit cheeky and does his own stuff', but he can't do scripts and things. Well, Jess was a scripts man, but he decided to give me a chance thanks to Jean, and I was in!

All I knew was that for the first time in my life there could be something really happening for me. But at the same time the idea of a scripted programme frightened me to death. After all, not being able to read and write, you can imagine how I felt. I just thought, where am I going to fit in? I could sing anything, but I was worried that I wouldn't be able to conform to what the show was going to need.

Bobby Bennett helped me. He was one of the stars of the show with Glyn Poole and Bonnie Langford.

Jean always helped out too. I found out later that although Jess really thought a lot of me, he had said he didn't want me anywhere near him when it came to reading scripts. Bobby went through it all with me learning it parrot fashion and he was such a help. He and Jean were my best mates on the show by a long way.

At first my *Junior Showtime* appearances were a bit of a joke. I'd asked all my friends in Hull to watch the show but for the first couple of months I was either dressed as a mushroom, lion, chinaman or rabbit, or something.

Mam said all she could see of me was my legs. But I was still enjoying being a part of it. I loved all the make-up and getting dressed up in different outfits. It was like being back in my gran's shop.

The programmes were made over a weekend in Leeds. I would leave Hull after going for a bath on a Friday afternoon at my Auntie Peggy's who lived in the centre of Hull. Then I would catch the train from Paragon Station to Leeds. There I would meet up with Penelope Keith, who was filming at Yorkshire Television at the time, and we would travel together. The funny thing was that I was there with a case full of scripts I couldn't read, which I'd been given the week before. There was really no point them giving them to me. We would rehearse on Saturday, record on Sunday and come back home Monday morning. Whilst I was in Leeds I would stay at my Aunt Rose's in Crossgates.

I had the scripts with me at home all week, but I couldn't even face looking at them. We had a really good club man in Hull called Ted Cuthbert. He worked for Carmichaels, the posh department store in Hull at the time, and he had sorted mam out with this perfectly decent case as a present for me. It really was lovely and it looked mightily impressive, but I still couldn't read anything that was inside. So I was there with a case full of stuff I didn't understand. Dad also had Yorkshire Television printed on to it. I used to hope they had got something that made life a bit easier for me every week.

Junior Showtime was so important to me because I knew this was my career. It was what I was made to do, and here I was performing on television already at 14 years of age.

Some of the others were probably only doing it as something to do. They were probably going to go on and do proper jobs. For me though this was to be my life. Thank God for Jean and Bobby, that's all I can say, they helped me through!

Typically, as you might imagine, I got into one or two fights with some of the other kids on the show.

I used to go in this room and every kid, I mean every kid apart from me, would know their lines. Some of them were really too clever for their own good and so I'd bring them down a peg or two. I'd say to this big lad from Barnsley, 'my mam says you look like Humpty Dumpty'. He'd then say, 'you want to tell thee mother she looks more like Humpty Dumpty than me.' That's when I'd go 'smack' and lay him out. It was childish I know, but we were kids and it was probably bound to happen if they threw a lot of us in together all from different backgrounds from all over our wonderful county of Yorkshire.

My first pantomime appearance was in *Cinderella* for Yorkshire Television just after I'd joined the show. This is how the *Hull Daily Mail* reported it: *'Pantomime TV spot for Little Joe – Hull's youngest showbiz personality, 14 year old 'Little Joe' Longthorne is to appear in his first TV pantomime. Little Joe, of 39 Woodcock Street, will sing and dance in the chorus of Cinderella to be broadcast on Yorkshire Television on New Year's Eve, after winning a Hull Corporation summer talent contest. Little Joe's greatest ambition was realised when he was given a chance to appear on television. He recently completed 12 recordings for Junior Showtime including a Christmas Special, which will be broadcast on Christmas Eve.'*

My most successful time on the show, I was on for two years, was as soon as I was singing on my own. But I might not have been as successful if it hadn't been for my Uncle Joe (Wilson). You'll find I have so many family members who keep cropping up – and Joe comes back in the story again later on. When you're part of the travellers' community that's the way it goes.

Uncle Joe is a real hard man; we're talking serious tough-talking traveller here. Joe was a dealer from Leeds and felt he could make sure I got to sing the right songs for me, the ones I was already good at. Jess had got me singing *I've Got a Lovely Bunch of Coconuts*, but Joe said, 'I want him singing *Marta* (which the Bachelors had a hit with). It was a very popular song for me at the time. I'd sung it in all the clubs in Hull and everyone liked me doing it.

Uncle Joe wasn't known for mincing his words. He told Jess, 'He's singing *Marta* or your head's going through that ****ing wall.' I'm not really sure whether Jess was swayed by that, but it seemed to pay off for me because Jess let me sing it and Uncle Joe even gave me a 'flim' (Romany for 'fiver') afterwards. Uncle Joe wasn't around all the time, but it appeared to me that from that moment on Jess gave me a bit more respect. I was no longer a mushroom or a Chinaman, I was now out on the front line.

In the end I was introducing the show with Bobby. Again, not bad for a lad who couldn't read or write! Jess was a master at writing the openers and closers to programmes and I just carried on learning everything parrot fashion from Bobby and Jean again. I cannot over express just how much of a help these two wonderful people were for me. I will forever be in their debt, because without them I probably wouldn't have lasted longer than a fortnight. And without Uncle Joe I might not have made it to the front line.

When I wasn't performing on the show I would be back in Hull either at school, or not at school when I should have been, or out 'calling' or playing the clubs.

One of my major moments during filming *Junior Showtime* was being asked to be involved in a programme being put together called *George Martin Presents*. I didn't know who George Martin was but suddenly there's Ringo

Starr on the phone to Jess – and Jess wants me to sing *Octopus' Garden,* which Ringo sang on The Beatles' *Abbey Road* album. The Bee Gees were on the show too, along with Lulu, Madeleine Bell, this big orchestra, and Pan's People. It was another fantastic show to be involved with.

Again the *Hull Daily Mail* reported it all: *'Aged 14, Joe is a TV veteran – A TV appearance with Ringo Starr on New Year's Eve was one of the highlights in the career of 14 year old Joe Longthorne of Woodcock Street. 'He was very nice to talk to and not at all big-headed, was Joe's comment on Ringo. Joe is rapidly becoming a TV veteran himself. He reckons he has taken part in about 14 Junior Showtimes so far. These are all pre-recorded. 'You never know which one will be coming on when you sit down to watch,' says Joe. Pint-sized Joe hopes to take up entertaining full time when he leaves Sydney Smith School. His current TV work does not interfere with his school work. 'I never miss school to take part in it,' he said.*

I was also to appear in a film! But don't get carried away here, because even I didn't remember it enough to put it in the first version of this book. I'll let the *Hull Daily Mail* tell you all about it. I'm still waiting for the call from Hollywood! *'Joe (15) in film – One of Hull's up and coming young entertainers, Joe Longthorne, has been busy in recent weeks. Along with his numerous clubland appearances Joe has just finished a fortnight's filming. He took the main role in a film produced by Mr Edward Little, a lecturer at the Hull College of Education. He and his half-dozen student helpers decided to make a film on the problems of a poor reader (was I typecast?) with the object of providing stimulus for discussion for students within the college. 'Do You Read Me?' was the title of the film and in it Joe had to play truant,' said his father with a laugh last week. 'He's never played hookey in his life!'*

And that was it for my big screen appearances! I don't even ever remember seeing the film! Looking back the whole thing was actually a ****ing sham! I felt as though I had been used in some form of experiment. I wonder whatever happened to the film!

All of my time on *Junior Showtime* was great, but none of it ever went to my head though because I felt as though I knew where I was going from the beginning. There was a time when I thought I had hit the big-time by being on the show, but the feeling didn't last too long. I knew there was a lot more to do before I would ever really make it as a real success in the world of show business.

I think you do believe you've got it made when you go back to school and all your mates say they saw you on telly and you were great. But I never came home and acted the big shot. I remember taking all my mates to a place called The Gainsborough in the centre of Hull, which was a big fish and chip restaurant at the time. David Whitfield once owned it. And that was the way I celebrated my success. Any of the money that was earned from *Junior Showtime* went straight into the bank, my mam made sure of that. Jess had told her that I should look after my money.

It was around this time that I started taking notice of other big-name singers, people who were to have a massive influence on my style and my future routines on stage.

As anyone who comes to my concerts or has seen me on television will know, Dame Shirley Bassey has been a huge part of my life. My impression of her on stage is one thing, but it should never be understated just how much I adore her singing style, and her stage presence. It's not all about getting a laugh out of performing as Dame Shirley. She is and always has been a fantastic performer. I have always looked up to her and thoroughly admire her work. Now don't get the idea I'm some kind of Dame Shirley 'stalker' here, but you will see just how much I think of her as my story unfolds.

In fact the first LP I ever bought was one of Shirley Bassey's. I just knew then that I wanted to perform and deliver songs as well as she has always done. Dorothy Squires came next to me, then Judy Garland. Later I also liked Charles Aznavour and then Sinatra came into my life. That was it, I didn't need any more. I had what I felt was the complete set of wonderful singers. Sure, there have been great ones before and since but these to me were the best.

I just love performing as Dame Shirley and whenever I perform as her I feel as though I turn into her for those few minutes each night. It is a wonderful gift to be able to 'Do Shirley' as my fans ask me to. There's a tingle goes right through me as I spread out my arms and extend my fingers.

Whilst I was being awakened to the show business people I wanted to learn from, my early TV career was about to come to an abrupt end in 1971. I hadn't done anything wrong except become 16 years old. That was the way it was with *Junior Showtime*. Once you reached 16 you were off.

The good news for me was that it meant there were no more scripts!

Let's take a little break from the early days right here. We'll pick it up again soon when my clubland career started going into full-time work, when I fell in love several times, when my son Ricky was born, and when I nearly landed up in jail. All of that is coming soon, as well as my elopement with a fantastically sexy woman, and my wonderful friendship with a lovely man.

There's such a lot to let you know about properly for the first time in my own words, but for now I don't know about you but I could do with getting a glass of something or other. Will you join me?

VEGAS

I've waited so long
To be with you tonight
Right now it seems – my hopes and my dreams
Have never been so right
I've waited so long to sing my song for you

Joe Longthorne   released 2002

'Where have you been all my life? I never thought I would see or hear anyone like you again. The game you're in, with the talent you've got, you're the tops baby.'

We've moved forward just a little bit, well quite a lot actually, because this is one of the reasons I'm so excited at the moment. And I just had to tell you now!

I've just come off stage at the Palace Hotel in Manchester where we have performed a 40-minute set for Engelbert Humperdinck's Variety Club Award. He has just been honoured with the biggest accolade you can get from the Variety Club of Great Britain. It's March 2009. I've always got on so well with him and Engelbert has said some really nice things about me throughout my career. He feels I'm by far the best entertainer he's ever heard, which is not only really nice, but amazing coming from the man who is known as the 'King of Romance'.

But these words at the start of this chapter? 'Where have you been all my life?' They are not Engelbert's. They are the words of an American who I have never met before. Someone I don't know from Adam.

I asked the man, an American, what he meant when he said he'd never expected see anyone like this again. After all, I'd only done 40 minutes. This wasn't all of my show by a long way.

'I'm the 'old man's' manager.'

He looked both a very gentle but at the same time very forthright man and I was taken with him. What I found thrilling was that he seemed to have 'got me' straightaway and understood that I was a genuine man too.

It still didn't click. I just said, 'Who do you mean? The old man?'

He said: 'Frank Sinatra'.

I wasn't impressed, I said: 'No-one calls Mr Sinatra 'the old man'.'

Then he introduced himself fully. 'I'm Elliott Weisman, Frank Sinatra's manager. I'm entitled to talk like that.'

That's when the excitement kicked in. I might have been in the world of show business for 40 years but I can still get excited. It really doesn't matter to me how many knock-backs I've had, or the disappointments, or the feeling that I've sometimes been shafted by people, I'm still hungry for success. I still want to reach the pinnacle, the top – and the top for me has always been Vegas.

I played there in the early 2000s, but not the big venues like Caesar's (Palace). Jean and Mal who got me those gigs, and who you will hear more of later, did well to get me to Vegas, but the venues were more like truck-stop shows with lots of guys wearing cowboy hats!

This was different. This was Frank Sinatra's ex-manager saying he wanted me in Vegas on 'The Strip'.

'You're coming to Vegas and you're going around the world with Engelbert. You and him, together.'

The tour with Engelbert might not be taking place, but America is certainly back on the agenda – and that could yet see me topping the bill in Vegas!

There are so many promises that turn to heartbreak in the entertainment business, so I'm not counting my chickens (of which I have quite a few by the way), but what I can tell you is that I'm looking forward to it all whichever way it turns out.

This book being released, you reading it, going to the States, this year's UK tour, more albums, the Australia tour - this really does feel like my time. I've been through so much and yet I'm now feeling so good. Even the leukaemia seems to be under control. Although I'll never ever say I've defeated it. I did that once before and let's just say it wasn't the right thing to announce. I don't want to tempt fate.

I just know that once I'm there – in Vegas – this time I can take it. I won't let go of it once I've got it. They will have to get some serious contenders in to shift me.

There – that's it – that's your up-tempo break, and mine too. Now it's back to where we'd left things. I've finished *Junior Showtime* and I'm back on the road with my dad. I'm also in love.

Making Love in the Daisies

So much to do, if I only had time, I only had time
Dreams to pursue, there are mountains to climb
They'd be mine…

Joe Longthorne *If I Only Had Time* released 1993

By now I had been packing out the clubs all over Hull throughout my teens. It seemed like I played every single one of them at some time or other, and I had still been playing them whilst I was doing *Junior Showtime*.

My dad was there for me every step of the way, especially in those early days. We had a few run-ins together over the years, like fathers and sons do, most notably when I made a mess of his prized possession, his Bedford truck, which I smashed up one day.

Looking back I was so lucky. I had my mam and my dad. My mam who had always believed in me and still does, who knew I had the talent and my dad who always worked so hard for me, making sure I got to the gigs and was looked after properly. I don't think there can be many in my business whose parents showed as much faith and belief in my ability.

After my two years on the TV show I was back on the road full-time. All of a sudden I was now an adult performer, playing every night in clubs, earning my living from what I always felt was where I belonged.

This was when the real travelling started. When Joseph Patrick Daniel Longthorne went up and down the North East, back to Hull, to the West Riding and York, and over to Lincolnshire.

What really changed was that I started going out and singing the songs that they wanted in the clubs. I shifted my emphasis on to more up-tempo and feelgood numbers like *Beautiful Sunday*, but I never left out the ballads. I've always been a big ballad singer. Songs like *I Believe* and *Till* (which Ken Dodd had a big hit with). I also loved Matt Monro. I always make a point of singing his songs even now, like *Portrait of My Love* and of course *If I Never Sing Another Song*. But back in the 70s I also put in a lot more that fitted with the era we were in.

When you listen to my earliest recordings, those I recorded around the mid-70s, you might hear a little bit of a nod to other singers around at the time like David Cassidy.

I did anything. I could sing anything – from ballad to rock, from soul to country. Some of the ballads I really wanted to sing at the time I felt were a bit too gay, a bit too camp, and they contained feelings I had about a man, even though I was with a lovely girl.

There was always a lot of talent on the clubland scene and of the other singers performing regularly in Hull at the time I remember Gloria Dixon being on stage at Jesmond Club. She really was like Shirley Bassey and she was a great singer.

It was when I started hitting the North East circuit that I really started finding my feet. I'd come off TV, but not being on-the-box hadn't bothered me.

What I found in the North East was that they had the best bands for accompanying singers like me. Back in Hull you often turned up and were backed by a drummer and organist. Up in Sunderland, Newcastle and all the other pit towns in the area you would invariably get a four-piece or five-piece band behind you, and to a singer like me that made all the difference. It always has for me. I'm a live performer and when I have a live band backing me we fly! That's perhaps why the North East remains so special to me today. I have such happy memories of my clubland days up there.

Playing the pubs and clubs was not just my main business by now, it was also my main happiness.

I think I have always needed to travel, it's in my bones, it's my heritage, and the North East was a wonderful area for me. Some of this country's finest artistes have come from there – The Animals, Alan Price, Sting. The furthest north I played was Ashington Miners Welfare Club.

Many people talk of working men's clubs being difficult places to play, but I didn't find them tough to crack at all. That doesn't mean you didn't get a hard word or two when you first turned up at a club that was new to you though. I would get some big fellahs and even children saying things like, 'Do you like your car, mate? Well, you'd better be ****ing good or it won't be there when you come back later.' I well remember that type of comment from some of the lads outside of clubs like the Downhill, and Redhouse Workmans Club in Rawmarsh Road, Sunderland.

This was the big era for clubland. Today working men's clubs are nothing like they were back then. In those days it was standing-room only by 7 o'clock at night with an hour to go before you went on.

Remember, those were the days when we only had three TV channels, no videos, no mobile phones, no satellite TV, no Playstations - this was the whole family's entertainment for the week and believe me people really wanted to be entertained. They had worked all week down a pit or at sea and if you weren't good enough they would soon let you know. I loved it.

My dad used to talk with the club committees to either tell them or suggest what they should do to promote me – especially if he had found that all they had done was scrawl my name in chalk outside. He was always very professional about how I should be promoted and would make sure they had a proper poster up the next time announcing 'Joe Longthorne – Direct from *Junior Showtime*.' He wouldn't stand any messing, but I guess you already worked that out earlier when the drums came crashing down and all of the club members launched into us.

Sunderland and the whole of the North East has always been a great area for me and I made some lifelong friends up there. Every time I go back it's like going home, it's really where my clubland career took off and it was particularly important because it meant I was going down well not just in my home city but further away as well.

One of my best friends in the business today is Roy 'Chubby' Brown. Roy comes from Teesside and he played that whole circuit too, including the Hull clubs with his band. I have always found that the people of the North East really are special, and those who come to my shows from there are very important to me.

I wouldn't say I was concerned about honing my act. Of course I was thinking about which songs to use, but I wasn't thinking about it the way I do today. I was just getting through, finding my way. I changed my show every week, building up an impressive catalogue of songs and impressions. I think it's called bobbing and weaving in boxing terms, but I've always been concerned about presenting a completely different show from one night to the next. If you come to my show today I guarantee the next night it won't be the same.

I was working for entertainment agencies like Bill Fredericks, Stage Space and Ronnie Lundy from Middlesbrough. They were some of the big names in the North East circuit.

As well as dad, I also had my brother-in-law Mick (Holliday), Lizzie's husband, take me to gigs. He used to work his arse off all day delivering coal, then he'd lock up his yard, go home and pick me up ready to get to somewhere like York for 7 o'clock. My suit would be on the back of his lorry, waving about. My sound system would be strapped in at the back too. We'd make for the Post Office Club or the Viking Hotel.

I still have a copy of a contract through the York & Leeds Branch Club Union of Clubs & Institutes which shows how much I was paid for an evening on Thursday 7 September, 1972 at Huntington WMC. It was £14. Don't tell the government will you! There was no mention of 'riders' in those days, asking for anything and everything else you wanted. You were paid the fee. That was it. The only thing with that copy of the contract is that the name of the artiste on it was Joe Longthorpe. I hope they got the poster right.

Most of my bookings at the time were handled through McLeod Holden. This itinerary for the end of October and going into the beginning of November 1972 gives you an idea of my work load at the time. I was 17. It was the year when Slade, T Rex, David Cassidy, Donny Osmond and Gilbert O'Sullivan all topped the charts:

Friday 20 October:	*Dixon's Arms, Woodmansey*
Saturday 21 October:	*Unity Club, Hull*
Sunday 22 October:	*York Street WMC, Wakefield*
Thursday 26 October:	*Teddy's Club, Withernsea*
Saturday 28 October:	*Wombwell British Legion, nr Barnsley*
Sunday 29 October:	*Hodgson's Club, Beverley*
Monday 30 October:	*Upper Healey WMC Club, Sheffield*
Wednesday 1 November:	*Gatehouse WMC, Clayton, Bradford*
Friday 2 November:	*Blackburn's Social Club, Brough, Hull*

They were the days when a pint of beer cost just 11p and a pack of 20 cigarettes cost 25p. When you put it like that it seems a long time ago now doesn't it?

Having the right stage equipment had become a priority for me and my first proper microphone was a Calrec, one of the first battery-enhanced microphones on the market. I had also invested in my own sound system. Before that it was often a case of using bingo microphones and what you sang and how it came out were two completely different things. I bought my system from one of Hull's finest musicians and entertainers. He's still performing today – Johnny Paterson. I recall him letting me have the gear without charging anything on the hire purchase either.

I had also soon learned that the bigger the star you were on the clubland circuit the less 'spots' you do on a night. So I went down from three to two, and then down to one.

Whilst my entertainment career was moving along nicely, my love life was about to become complicated.

Pauline (Jubb) had been my first love, like I said earlier, and we had been great friends. My next girlfriend was the lovely Janice (Brown). Janice has done very well for herself at Hull Royal Infirmary. We had some good times together and she was a really lovely girl and is still in my heart today. I had some beautiful girlfriends. Denise (Santos) was gorgeous too.

It was Susan (Moore) who was the first girl that made me think I ought to be within a relationship, like my mam and dad. I thought it was right, her and me, but in the end I was wrong. This is really important, this part of my story, because it involves Ricky, my son, who means so much to me. I didn't have any contact with him for many years, but in the recent past we have become much closer and I now see him and his family regularly. That has been a real joy.

At the time I thought Susan and I were made for each other. I honestly believed we were going to have more children than just Ricky. At 17 I was enjoying what it feels like to make love to a woman. There's a cheeky side of me that wants to tell you all of the intimate things I wanted to do, but let's keep this a family book where we can – at least for now. Now don't you go skipping any pages!

Susan was beautiful. She was just a year older than me and lived in Cholmley Street, not far from our house. I was always with her. I really respected her because she was the eldest in her family and had brought up the other children, as her mum had left them and her dad was at sea for weeks at a time.

Her father, Tom, was a massive Frank Sinatra fan, so we got on really well when he was back. He was also a very hard working man who spoke a lot of sense.

When Susan said she was pregnant there were three thoughts, if I'm being truly honest, that came into my head. The first was just how lucky I was that I was to be the father of a son or daughter. I thought, that's it I'm straight. Not gay, not bisexual. This is what you do, a bit of singing, come back home to your wonderful wife, although Susan and I were never married.

The second thought was, 'I really don't know who I am'. I didn't know whether I was gay or straight. Then I knew I was gay. Then I knew I was bisexual. I didn't know what was going on with me. Some of that might have had something to do with drinking two bottles of cider every night though. But seriously, at that time I didn't know whether I was Arthur or Martha. It was only years later that I realised I was actually a bit of both!

My third thought, and it probably won't surprise you, was 'what happens to my career now?' But just at that moment none of this seemed to matter because I was so excited about being a father. Susan was growing bigger and bigger and I loved coming home and wrapping my arms around her tummy like any man would. It doesn't matter whether you're gay, bisexual or straight, it's still the same feeling.

Ricky was born on 12 November 1973. I was 18 and in my local pub, Rayners on Hessle Road, at the time. I was there half an hour after Ricky was born though, cradling him in my arms. I felt like Champion the Wonder Horse. It was one of the proudest moments of my life, as it is for any parent. Susan and I were still alright at the time, but that was soon all about to change.

I loved Susan, I really did. She was a very sexy young lady. But she didn't see things the way I did. I think she liked the idea of stardom, but she thought that stardom was more like Diana Ross and the Supremes and the Temptations than me. I could see where she was coming from. It's sometimes hard to imagine that someone you know will be able to reach beyond your own area and become far better known.

I really don't think Susan felt I had any place in all of that. I don't think she ever thought I had that much talent and all of a sudden, now that we had a son, the issue of show business was a problem for her, maybe deep down it had always been a problem for her. I was forever travelling, earning a shilling out of town, but I always knew where I was going.

My dear sister Anne didn't like her because she felt Susan was treating me wrong, she could see her taking me from being an entertainer to being an at-home-all-the-time daddy. I felt it too, but I didn't blame her for it. I think it's only natural for most women to want to get married and have a happy family life. I think that's what Susan really wanted, but I couldn't give her that commitment. I knew it could never be just me, Susan and Ricky. I knew I had to be back on the road, doing what I do best.

When I parted from Susan it wasn't anything to do with falling out with her, or not loving Ricky. I told Susan, and I hope she remembers it this way because even if these are not the exact words it's how I'd like to think I said it. 'It's not that I don't love you. I do love you, but I'm not IN love with you.'

I was headstrong. I was probably thinking more of myself and my career, but I also like to think that I'm a good man. We've all got our faults and I know I've got mine, so I'll never come out and say something was wholly somebody else being wrong. Things aren't that simple. Susan was a woman who needed her man to be with her more than I was ever going to be, that's all. Of course I had all sorts of other things going on in my head too, but that's all it really came down to. We weren't meant for each other after all. We still keep in touch today.

Sometimes there are things that just happen and lovers who just come into your life when you least expect them. For me that was a young man. I can't name him because it just wouldn't be right, even now. And if I gave any clues his family and friends would work it out very easily, so no clues. There was this young man.

How it happened was like this. I was with Susan, living with her in her dad's house, when I met this young man in a local pub. Bang! That was it. I fell in love with him instantly. The trouble is that I do fall in love that way, and with both sexes. I couldn't hide the fact that I was in love with someone else and anyway, I think she knew straightaway. Women do don't they? It's female intuition.

Like I said, I still loved Susan, but I had also fallen in love with this young man. I ended up spending two years with him, but it wasn't sordid. We were just two blokes who got on well together.

I had still hoped to look after Ricky financially with whatever he needed and be with him whenever I could, but I had moved out of Susan's house where we had been living together so that wasn't easy. Ricky was a beautiful baby boy, with blond hair like me, and I was still feeling good about being a father, in fact I've always felt good about that, I've never once wished Susan and I hadn't had Ricky.

Did I feel bad about what was going on? I actually felt quite relieved. At least Susan knew that we weren't going to make it as a couple, because we'd been living under quite a bit of tension as you can imagine. We were getting further and further apart as time went on. My life was with him, or so I thought at the time. So was I gay, or was I bisexual? Do you know? I still didn't know for definite. Yes, of course I had feelings but knowing exactly who you are and what you are is sometimes very confusing. It certainly confuses others!

There was no big announcement anywhere. I didn't advertise anything. That's because I think I always knew I was bisexual, rather than purely gay.

It wasn't as though I hadn't been around girls whilst I was up in the North East, and I certainly wasn't oblivious to the ladies, as many readers will know. Fortunately, I've always been a fairly good looking guy and I have made wonderful love to a number of beautiful women in my life, including a contestant from the Miss Isle of Man contest one time. Maybe that's why I usually sing *To All The Girls I've Loved Before*.

You hear of people losing their minds over working out who they are, trying to understand their sexuality, but none of what happened did anything to my head. I still knew I was a singer, an entertainer first and foremost. That was always there over everything else.

In brief terms, how the move from Susan's house happened went a bit like this, although I'm sorry if I've got any of it wrong if you're reading this Susan:

After Ricky was born I felt that Susan was blanking me. Within six weeks I was on tour, back up in Sunderland and the North East, and both Susan and Ricky were with me. The truth is Susan never wanted to tour and when we came back it was time to move out and I ended up living with two lesbians in a flat as well as my new partner.

My partner (no names, like I said) very rarely came to my gigs, because he wasn't a gig type of person. He was a college boy and liked fast cars. I had a big gold Ford Zephyr at the time, which my mam had bought for me, and it went like a bomb. We had two fantastic years of being great mates. It was wonderful, but then it just frittered out in its own way.

I can't even give his first name because someone in Hull would be bound to work out who he is, and like I said that's not fair. I hope he's still around though.

But that's just the start of the heartaches, break-ups and love affairs! I'm only just getting under way here and thinking back to my past loves from Pauline Jubb onwards is giving me a very pleasant feeling just thinking back to them all! That's because, truthfully, everyone I have ever fallen in love with I am still in love with in some way today.

It wasn't all about falling in love though, some of it was pure, unadulterated lust as you're about to find out next! We'll keep the book right though. I'm not about to turn it into something smutty.

Let's stick with the love life a while longer…

Like I said, when Susan and I parted I had two fantastic years, but they weren't all just with the young man who cannot be named.

I was also seeing Sandra!

What can I say? I was young, virile and Sandra wanted me, and wanted me a lot! She knows she did. Her husband John didn't seem particularly bothered by it. They ran a pub in Hull. Sandra was ****ing gorgeous, extremely sensual, had really firm breasts and boy could she make love! We had some fantastic lovemaking and neither of us could stop. It is one of the best drugs you can ever have when it is like that. Sandra was my dream sexual woman.

Have you ever made love in the daisies?

I have and it's not too uncomfortable. What is more uncomfortable though is when half of your family and friends turn up whilst you're doing it! This has to go down as one of my most embarrassing moments, although I've had a few! TV programmes like *Shameless* are nothing compared to some of the things that have happened in my life!

I used to go diving in the ponds at Brandesburton, which is a little village going towards Bridlington from Hull. I would go there when I was younger, with one of the greatest boxers England ever had – Ricky Beaumont, a really good Hull boxer. No, it wasn't him I was with in the daisies!

I was with Sandra.

It was a beautiful summer's day in what must have been July and we had gone to Brandesburton. We went out for the day to talk about our future together. We used to go round to her mother's place whilst she was out and enjoy ourselves. I'd pick her up from the pub and we'd go straight there. Anyway this particular day was lovely. Brilliant sunshine, everything was right with the world.

Sandra was an absolutely fantastically sexy lady. She was both beautiful and stunning, and she certainly confirmed a lot for me about my manhood. Susan had already confirmed that earlier of course, but Sandra was at me every minute and we had such a good time.

Anyway, back to Brandesburton! It was a beautiful July day. One thing leads to another and we're doing what comes naturally! It certainly did to both of us at any rate. We were making love in the daisies when all of a sudden, a bit like the Battle of the Little Big Horn (no pun intended) the 'injuns' come over the hills and surround Custer on his last stand (again, no pun intended).

The 'injuns' in our case were none other than half my family, popping up from over the hill. I couldn't believe it. Loads of travellers all looking at me and Sandra in all our glory!

Amongst them was 'Knockie' Windass. His son Willie is now married to my beautiful niece Theresa. There are times when you'd prefer it not to be the small world everybody says it is. This was definitely one of those. All of the travellers were saying things like, 'Now then charver ('mate' in Romany) how's it keeping?' Honestly, how can you allow for things like that happening?

You're probably thinking now that I was cheating, by being with two people at the same time. I guess I was in one way, but as I said, my relationship with the young man wasn't the same.

By now you might be wondering just where the career had got to in the midst of all of this sexual activity with Sandra and falling in and out of love. Well I was always busy musically too, continually playing the club scene.

Then another man entered my life when I was 20 – my sound and lighting engineer. We never had a sexual relationship at all. It was purely business and real companionship – we were to be best mates for years and years. For personal reasons I've kept his name out of this book, but he was with me on the road for 17 years and is now married to one of my nieces. They have a lovely family too.

We formed a bond and became great friends, constantly in and out of tricky situations, sharing the laughs and at times the despair that comes with the entertainment game. Throughout our time together I could never once fault him over our friendship.

It was outside the Cholmley Club that I first met up with him. Susan lived directly opposite.

'That didn't sound too good in there,' he said.

I came out with the reply so quickly. 'Tell you what, you do it for me then.'

I didn't muck about in those days and if he was giving his opinion and reckoned he could do better then I was up for it. That was it the die was cast.

We were great working together. He made sure I was okay wherever we went and we were a team. I probably love this man more than most of the people I have ever loved simply as the man he is and because of the times we had together. We spent so much of our lives travelling all around the world over the next 17 years that he probably knows me better than most will ever do.

Now, back to Sandra…

Whilst Sandra and I had gone to Brandesburton to discuss our future we actually went much further than that in the end – and I'm not talking about what happened in the daisies!

At this point, and we're talking around 1974-75, I'd only ever travelled as far as places like Sunderland, Leeds, Barnsley, York, Lincoln and New Holland. Then suddenly everything pointed to Jersey.

You'd better get ready, because if you think things have been getting pretty hot at times up until now they're about to pale into insignificance with some of the stories that took place over there!

But we haven't got there just yet. There's still 'Lock, Stock and Two Smoking Barrels' to tell you about.

First I've got to introduce you to a new character in this book, someone I've not mentioned up until now. His name is Mr B – or at least it is here, for legal reasons. He was one of the finest singers I have ever heard and let me tell you, when you had Joe Longthorne and Mr B together you really did have some night! It was him who really taught me how to sing. By that, I mean he taught me more of the technique of classy singing. He showed me how to use the tools of my trade properly. He was very smart and had a great voice. I worked with him in the clubs several times.

Somehow Sandra had got me an invite to go out to Jersey to meet a man called Jim Lamey who owned five hotels. He also owned all the tugs on the Mersey and he was on the board of the Variety Club of Great Britain.

It was all part of Sandra's plan for us to elope, but for me to go out first and meet Jim. Sandra had said she'd make things work for us. She was managing me at the time too.

Mr B was sick of the woman that was effectively his mother-in-law. He wasn't married but his partner's mother was doing his head in. He'd had enough. We knew it wasn't the right time to go to Jersey in some ways because it was now November, not the main season. But it did give us chance to go around auditioning for Jim's hotels.

At that time you couldn't get summer season bookings in the UK if you were just a clubland act. They wanted big names on the posters, people who had been on TV.

I'd been happy going around and around the clubs for the past four years since *Junior Showtime* had ended for me, working hard, but you can only go round doing the same clubs so many times. It was time for a change, to go somewhere different.

Before we left – and before we get to 'Lock Stock and Two Smoking Barrels' – I had gone into a recording studio for the first time. The first session had been in 1974, with two further sessions in 1975.

Fairview Studios was one of the few recording studios outside of London at the time that was fully equipped. It is still going strong today, run by Keith Herd in Willerby just on the western edge of Hull.

Keith had played the clubs himself in the 60s and 70s but had started earning a really good reputation for his recording of clubland artists, as well as recording some of the best UK singers. At around the same time as I was in recording my first tracks he had Ronnie Hilton recording a single, and country singer Tammy Cline with her Southern Comfort Band.

The Housemartins, Beautiful South, Joe Cocker, rock band Def Leppard and Barbra Dickson have all recorded there too.

The main thing I liked about the studio at Fairview was the atmosphere. Being a fellow musician and singer himself he always looked after every act as if it was his own. The demos we made were well worth it and have never been released up until now. They were my very first recordings in a studio. Dane Morrell was the drummer and I think there was a big lad called Danny who was on the organ/keyboards. I may be wrong but I think his parents had The Brickmakers Arms down Walton Street.

Peter Green played guitar and Steve Powell played keyboards. They all played in a variety of other bands in the 60s and 70s. Peter played in The Telstars, The Sunsets, Hammer and Tomorrow's Topic. Dane was one of the finest drummers I have ever worked with. We used to go to his house and he wouldn't have your typical drummers' favourite tracks on the stereo, he'd have Sammy Davis, Frank, Dizzy Gillespie and Judy Garland. Steve Powell wrote and arranged some of the songs we recorded, one of those was *Can't Get Enough*.

My first ever recording was a song called *My Life Is Just Like A Symphony* which was written by a local man called Gary Nicholson.

Keith was so conscientious with his record keeping that he has recently sent me the tracks I recorded. My first session in 1974 saw me record two demos: *The Way We Were* which both Barbara Streisand, and later Gladys Knight had hits with; and *My Life Is Just Like A Symphony*. The second session brought about four songs: *Hurt* which I still sing today, the Timi Yuro classic; *Crying in the Rain* which Keith tells me came from a demo by a chap called Vince Everitt in the North East; a song called *You You You* also written by Gary Nicholson, not the Alvin Stardust song of the same name; and a fully worked up version of *My Life Is Just Like A Symphony*.

I have recently spoken with Gary for the first time in years. He is still writing songs, still lives in Hull and one of his songs is just about to be used in a promotion on American television. When I heard the song *My Life Is Just Like A Symphony* whilst writing this book it struck me just what a brilliant song it would be for the young man who has just won the latest X-Factor, Joe McElderry. It probably needs a bit of work on it to bring it up to today's production values but maybe I should give Simon Cowell a call.

My final session was on 4 November 1975. It must have been just before we were heading for the plane to Jersey. It included my version of Gilbert O'Sullivan's Number One *Get Down*, and on reflection sounds to me like we did it a bit fast; plus the song I've already mentioned called *Can't Get Enough* which wasn't the hit by rock group Bad Company that was released around the same time and actually has a bit of a Wham/George Michael feel to it; and *Until It's Time For You To Go* which was written by Buffy St Marie and recorded by both Willie Nelson and Elvis.

Keith recalls that I also helped out with financing a recording by a local duo, Ruth and the Rudens who sang *Crazy* and *Good Love's Gonna Go Bad*. Keith also remembers a row of 'scary' ladies who just sat and stared whilst I was recording. I think that must have been my mam, Lizzie and Anne. Scary indeed? It was the beautiful ladies of the family. Formidable may have been a better way to describe them, Keith.

The date of the last of these recordings is just at the time Mr B and I were about to go to Jersey, so it's likely I was using them as demos for future gigs on the island and elsewhere.

Are you ready now for 'Lock Stock and Two Smoking Barrels'? You are? Here we go. We are heading for Mr B time!

I had my bright orange Granada Ghia with the Everflex top, and I'm looking like I'm a big time Charlie. I picked up Mr B, who said the one thing he wanted to do before he left was a little bit of business. Well I didn't think any more of it, I just thought he was joking and that we had to go round before we set off. Little did I know just how much he meant what he was saying.

Mr B got me into a lot of trouble in Jersey, but maybe I should have known he was a bit dodgy based on what took place next before we'd even set off from the tarmac.

We're on the Orchard Park Estate in Hull, only a short distance from his mother-in-law's place. Everything is going fine, we're chatting away about Jersey, when suddenly ... and legally I can't tell you what happened next except for the fact that I'm driving the 'screeve' (Romany for 'car') and I'm saying 'Do me a favour'. I sound like the late Mike Reid from when he was in Eastenders, or Bob Hoskins in any film he's ever been in.

'Just drive around the block', he says.

I'm thinking more about getting to Leeds/Bradford Airport, as well as hopefully living for at least a short while longer since I now have what appears to be a man with a vendetta alongside me. Then, as we go around the block I can't believe what's happening. He's only forgotten to wind the window down and our car window is shattered. There's glass everywhere, lights going on everywhere… Jersey here we come!

> *Yes, we're different – worlds apart, we're not the same*
> *We laughed and played, at the start like in a game*

Joe Longthorne *Until It's Time For You To Go* recorded 1975

I'd never really been anywhere until I went to Jersey. The nearest I'd been to going abroad had been sailing on the Tattersall Castle ferry across the Humber.

The only thing I seem to recall about Jersey was that I think my Aunt June got married there.

When I got on the plane for my first ever flight all I was thinking about was whether we were going to stay up in the air. I was frightened to death. I seem to remember it was a Viscount, a turboprop, which had four propellers. I've flown a lot since then and I like jets, but I always make a point of getting into something that has at least two engines.

We caught an early morning flight and it was ****ing freezing when we got there. It was late Autumn and way before Bergerac became the most famous name on the island.

If Sunderland and Hull had been my clubland version of a school education, Jersey was about to be my cabaret version of a college education. It also brought me into contact with some of my greatest pals in the business for the first time – and, just to complicate matters further, it was also to be the place where I met yet another new love!

But before we go there let's set the record straight about an issue that has kept coming up over the years. Then we'll start on Jersey.

CHAPTER SIX

RICKY

If a man could be two places at one time,
I'd be with you.
Tomorrow and today,
beside you all the way.

Joe Longthorne *If* released 2008

About Ricky.

There have been a lot of rumours going around for a long, long time questioning whether I am Ricky's father or not. I have always believed I am his dad. Susan and I certainly made love many times. I was there when he was born, I loved Susan and we had some wonderful moments. But there are always rumours and when they come back each time you find yourself asking those same questions again and again.

What I can say is that whether I am Ricky's real father or not I have always taken my responsibilities very seriously. I call him my son and he has had everything he could ever want, even if for a number of years he didn't want to see me or get to know me. I've helped him along the way. I gave him his first trials bike as a present when he was 12 years old. I followed him in my yellow Roller as he rode it through the woods.

I suppose there are always going to be doubts as long as rumours persist and unless we get to doing one of those tests, which I refuse to do, I suppose we'll never find out for certain, biologically.

My point is what good would a test do now? Isn't it better that he's my son rather than opening up a can of worms if he isn't? I think it's the right thing and I know I've always loved him right from the start when I cradled him in my arms at the maternity hospital. No-one wants to give anyone any unnecessary heartache surely? I know I don't and I'm happy with the way things are.

Susan and I did split up for a short while and it could have been around the time of conception, that's the honest truth – and that's why there is some conjecture over Ricky's parentage.

Ricky's really happy with his lovely wife Alexandra. They have a son, Dominic, and a daughter, Megan. He also has another daughter, Chelsea, who I haven't seen for years. She will be about 19 now. He had Chelsea with another woman. So I've three grandchildren. Why would I want to have a test to find out that I'm not his father when I'm really happy being his dad?

There was a time when Ricky sold a story to a national newspaper about the doubt and the rumours. I was disappointed. I thought he'd let me down and that he had also made things embarrassing for Susan. I never mentioned a word to any newspaper or any form of media. This is the most I have ever said publicly about it. No-one gets me on the phone before coming through James or Chris (my PA). In fact this is as far as I have gone at any time in talking about it, because this is how I really feel and I wanted it to be clear here.

Ricky was very forward about why he went to the papers, which I think was champion really. He told me, 'Dad, I just needed the money.' He was going through some tough times and he saw it as easy money. Like I said I was disappointed, but Ricky knows he has always been and always will be a big part of my life. He's got a beautiful family and we make a point of seeing each other. They come over to Blackpool and I see them when I'm in Hull. My grandchildren Dominic and Megan are lovely adorable children. As I keep saying, no matter what has happened to me along the way, I'm actually a very lucky man.

There, that's it. You've got it straight from me now. It's quite therapeutic writing your own life story, you know. Let's try some more. Let's fly, pack up let's fly away… to Jersey!

CHAPTER SEVEN

JERSEY

Feelings, nothing more than feelings
Trying to forget my feelings of love

Joe Longthorne *Feelings* released 1977

Rupert the Bear, Pancho Villa, a massive fake lottery win, living in a shed for months, detectives running all over the place - these were just some of the acts and bizarre moments I experienced on the beautiful, wonderful island of Jersey. Although I didn't know it at the time, this was to be pretty much my second home for the next five years.

Jersey was where I really learned my craft, because up until then I had been performing, but not watching how others performed. On Jersey I got to see some very talented entertainers, people who have gone on to do big things in the business, like my dear friends Cannon and Ball. Bobby (Ball) produced my summer shows in Blackpool last year (2009) and he regularly pops round for a cuppa and a chat. His sons The Harper Brothers are an impressive double act in their own right and were part of that show.

It was also whilst I was in Jersey that I tried out for the TV talent show *New Faces*, failing miserably, and then, the one that gave me my first real break as a professional singer and entertainer, *Search for a Star*.

When Mr B and I had first arrived in Jersey we headed straight for the Woodlands Hotel. It was one of Jim Lamey's string of holiday establishments. Jim has since passed away but I'll tell you this: the top three men I have most respected in my life are my dad, he's number one; my brother-in-law Abdul, who we haven't got to yet, but he's on the way; and Jim. If you hear me mention them several times in my life story I make no apologies for doing so. All three were, and still are, so important to me even though all three are no longer with us. All three have made such an indelible impression on my life and I really wouldn't be anything like I am today without them. I thank the Lord for the time I had with them and I can feel the tears welling up in my eyes as I speak about them in this way even now.

Jim was one of the finest, most wonderful, likeable and courteous men I have ever met. I'm sure anyone who ever met him would say the same. Jim was always immaculately dressed wherever he went and never once treated me less than wonderfully well.

I remember getting up and singing for about 150 of his people, so it wasn't an audition where you're singing to just one or two.

Jim seemed to take a shine to me straightaway and said he would use me, but he didn't just leave it there, he also put me on to Maurice Segal who ran the Modern Hotels Group, which was made up of a huge chain of hotels.

Maurice was also hugely instrumental in the building of the great Fort Regent complex, Jersey's largest and most fantastic conference and leisure centre at Mount Bingham in St Helier. It was originally the site of a Napoleonic fortress, which is why it is named the way it is today. The views from there are tremendous.

I played there regularly throughout my time on Jersey – often with Rupert the Bear, maybe he should have been renamed Rupert the Bear who was fond of his drink. More of him soon.

At first though, because it was out of season, I just seemed to be singing to Germans all the time. It was coming up towards Christmas and Jim had put me on at the Woodlands. Mr B was with me as well so we put on some show! But he then went off to be in a band, one of the show bands like the Barron Knights or Black Abbots, something like that.

Once I'd got sorted with the hotel bookings I went back over to Hull to tell Sandra that I'd landed a job or two in Jersey, and that her contacts had come good. I told her that I'd got the summer season sorted out, through Jim, to play at Maurice Segal's hotels.

We'd talked about eloping before I'd left for Jersey the first time with Mr B. At least that's what we were meant to talk about at Brandesburton that day when we had been interrupted by half the travelling clan!

Sandra was ready to come with me. After all, since she was managing me, it was she who had told me it was time I left Hull, and that I needed to move to get anywhere in the business. She just said, 'I'm coming with you'.

What happened next was not quite what I'd expected though, and it caused quite a bit of bad blood with not just John, Sandra's husband, but also another man, who just happened to be in the local constabulary back home. In fact he wasn't just any policeman either, it turned out he was one of the top men in the Humberside Police Force!

It wasn't the best laid out plan in the world looking back, but Sandra really was a very sensual woman, like I said earlier, and well, when you've got that kind of attention from someone like her what was I to do? I'm only flesh and blood.

I left Hull to go to Jersey for the second time. This time it wasn't dramatic in the sense of shotgun fire as we left, but it might as well have been for the impact it made back home.

You see I didn't go with just one beautiful, gorgeous, incredibly sexy woman, but two! Sandra had brought her friend, another sexy lady and we all eloped together. You couldn't make it up could you?

The big problem with it all was that her friend just happened to be married to this top dick detective! I know it doesn't sound like the brightest career move I've ever made, but I was just living for the moment. To me it wasn't a problem, it was Sandra who I wanted, and she wanted me, and we wanted each other constantly!

Having got back to Jersey, that's me, Sandra and the top dick detective's wife we booked into the Woodlands, one of Jim's hotels.

At first everything was okay but back home, perhaps not surprisingly given the circumstances - his wife having run off with an entertainer – John was not happy back in Hull. I'd been told he'd gone barmy. Also, it turned out nobody had told the cop, whatever role he was in the force, where his wife had gone, so after a couple of weeks they both went back. Sandra went back to sort the pub out. Then she was due to come back over to Jersey once that had been done. The wife of the copper went back and I never heard from her again.

Sandra did come back, but by that time I'd met Rita, Jim Lamey's daughter and my next true love. We're now into the early part of 1976. It's not the summer season yet, which I'm looking forward to. I'm playing at the Woodlands Hotel.

Rita came down the staircase. I was singing Morris Albert's *Feelings* which was really big at the time. I was playing the piano in the reception area. Rita and I got eye-to-eye very quickly and we really hit it off together. She was always a wonderful, warm and compelling woman – and I'm sure she still is even though we haven't seen each other for a long time now.

When I met Rita it was to be the start of a relationship that would last well over 20 years, the longest relationship I've ever had with a woman. Rita was with me through all of my TV years, she ran my fan club too, and she ran it majestically, but there was so much more to her than that. She believed in me, she talked with me properly. It felt so good. I felt so very comfortable with her.

Feelings was also my first ever single release. It was backed with *This Ol' Heart Of Mine* and *The Way We Were* and it was released whilst I was on Jersey in 1977. It went out on the Arny's Shack Records label. I had recorded it at Tony Arnold's garage studio in Blandford, near Bournemouth and it was distributed by Pye Records. I am grateful to Christine Whitnall, one of my many extremely long serving fans, for that information.

But let's get back to Rita. Talent, whatever talent you have, is always a hook for bringing people closer to you and I don't just mean my talent. Rita was a very talented and very knowledgeable lady and I loved her dearly. I'm still in love with her now. If I say I loved her brain don't get the idea I didn't love her sexually as well, because I did. We had an extremely intense and passionate relationship. I think she knows I still love her, I certainly hope she does. Rita, if you're reading this I really do mean every word. You continue to be a part of my life even now.

Rita was and still is a wonderful woman. She wasn't after anything from me.

Susan had wanted a family man, Sandra had wanted raging sex, others had wanted me just because I was a singer. None of those are bad reasons at all but it was good to have a girlfriend who was interested just in me as a person, someone who wanted to get to know me properly for who I was and who I am.

She wanted me for being me – and she wanted to help me in any way she could. Rita was what I have always loved in a woman - intelligence, regard and love-making, of course. She also taught me how to be as eloquent as I could be. I had a lovely time with Rita in the 1980s and throughout most of the 1990s too. I will love her until the day I die. She made me feel like a man, a complete man.

Both Rita and her father Jim were so significant in me getting on career-wise and I can never thank them enough. You'll hear that line a few times in this book too. One thing I have learned along the way is it is always important to thank those who help you. I'm not one of those who just thinks everything is down to me.

Like I said earlier, this is not meant to be a 'me-me-me' book even though I know it's my autobiography. So many people have touched my life for the better. Forget about those who have touched it for the worse, they're not important. The people who have helped me along the way deserve the very best from me. They are the ones who it is important I mention in this book.

I know some people might think that the only reason I got on with Rita was because she was a multi-millionaire's daughter, but it wasn't like that at all. She had charm, intelligence and I found her exciting. We didn't just jump into bed together. We courted. We laughed together, we enjoyed each other's company. I liked all of that.

Rita spoke nine languages and had been educated at the Sorbonne. Me? I was just a lad who didn't understand reading or writing in English very much, let alone all the other languages. Her head, her brain turned me on completely.

I had to go back to Hull before the summer season started in Jersey, because I needed to honour a few verbal agreements to play back there.

Over the past 40 years I might have had to cancel shows from time to time for a variety of reasons, mostly down to my health situation, but wherever I have been able I have always tried my best to fulfil what is on the schedule. That's why I went back from time to time. I don't like letting people down so I always try to fit everything in.

Sandra went back as well, this time for good. We had finished. She had things that needed sorting out back at home. I don't know what she's doing now but I think she still lives in Hull. She will still be a stunner, of that I have no doubt. She was certainly all woman! The last I heard she had split up from John. He now lives in Perth, Australia and came to see me in concert at the Burswood Casino.

Sandra was more than just a vivacious, sensual woman though. It was thanks to her that I got to Jersey, and it was her approach to Jim that set the ball rolling for me further afield than the clubland circuit of Yorkshire and the North East. So I've a lot to be grateful for from Sandra. So again, if you're reading this Sandra, I do hope it gives you the same tingle thinking about those times 35 years ago. It's such a long while now isn't it? But I still think good thoughts about when we were making love. Sandra put me in what turned out to be the right place at the right time. The only thing she might not have counted on though was my relationship with Rita.

In show business the press is always interested in stories about entertainers and I don't know whether Sandra went to the newspapers about me or they approached her, so it would be wrong to jump to conclusions but a story was published. What I can tell you though is that far from being annoyed with what had been printed, I was more than happy with the way Sandra's story came out in the press. In fact it wasn't bad for my reputation at all. She was telling everyone I was like a stallion. There really is some truth in any type of publicity working for you. Who knows? Maybe Sandra was still managing and promoting me with that story. It certainly worked out that way.

My sound and lighting man, but most importantly my good friend too, hadn't come over with me at the start.

I had asked him to fly out with me when I first went to Jersey with Mr B, but he'd said no. When I'd got the bookings I contacted him again, telling him I needed him. Good sound and lighting men are hard to find, but I needed a good mate too, someone I could rely on during the performances. All I said was that Jim had got me the shows and that if he wanted to come over I'd meet him on the tarmac at the airport the following day. I left it up to him. The tickets were there. He came and he ended up being my light and sound man, as well as the perfect friend and all-round good mate. His friendship and our working relationship has always meant so much to me. I think of him every day too, of the scrapes we got into, and how together we made it from me being a clubland act to hosting our own TV shows. He was with me every step of the way throughout that time.

He had such a good ear. I know that's what you'd probably expect from someone whose job was to make sure that the sound was right, but he really did know what was what. I once asked him how he did it, how he always got it right, and he said, 'I just listen.' He did everything. He put the equipment up, he roadied, he was the one person I could always talk to before and after the gigs. He would always tell me straight about anything. We used to travel all over Jersey doing shows at different hotels on the island.

Paddy was my road manager, I think he now looks after a theatre in Tunbridge Wells. He drove us everywhere in this Volkswagen van – me, my sound and lights man, the organist, the drummer and the dancers called Rusty and Nova. We were doing three shows a day on the island to audiences of French, German and British people. We would do about two hours at each hotel.

It certainly wasn't the glamorous lifestyle that people might think who aren't in the business, but Jersey really did give me a fantastic showbiz education. I found out the difference between performing in clubs, hotels and theatres, what skills were needed for each, how different audiences reacted, and I got changed in more kitchens than Gordon Ramsay has ever sworn in.

I learned about audiences, especially audiences that were a little bit more on the posh side. For those I was singing more as after-dinner entertainment and finding out what they liked. They wanted to laugh not just listen to a singer, so my comedy routines became bigger. They wanted more of a 'Las Vegas' feel to their holidays, so I gave them that too. I also found that certain songs and parts of the act were now becoming more permanent. My 'Shirley Bassey' stayed, as it has always done to this day. I can't imagine a time when I won't be asked for it. But I was expanding my routine all the time with even more singers.

One of the changes that I eventually made to the act was that I had originally dragged up for the female singing impressions – wigs, dresses, the lot. I had then moved on to purely using wigs. By the time I'd finished on Jersey I wasn't doing Shirley other than as an impression, with no props at all.

That's the way it's always been since then. Tom (Jones) stayed, as he has always done too, as well as Frank (Sinatra) and Willie Nelson. I was doing Timi Yuro at the time as well, and still do her *Hurt* today. *For Once In My Life* – the Sinatra version was in there too. But I was adding other hit songs of that time as well, it wasn't all about the big ballad singers.

I also learned a little more about how entertainers were treated by people who weren't as gentlemanly as Mr Jim Lamey. We're talking accommodation here.

My first impression of where we were to be put up didn't seem at all bad, but I was quickly to find out just how wrong a first impression can be.

Dick Wray was the 'guvnor' of the island's entertainment scene and I was on £100 a week with him. He had a lot of property in Jersey and he owned the Opera House. He had venues throughout the island.

Working for him was Dave Marshall who picked us up from the airport and take us to where Dick had arranged for us to stay. The idea was that it would be cheaper than staying in one of the hotels.

It all felt good to start with. Dave picked us up in this big white Jag. He took us to this big house and we both thought that it would do us fine. We thought we'd fallen on our feet. What we didn't know was that he was going to walk us right through the big house, take us out of the big back door and then tell us about our humble lodgings. Actually the word 'digs' is used to describe where performers stay when on tour. Never would it be a more accurate word than now – we were to live in a shed! So these 'digs' even included the spades.

'That's yours', he pointed at this hut for us both. We couldn't believe it. We just looked at each other in amazement. So I was on £100 a week for Dick Wray and we got £16 knocked off the rent for cutting the garden and clearing the trash. I know I come from a travellers' background, but a shed? It wasn't my idea of accommodation. The thing is we couldn't afford to lay out £38 a week to continue staying in Holden Hotel in St Saviour's. At least I knew that much about money.

So here I am, supposedly the star of the show with a wonderful little band and some beautiful girl dancers - and I'm living in a shed in someone's backyard of a beautiful Victorian house in Beach Road, alongside a row of dustbins and expected to do the gardening.

Fortunately 1976 was the hottest year on record and we had a fantastic summer. We stayed in the shed for about a year and then a Portugese man called Clem Freer took me on, and away from Dick Wray. We moved into far better accommodation and I worked for Clem and his wife Ann at a place called El Rancho.

That's not to say the accommodation was brilliant. One night when I was on the toilet I saw a rat walk between my feet and was quickly followed by a whole army of them. Sound and light man, Rita and I were all stopping in this place with three great dancers called Charade, but this was no charade, the rats were for real.

I was performing at El Rancho in 1977 when Elvis died. I had never really sung Elvis songs as impressions. I had just sung them as me, singing songs like: *The Wonder Of You* and *Always On My Mind*. Today I sometimes sing *American Trilogy* with my collar hitched up out of respect to the great man, and one of my own personal favourites, which has also become a favourite with many of my fans is *Mary in the Morning*.

Before we left the shed we had a bit of fun at Dave Marshall's expense though. We doctored the aerial for his television in the big house he had tempted us with before showing us the shed, so we kept changing the channels he was watching. That messed with his head a bit. We saw him getting madder and madder inside the house as he tried to watch one programme only to find seconds later that his television had automatically switched channels!

The best moments came when he would be watching a football match. We would try to make sure that if it looked like there might be a goal, he would suddenly be watching something like Panorama. One day, just before we left, a guy came to fix it for him and told him someone had sabotaged it. I think it cost him quite a bit to have it fixed. I don't believe in people just getting away with things, and he had been a bit of a naughty lad to us by tempting us in the first place, but we did him in the end.

Dave Marshall really upset me when he told me that, with our travelling show, I would top the bill one week and then someone else would top it the next week. It was just a way of giving everyone top billing and making sure the show looked different every week, but I wasn't having it. We had me, Pancho, the girls and Welsh comedian Bryn Phillips touring around the island.

'Pancho 'b***ard' Villa above me on the billing?' that's what I said. All Dave would say was that the others had to top the bill sometime. I said, 'do they?'

Funnily enough I have met Dave since and we now get on well.

When I'd been appearing in Hull, just before going over to Jersey, I'd got up to about £15-£20 a night and I'd played every night there was available. Over here I was working harder than ever for probably the same amount of money in the end, but to me it wasn't about the money, it never has been.

Sure I've enjoyed the money I've had along the way, but that's not what thrills me. It really isn't. The audience, my fans, they are what give me the thrill. Just walking out on to that stage every night and hearing the applause, then delivering the best performance I'm capable of. That's the adrenalin rush I get.

Before I gave up with the costumes I used to get dressed up as Cleo Laine, Dorothy Squires, Barbra Streisand and Shirley, as well as plenty of other famous singers, including Demis Roussos. I looked fabulous, or at least I thought I did, but there was one time when Rita and I saw a poster of me that made me look like a docker trying to be a drag queen. When we saw it we immediately went all around the island and ripped down every poster. That was the start of me getting rid of the dressing up, the dragging up. I knew by now that I didn't need it. But before I got rid of the props and the dresses there was to be an incident that helped my decision quite a bit.

I think it's time to introduce Rupert and Pancho properly here...

Rupert the Bear liked his drink a little too much in my opinion. I still don't know who he really was to this day but he was dressed like the character and his act always started with him singing 'I'm Ru-u-pert, Rupert the Bear, everyone knows my name.' During one performance at the Fort Regent, just before he was to go on, he stunk of brandy. It wasn't the first time I'd seen him in that state, but on this occasion he was far worse than normal and he was in a pretty bad way. He could hardly stand.

I was just about to say, 'Roope, you can't go on like that,' when he lost his balance completely and fell the whole length of the stairs. Rupert became a bit of a fall-guy after that. He even got in the way one night when I was in a bit of a temper about something and ended up falling down the full length again. Maybe it was part of his act in the end.

Whilst Rupert may have been fond of the tipple, Pancho Villa was an absolute imposter! He always over-ran, which is criminal in the entertainment world when you're in the early part of the show – and he sang too, because he thought he was an all-rounder. He wasn't. That was criminal as well. He was a comic, and actually he was a pretty good comedian, but singer? No way. He also pinched my material. We all do it a bit, we hear something somewhere and then incorporate it if we think it fits for us and we can do it. But he wouldn't toe the line at all.

But what really topped it for me one night was when I was waiting for Pancho to come off stage.

He's over-run, yet again, something I've never done when there are other acts which have yet to come on. It just messes up everyone's timing. If an act over-runs it is really stealing the time off another performer.

I know my act isn't going to work now. I'm dressed up in the full kit as Demis Roussos and I need the smoke machine to blast out fog as I sing *Happy Together On An Island In The Sun*. It's supposed to be all about welcoming the audience to Jersey. But his act has gone well, so he's chosen to stay on, which isn't fair to your fellow professionals like I said. He's nicked my time. Not only has he done that but the fog machine has now blurted out liquid on to the stage, which fog machines used to do. It's something to do with the time at which it was plugged in, to the time of me going on stage. Things are starting to gang up against me and I'm already thinking, 'Panch, I'm going to kill you for this'.

I go on stage, full Demis Roussos outfit, flowing robe, wig, the lot. My feet go one way, my arms another, the wig flies off, I split the outfit and I go down, arse over tit. The audience are laughing, but not the way I'd intended and I know I've got to go back and sing sentimental stuff like *Danny Boy* and finish as Shirley yet, when all I want to do is get hold of Pancho and wring is ****ing neck!

We're at the Lido de France in St Helier.

There are probably still people around who remember it. I'm sure many of them will think it was hilarious – and probably one or two who think it was all part of the act. But it wasn't. I'm not some kind of slapstick, knock me down and I get up again, kind of performer.

The producer had told me before the show that he wanted me in drag for Bassey, with 20 minutes at the end to appear as myself. But when I went down I remembered there was a thing in the programme that said 'this show could be changed at any time'. It's a thing that all production companies put in just so that people can't claim their money back by saying that what they have seen was not as it appeared in the programme.

I used that line myself and changed my show, right there and then. I changed the whole show, the props and costumes were thrown out and I went on as me. I still did the impressions but without the props apart from one or two incidental ones like caps and wigs and I went on to win the Best Top of the Bill award in Jersey that year, so it was the right decision.

That didn't alter what I felt about what Pancho had done to me though, and after the show I had some seriously unfinished business. I finished the act, went straight to Pancho's dressing room and knocked him clean out. Bash! My sound and light man was as mad as I was about what had happened. It had screwed up all of his lighting arrangements. We both took care of Pancho that night and he never ran over his time again.

I'd been doing drag in the first couple of years on Jersey in 1975 and 1976. It was camp and I enjoyed doing it, but I also felt that maybe it showed me trying to hide away from who I was. In the end I just realised that I could impersonate everyone without the need for props apart from the little ones I use occasionally today. A hat for Steptoe, but the rest of the time I either just move my hair a bit, for Ken Dodd; my sleeves, for Barry Manilow; my collar, for Elvis; and slip my jacket off my shoulders, for Shirley.

Maybe Pancho did me a favour in a roundabout kind of way, but he's one person I'm determined not to give any credit to. It still irritates me now that I'm thinking about it again. I have pride in what I do on stage, but that night he just made me look stupid.

I rescued the act of course, and the night was still a success, but no thanks to Pancho. So wherever you are Pancho, I hope you are not over-running today.

There were some tremendous acts appearing in Jersey during the time I was there. It was an era when a lot of the talent that was to appear on television in the coming years all seemed to be on this one wonderful island. One of those great performers was Dustin Gee, who came from York originally and was a fabulously talented man. He worked with Russ Abbott for many years and formed a great TV partnership with Les Dennis.

Dustin died tragically early, of a heart attack, when he was just 43 in 1986. He was a brilliant impersonator and he dragged up too. I remember when Cannon and Ball first came over and Dustin was top of the bill at the time. There was some pressure from the agents and managers to get Dustin out. I don't quite know why because Cannon and Ball were just an up and coming act and Dustin was already established.

Around that time, from what I can recall, Dustin's boyfriend jumped through a window. Dustin went mad, and then I believe what happened was that the cops found some marijuana in Dustin's dressing room. That was it for Dustin. His time on Jersey was over and he was banished from the island.

Cannon and Ball were top of the bill at Behan's the next day. They deserved it because this was their time. They were on the brink of making it really big and they were murdering him on stage. It was real dog-eat-dog for billing at that time and the competition was great, because all of the headlining acts were quality performers.

One of the best and funniest acts on the Jersey scene at the time was The Grumbleweeds. I would go and see them and learned from their stagecraft. They were a great show group. Graham Walker and Robin Colvill are still going strong today. Maurice appeared with me again just recently but Carl and Albert gave up a while ago. Tony Jo, who I know very well in Blackpool these days was with them at one time too.

Yes, alright, I was a script-nicker as well. We all were. We all took bits that we thought would work in our acts and I took a few lines from the Grumbleweeds. They were a great set of lads, I went go-karting with them sometimes.

Mr B was still around too. With his voice he could never be ignored – and he really was one of those larger than life characters. I hadn't seen him for a while, but with Mr B you never knew what would happen next. One day though, whilst we were still living in the shed he turned up in this big flash Merc. He was excited and pretty pleased with himself. We had always got on well together.

'I want you. Get in the car!'

I got in. He was in such good form. You couldn't not do what he said when he was like this.

'I've only won the ****ing lot haven't I? I've won the Pools!'

At first I couldn't believe it. 'You've what? Well, good luck to you.'

He said: 'I'll get you some new kit, some new clothes. Come on.'

So he took me to the most expensive shop he could find in St Helier and bought me three amazingly expensive outfits. Shoes, shirts, trousers, ties, he didn't skimp at all, and we bought the lot. I asked him why he was doing it for me and he just said he'd won it and wanted to share it. What's more, he reckoned I deserved it, probably for bringing him to Jersey in the first place. He took me back to the shed and off he went happy as Larry.

Next thing I know is that I'm back home in the shed. There's a knock on the door. It's Detective Sergeant Charles Quinn. Well it was too early for it to be Jim Bergerac wasn't it. He wasn't invented then. He first appeared in 1981, by which time my Jersey experience was over.

What I quickly found out was that Mr B's 'Pools win' wasn't all it had appeared. Don't ask me how he got the money. Why he then came along and bought me what he did I'll never know. It was still good of him to look after me, but with the police coming around he had also put me under a lot of unnecessary pressure.

Charlie Quinn, who I went on to be really good friends with, gave me a hard time at the start. He looked in my wardrobe and saw all the brand new clothing. Boss stuff, shoes, shirts. He knew I didn't have the money for all that kind of gear. He'd seen my shows with his wife and I knew she really liked me. I told him 'Sergeant Quinn, as sure as I am standing right in front of you now, I do not know anything. I'm just a singer. I'm busy singing, performing. All I can tell you is what he told me, that he'd won the Pools.' Like I said, Charlie liked me and he told me he wouldn't take the clothes in as evidence, so all the stuff Mr B got me stayed with me. Maybe Mr B was a modern day Robin Hood looking after the modern day minstrel like me.

The last time I heard from Mr B was about 17 years ago when I was playing eight weeks of cabaret in London. He phoned me, out of the blue, said he was calling from Stockport. He wasn't doing too well. I said that from what I had gathered he had upset a few people back in Jersey and he hadn't done me too much good with the police – even though I had a new wardrobe out of it. He apologised – and put the phone down.

Within a minute there's a knock on the door and in walks the man himself. I said that I thought he had told me he was in Stockport a minute ago. He just said he had to be very careful wherever he said he was. I'm certain there were people after him, but knowing him it could have been anybody – even his mother-in-law. I've never seen him again, but I still love him as a singer. He was a great singer. What a waste of talent.

There were some even stranger characters on the island. One was Ian Parker, heir to the famous Parker pens fortune. I worked for him for a while in one of his hotels – the Hotel De France. I think he'd been sent out to Jersey and been given millions of pounds to spend out there just to keep him occupied. I always thought he was quite eccentric for someone who was hosting entertainment in a hotel. It didn't matter which act was on in his venue, he used to say everything was too loud. One night I went on stage only to find he'd cut all the microphone cables!

My five years on Jersey wasn't continuous, by that I mean that I didn't just stay there throughout that time. We would be on the island for six months then we would come back for me to play the clubs back in places like Hull, Sunderland, Sheffield and Barnsley. Anne would come over to Jersey quite frequently and so would mam, but dad never came. He wouldn't fly, but I still saw him every time I was back in Hull.

I will always be grateful for what Jersey gave me. It transformed me from being purely a clubland entertainer to a much more rounded performer. I had seen different acts, fabulous other singers and comedians and I had learned much more about my own performance. I had also learned so much from Rita, as well as having a wonderful time with her.

The people on the island didn't want me to leave. They invited me to take up residency there, which was very flattering. Along with cabaret singer Stuart Gillies and actor John Nettles there are few others who can say that. But the time had come for me to make a choice.

Did I stay on Jersey or did I go elsewhere? I chose to go. It would be a decision that would eventually see me team up with one of the biggest family entertainment acts around, and saw me hook up with the manager and promoter who looked after me better than any other.

But they didn't come along just yet.

There were a few years to go before all of that started. First there was a little matter of a TV programme that would launch my broadcasting career and lead on to so many good things.

You see Sandra really did set me on my way, because if I hadn't gone to Jersey I would never have had a man called David Bell come to see me. David was a TV producer. He was working on the TV programme *Search for a Star* at the time. I had already failed two auditions for the popular ITV show *New Faces* whilst on the island, plus one for another programme called *Starburst*. Add those to several auditions with Hughie Green for *Opportunity Knocks,* which I had whilst back home as a teenager and you can see why I wasn't particularly taken with auditioning. All I wanted was for people to come and see me in concert, doing what I did every day and every night. Funnily enough, that's exactly the way it happened with David.

But let's hold it right there.

After all, following all that activity on Jersey you're probably not quite ready for when the breaks started going bang, bang, bang! So let's take another time out in the story. It's about time you recharged your glass isn't it?

You know I don't look myself but I understand a regular feature on the various websites and Facebook sites about me is which songs are people's favourites. I thought that here would be the perfect place to tell you about some of the songs I sing, why I sing them and what they mean to me.

CHAPTER EIGHT

SONGS

Nothing's quite as pretty – as Mary in the morning
When through the sleepy haze I see her lying there
Soft as the rain, that falls on summer flowers
Warm as the sunlight shining on her golden hair...

Joe Longthorne *Mary in the Morning* released 1999

Mary In The Morning has been a part of my show for many years now. I cry when I listen to Elvis doing it. There are two Elvis versions and I particularly like the one where he cries when he's singing it. He has a big towel around his neck and it was recorded in his house.

I don't know how many people notice, but I sing it slightly differently every time. I love it. It's such a passionate song. When I sing, 'I want to kiss her face so softly..' I'm actually thinking I want to kiss her on every part of her body whoever it is I'm thinking about. And I am talking female here, let there be no doubt at all.

The amount of emotion Elvis gives to the song comes out far, far greater than anything I have ever heard or seen. I feel the emotion too when I sing it. I think that's why my fans always want me to do it.

My top three songs I have sung over the years, just at the moment, would be *When You're Smiling*, *Smile* and *Cycles*.

When You're Smiling is such an obvious choice for me because it sums up everything about entertainment. It's a song I've sung from being very young and it is one that everyone knows and enjoys. It was also first made famous by Asa Joelson (Al Jolson) who was one of my first ever impressions.

Smile fits into a similar vein. But what I would like to know is how could Charlie Chaplin be so gifted as to write a song like that as well as be the world's greatest clown? He could do no wrong at all in my eyes. You know just how good a song is when so many artists have covered it over the years. Nat King Cole, Frank Sinatra, Diana Ross and Hull's own David Whitfield to name but four, have all recorded it and I also put it on my studio album in 2008. It's a beautiful song and the lyrics are particularly poignant for anyone who is ever going through any heartache.

Life is like the seasons, after winter comes the spring
So I'll keep this smile awhile and see what tomorrow brings
I've been told and I do believe – that life is meant for living
And even when the chips are low there's still some left for the giving…

Joe Longthorne *Cycles* released 2008

Cycles is one of my all-time favourite songs from Frank Sinatra and was written by Rod McKuen. Sinatra sang it on his *Cycles* album released in 1968 and I finally got round to recording it on my *You & Me* CD released in 2008. It was my first all new studio CD for nearly 10 years. This was a real challenge for me and my interpretation is once again fuelled very much by what has happened to me. Even when my chips have been low I've still had something to give.

There have been lots of 'live' CDs over the years and lots of compilations constantly going into my back catalogue of hundreds of songs, but it has been a real pleasure to be back in the studio in recent years. I'm now recording my next album at the same time as writing this book. It really is a busy time for me just at the moment.

In fact a number of my recent favourites are on *You & Me* (the 2008 recording). They include the title track itself, another song recorded by Frank Sinatra; *If* written by David Gates (not Bill!); and *Let Me Try Again*.

You & Me was written by one of the men who I consider to be amongst the best songwriters in the world, Peter Allen. He wrote some fantastic songs and I love everything about *You & Me*. It was a sad loss to the world when Peter died.

The David Gates song *If* has become a really strong part of my shows over the past few years and I have Andy Mudd, my musical arranger and currently my on-stage partner and musical director to thank for that. It's a very special, tender and yet powerful arrangement and has become a fantastic production number.

Let Me Try Again is yet another of those songs where I can put so much feeling into it because of what I have experienced over the years. I think everyone who comes to my shows understands the emotion that I try my best to put across.

One of the things BBC Radio 2's Chris Evans has said he always likes about my act is the big finishes I have always done. I once appeared on his Friday night TV show *TGIF* on Channel 4 and all I did was finish a few songs with my band. The audience loved it.

Somewhere from *West Side Story* is an all-time favourite of mine for just that. In a number of my shows I used to come on and the first song I would do would be the final part of *Somewhere*. It still gets a great reaction from the audience when I do it now.

I couldn't go through this chapter without mentioning this next number: *If I Never Sing Another Song* has become another of those songs that those who come along to see me constantly request. It's probably the main song that people now who come to my concerts associate me with for what I have been through. Of course Dame Shirley recorded it and the wonderful Don Black wrote it originally for Matt Monro. But when I sing those terrific lines it's almost as though Don wrote it especially for me. I've rested it a little over the past year as it has been a main part of the show for so long but I know that many in the audience still love hearing it and I really enjoy singing it again and again. I have recently been finishing with *The Impossible Dream* which is absolutely wonderful and another really great close to the show.

Recently I have added *I Started A Joke* and *The Morning Of My Life* which have become two recent favourites of mine. They are both Bee Gees songs from the 60s and it was my great, great pleasure to be able to sing them for Robin and Barry's special Variety Club Silver Heart award. Ever since then they have become a popular new addition to my show. Sadly Robin passed away as we were getting this edition of the book together. My heart goes out to the Gibb family. They are truly one of the most important families ever in the music business.

I know my loyal and very loving fans have their own favourites: *As If We Never Said Goodbye* from *Sunset Boulevard*; *As I Love You; If I Loved You* from *Carousel*; *Hurt; Danny Boy; My Mother's Eyes; I Wanna Be Where You Are; I Will Drink The Wine*. I'm sure I've missed quite a few more but these are just some of the ones I hear being called out during a concert. I love singing them all.

Right. Where had we got to? We've all had our little intermission. Is that glass fully charged? Come on now, you're lagging behind. Now it's time for the real breaks. The ones that saw me become whatever it is I became!

CHAPTER NINE

SEARCH FOR A STAR

Fool yourselves if you will
You can hold out your hand
I'll give you back your flowers
I will take the land ...
You can drink the water,
I will drink the wine

Joe Longthorne *I Will Drink The Wine* released 2003

Actually we're not quite off Jersey just yet, because my first big break, as I mentioned a short while ago, was to start happening whilst we were still on the island. David Bell was a lovely Scotsman who helped my career enormously and not just by scouting me for the talent show *Search for a Star*. We went on to work together a good deal on further TV programmes over the years.

David had worked on Scottish Television. He had worked as producer for many of Stanley Baxter's great shows and had come down to work for London Weekend Television with two other producers. Their flagship production was to be the talent show *Search for a Star*.

By this time, in late 1979 to the early part of 1980 I was coming to the end of my time on Jersey and had been signed up to play summer seasons at Pontin's Holiday Camps throughout the UK.

I had got a bit fed up of failing auditions. I knew that auditions weren't what I was particularly good at and I felt that producers and TV programme makers would get a better idea of what I did and the potential I had by sitting down and watching one of my shows. I'm sure there are many other performers who feel the same, but I just knew that once they'd done that they would know what I was really capable of providing.

I'd failed those four Hughie Greens (*Opportunity Knocks*) when I was in my teens. Me and my dad used to follow him around in his Rolls Royce just making sure I was seen. There was one time when I actually heard him say, 'Not you again!' We gave up in the end.

Probably the best audition I ever did was the one that David Bell saw – and it wasn't even an audition at all! That's also the reason why it went so well. As I've said before I don't do auditions, I do performances. I need an audience in front of me, real people where I can see their smiling faces.

Nearly everyone else had to go to London to try out for the show. There wasn't a Jersey audition so far as I know, and it certainly wasn't anything along the lines of *X-Factor* auditions, where they have thousands of people turning up these days.

David Bell had come over especially to see me. He'd heard about me and how well I was doing. He particularly wanted me because I was different – a singer impressionist. There have never been too many of us in that line. David Copperfield, who had his own TV show with Tracey Ullman and Lenny Henry, was pretty good, but after that you would struggle to name more than one or two. So I was different, just as my mam had always said. I had something that made me stand out from the rest – and by now I had served quite a bit of my apprenticeship in the clubs of Hull, Sheffield, Lincoln, Sunderland, Newcastle, York and Barnsley. I had proved myself on the cabaret circuit of Jersey and was about to do the further hard graft of getting around all the Pontin's resorts. I was still only 24 when I met David for the first time but I was ready. He came over to see me at El Rancho.

I remember David telling me: 'We don't usually do this sort of thing you know, coming out to see acts. Normally we get those who we are interested in to come to Waterloo. You know I shouldn't really be here. But we've heard a little bit about you.'

If he'd got me to go over to London, to Waterloo, maybe I would never have got on the show, but he did come over without me knowing. He saw me in action, the right way, and he signed me up for the show the same night. It was a done-deal, I was about to be back on the box!

London Weekend Television did three series of *Search for a Star*. The first was started at the end of 1979 and went into 1980. The second was near to the end of 1980, with the third and final series – the one I was in, starting just before Christmas in 1980 and finishing with the final on 31 January 1981.

I didn't appear on the show until 1981 so by the time I was back on TV for the first time since my *Junior Showtime* days 10 years previously I was off the island and touring all over the UK.

It really was a fine talent show and it launched the careers of several entertainers who went on to do wonderful things in the business. Many of them are still around, like me, today. I think that's because David (Bell) knew what he was doing with the show. He knew he wanted good acts from day one and he also had the fantastic Alan Ainsworth and his orchestra who were just brilliant.

Lenny Windsor – a great comedian who went on to write scripts for Benny Hill – won the final. He regularly plays the cruise ships today and is a sought after speaker at corporate events right across the UK. I read somewhere that he was touring with The Temptations a year or two back.

Paul Rafferty, who is now lead singer with Billy J Kramer's band, The Dakotas, was in the same final, I think he sang *Guilty* with Annie Noel who I understand is still singing jazz with her own Annie Noel Swingtet in Torbay.

Quite a few of the northern clubland scene were on the shows too. I was up against Bobby Knutt, a very popular comic who went on to appear on TV's *Emmerdale*, in my first round on 10 January 1981. Tammy Cline, the lovely country music singer from my home city of Hull, who was recording at Fairview Studios at the same time as me, appeared in the same series too. She went on to do really well over in Nashville, playing at the Grand Ol' Opry and had a successful radio career.

Comedian Jimmy Cricket had reached the previous final and some of the others who took part included Wayne Dobson, a fabulous magician who was later to become a regular on my own TV show, and there was also the really popular Irish singer Rose Marie. There were also some strange sounding acts, probably none more so than Gutbucket & Camelfoot, a folk music duo.

I've done my research on this you know, because I honestly couldn't remember all those off the top of my head. Looking back there was also Gordon Haskell, who went on to have a massive hit with *How Wonderful You Are* from his album *Harry's Bar* in 2001. He took part in one of the early rounds in my year.

Scriptwriters would work with you on new scripts, or they would help hone your existing material, if you wanted them to. There was clever direction. The wardrobe department couldn't do enough for you. Suits, dresses, whatever costumes you wanted you got.

There was no way you could fail if you had the right act, and mine was there just at the right time. All of those nights on Jersey, all of those nights up and down Yorkshire and the North East, had given me such experience that I felt ready for anything. One of the main differences between then and today's *X-Factor* was that everyone involved was a working entertainer. We were all involved in show business, so it was already our profession.

I won through the early round and David was privately telling me, 'Joe, you've won it here. It's in the bag.' But that didn't prove quite right.

The voting in the final was different to the early rounds, as it was a 'live' show. The others were all pre-recorded. It was conducted a bit like a Eurovision type of thing where votes were cast by areas. There were only five areas in all – London, Leeds, Glasgow, Cardiff and Belfast.

Where I came unstuck was with the Irish vote after being hotly tipped to win, and not just by David and his team but also the national press.

Everyone, it seemed, loved my Shirley. For many it was the first time they would ever have seen me do it and I'd worked on it even further.

David had been fantastic about the way I did her and having watched me in Jersey he had pointed out things that no-one else had ever noticed. It is David's comments that helped me take my impression of her to a new level. I cannot possibly tell you all that he told me. It's what you call a trade secret. He certainly taught me how to do her properly though. He said to me, with his arms outstretched and fingers spread, in his wonderful, camp Scottish accent, 'Joe, darling, this is how you should play Shirley.'

I came third in the final. Apparently the Irish vote had said they didn't give any points to people who weren't using their own voices. They thought the voices I was doing just had to be mimed. I suppose I should have accepted it as a compliment to what I was doing that they felt I must have been miming, but I have to say I didn't feel that way out at the time. David's comments had led me to feeling that I really was going to win.

Next day the story was all over the newspapers, and even though I hadn't mimed in any way there was still a big hoo-ha about it all. I really didn't mind by then, there's nothing you can do about it after the event. I knew I'd done okay.

Once again bad news hadn't done me any harm and it was about to lead me on to my next big break. Things were starting to happen – although they didn't really pick up until after we had seen off a few vans. Read on!

PONTIN'S

We seem like passing strangers now
Funny how things can change, we were so inseparable

Joe Longthorne & Liz Dawn *Passing Strangers* released 1994

When we had come off Jersey we went back home to Hull and from there to Bournemouth. It was where the work was.

I'd been involved with people from around Bournemouth both before and whilst I was on Jersey.

Whilst we were together, both in Hull and on Jersey, Sandra had done anything she could to get me better known. She was always on to Radio 1 and the TV companies about me and one time she got Don Jones, who you'll hear more of very soon, to come and see me in a talent show at Tiffany's nightclub in Hull. She also introduced me to Harold Shampan, who was a children's writer. Harold then introduced me to record producer Dick James who asked me to sing *If You Look For The Lord*. He told me he didn't want me to sing it like Tom Jones and that if I could do it he'd record me. Unfortunately it didn't happen, however the contact with Don did lead me to recording my first LP *Only Once* as well as my first two singles.

Search for a Star hadn't started for me at that time and I was managed by a man called Keith Johns, who lived in the town. He used to have The Round House Hotel, which had earned a great reputation and was quite famous on the south coast. Keith was to be my manager for a while before Don Jones took me on. But it was actually Don who met us when we first arrived in town.

We turned up in Bournemouth, from Hull, with nothing, just the clothes we stood up in. As you will constantly hear me say in this book, I'm really not good with money. Whatever I have I spend and not necessarily on myself either. Money has never been what I'm about. Of course I like to look good and I know that things cost money, but I guess I'm just not cut out to look after myself in that way.

That's where James does such a good job with me today and it's also why I've managed to get back on my feet and start all over again since the nervous breakdown, the bankruptcy and the bone marrow transplant.

So what can you do when you've turned up with nothing, apart from what you're wearing at the time, and you really do have no money. Well, we blagged it didn't we? Yes, we did. We had our story ready. My sound and lighting man and I were by now a highly competent double-act on tour and we knew the kind of act that was needed on this occasion.

We said something along the lines of: 'You'll never guess what's happened Don. On the way we stopped to get some petrol and someone's taken all of our clothes out of the car.' I had a Mercedes at the time, but don't get any ideas about it being flash. It was an old Merc and had only cost us £200. Anyway, back to our little 'scam'. I know it was a pretty feeble excuse looking back, and I don't know whether Don ever believed us or not, but he was more than helpful.

He took to us right from the start and was kind enough to take us into Bournemouth where he made sure we got some clothes from the famous Four Seasons shop. Don was a gentleman.

I loved Bournemouth, and I still do. It is a very attractive town, has a wonderful university and the place did me proud. I met up with some very talented musicians and entertainers there. One act, The Lyndrics, which consisted of Eric and his daughter Lynne, were a scream. They were illusionists of the old fashioned variety. They did all the magic tricks with pigeons and doves everywhere. Eric would put Lynne in the box and saw her in half. You know how it used to be. They were a great fun and really well known in the area.

The Majestic Hotel in Bournemouth was the home of a great jazz club. There were quite a few others at the time, but the Majestic was the top one. I loved it in there. Whenever I wasn't performing I'd go and see who was on. I'd perform in all the jazz clubs and hotels in the area.

The only thing about jazz, with me, is that I can't just listen to a piano solo forever.

Bournemouth was also where I bought my first house. You know I've only ever been to see a bank manager twice in my life and the first time was whilst I was in this lovely town because I was about to buy my first property and I went into Williams & Glynn's. I've had times when bankers and other money-men have come to visit me, although for not quite such happy reasons!

By now you're probably starting to wonder when the first thoughts of cancer, or lymphoma, CLL, or whatever started kicking in. Well at this stage in the story we haven't touched those really awful, distressing times just yet. At this point none of that was on the horizon. I haven't yet found out about cancer, leukaemia, haven't yet gone bust or broken down, although it is likely that I had CLL all of this time without ever knowing.

These are still the early years, the times when I was finding my way, learning my craft and learning more about who I was.

Up to now there has been drama, there's been humour, there have been fights, there's even been a certain amount of success – but we're getting closer to all of those real highs and the lows.

I haven't even introduced you properly to Abdul yet either. Well, he's on his way!

Our first accommodation in Bournemouth was above a Chinese restaurant in Lansdowne Road. It was at least a step up from a shed in a backyard on Jersey although it provided its own drama.

We played all of the hotels and clubs of Bournemouth and the surrounding area. Looking back we had a fabulous time playing there, all that is, apart from when a girl was murdered upstairs in one of the flats where we were staying.

Ironically the first place I worked after I'd signed up with Don Jones' organisation was Keith Johns' Round House Hotel. As well as jazz they also used to have cabaret there. Neil Martin, who had won on *Opportunity Knocks* in the 70s was also there regularly. He was one of Keith's acts. I always loved Bournemouth from the moment I got there and still return regularly. It was to be my base for a while during the 1980s.

But now we're heading for Pontin's, whilst still living in Bournemouth, and two years of almost constant travel throughout the UK, and some of the funniest moments in my life. It's also now time I introduced you to Abdul.

Abdul 'Shahid' Shaibi's picture hangs above my mantelpiece in the lounge at home in Blackpool. He's with me now even though he passed away years ago. I think about him every single day too. This man meant so much to me. He taught me so much about family, respect, honour, all of the good things you can ever imagine. He knew I was bisexual and he knew that didn't really fit in with his religion, but he never once crossed me about it. He was an absolute gem, a man you could always look up to.

He married my sister Anne. He looked after her better than any man could ever have done. They met in Attercliffe, Sheffield where Abdul ran a little café called Arab House. Anne had been having a few disagreements with my dad at home, and Abdul's one concern was that she went back to see mam and dad, to make things right. He believed in families being together and in families sorting out their problems. Family was always the most important thing to him, as it is to me. Whenever there were arguments the children always went to stand alongside this wonderful man.

Abdul had come over to Jersey a few times. He loved it and he went everywhere with me. He was such a steadying influence on me and he was always on to me when the bigger money started coming in, telling me that some of the people around me were only ever interested in my money, not me. He was only about 5 ft tall but he was the biggest, most warm-hearted and wisest man I have ever met. He also had a wickedly funny sense of humour too.

When we were working the Pontin's holiday centres he was with me all the time. There was me, the sound and lighting man and Abdul. Rita was never out of the picture either, but she preferred to stay at home, whether that was in Bournemouth or attending to some of the business interests for her father on Jersey.

I also now had a musical director for the first time, Nick Potter. He had ginger hair, a bit like an afro-style and wore a purple catsuit on stage. He now lives in Australia. Nick was my first ever touring band. In the van there would be me, sound and lighting man, Abdul, Nick and three girl dancers. Abdul did all the cooking.

Everything about Abdul's cooking was so clean. You certainly didn't touch anything whilst he was on with it.

We were doing something like 18 shows a week for Pontin's, for what amounted to next to nothing! All those people who queue up for the TV talent shows of today, and who just want ready-made success selling millions of CDs should see what it's really all about. I don't begrudge anyone anything though so I'm not having a pop. After all, I got my chance through a talent show as well. But for people like me this was the way we learned our business.

Humour was never far away when we were on the road – and I don't mean just on-stage humour. We didn't think too much about the money. It was all still about having a good time.

Now, about Abdul's wicked sense of humour, are you ready? Prepare yourself for a laugh here.

We also had a magician on tour with us at one time, so add him to the passengers in the van. His name was Mike Danatta and I believe he went on to run a sex shop in Bournemouth. You can just imagine how that would go down today if he was still playing the holiday resorts can't you? Anyway, as part of his act he had some doves and a chicken.

At that time the food at Pontin's left a lot to be desired. It was way before Burger King and MacDonalds took over everywhere and things like scampi-in-a-basket, garlic bread and chicken kiev were the 'new' foods.

Muslims are quite careful about what they eat because of their religion.

Having mentioned the magician's act I guess you're already a bit ahead of me here aren't you?

Mike's on stage with his act. The doves are coming out – one, two, three. The rest of the act is going well. Everything's going to plan. Then Mike comes to the wings of the stage.

'Where's the chicken? Where's Friendly?' He's panicking a bit, you could see the sweat just coming up in beads on his forehead. 'Did you feed

Friendly?' That's what he called his chicken, and Abdul would feed him each night. That way he would be ready the way Mike wanted him.

But Abdul had been hungry that night. The meal we'd eaten earlier had been, you've guessed it … chicken! : 'Friendly, love? Friendly in your ****ing stomach, love.' We had all eaten Friendly. And the magician had helped eat his own act! Mike turned yellow at that moment.

We were going round and round the UK like a Ferris wheel playing all these gigs. It was no wonder things got a little heated sometimes. In 10 weeks we had 18 transits that had failed us. Inside the van with sound and light man, me, Abdul, Nick, the dancers and a magician (now minus his chicken!) things occasionally boiled over. One of the arguments saw us dispensing with one of the girls – and no, Abdul didn't eat her.

The argument was all about why Abdul should be in the front of the van instead of her. So I said: 'All you've got to do is get out if you don't like it.' I'd had enough of her. She was getting on everyone's nerves at the time. We were on the Dorchester-Bournemouth bypass and she was all dressed up in her show gear. She looked like something out of a Danny La Rue show. She took me to my word and got out. I don't think she expected us to drive off, but that's exactly what we did. Well, she was stroppy at the time.

There was also one Pontin's holiday park where they charged a little bit more. It was Barton Hall in South Devon. Each time we played there I couldn't help but think 'they pay extra for this!' It was no different in my eyes to anywhere else we were going. I got myself into such a laughing fit over it. But I didn't get tired of Pontin's as such, the people we played for on their holidays were lovely and many of my fans today remember seeing me at the different resorts.

The travelling was tiring, especially with the sheer number of gigs and mileage we were getting through. To say nothing of the vans we were going through as well! I had the energy, that wasn't a problem, it's just that after a while I didn't feel as though I was getting anywhere.

I suppose I could have taken up other jobs like being an entertainments manager for one of the camps, like some do, to be able to stay in one place but I knew that it wasn't for me. I never saw myself as a bluecoat or redcoat. That kind of thing might have been alright for others and a number of top entertainers have done that, but I always saw myself as an artiste, a singer, an entertainer - nothing else.

Everyone in the entertainment world accepts that travelling is your life when you are a performer and I love going to all of the places we get to. It's great to see all those fans who really feel you've done something special by coming to their home town. I've never been one of those who feels that the whole world revolves around just one city, but the time was coming for me to spend some time in the city where everyone tells you it is important to make your mark in the UK – London.

But before we leave the south coast I have to tell you about another landmark in my life.

During my time in lovely Bournemouth I spent several days at Arny's Shack making my first ever LP release.

My recordings with Keith Herd at Fairview Studios in Hull, had been back in 1974-75. I had recorded the single *Feelings* at Tony Arnold's studio, which came out in 1977, but I hadn't recorded an album until 1980-81 when I put together the LP called *Only Once* on a record label called Roxon. It featured one of my own compositions, which I co-wrote with my Musical Director at that time, Chris Summerfield, *To Live Without You*.

The LP included several well-known songs of the time – *Fame, You To Me Are Everything* and *Ain't No Stopping Us Now*. It was also the first ever recording of my impressions and included Elvis, Barry Manilow, John Lennon, David Bowie, Stevie Wonder and Neil Diamond.

This is what I wrote as my sleeve notes to *Only Once*:

'A big hello to all my friends! I hope that you had a great evening (because the LP was sold after the show) and that you enjoyed the show! We thought that it would be a good idea to record something to enable you to take a little bit of the show home with you – and we came up with this, my debut LP. I thoroughly hope that you will enjoy listening to it as much as I enjoyed recording it.

There's a bit of something here for everyone, from up-tempo numbers like Fame *to my version of that great old standard* What Do You Want To Make Those Eyes At Me For? *(Emile Ford & The Checkmates) – and I think that* Only Once *should get a mention too, because that's one of my great personal favourites!*

At this point I would like to take the opportunity of thanking my faithful 'team', the unsung heroes who travel everywhere with me. My personal Musical Director, Chris Summerfield, who is to be found behind me on-stage, enthusiastically directing the musicians, plays keyboards with superb proficiency, and is also a very talented songwriter. He co-wrote with me To Live Without You.

Something that people tend not to notice, unless it is bad, is the sound and lighting in venues. The man who sets the mood on stage for me is my good friend the sound and light engineer (I did use his real name in the notes).

And last but not least, a big thank you to my manager, Ron Page, who handles all show production and pulls everything together, taking the worries away, leaving me to my singing!

What more can I say, except to leave you with all my good wishes, and to hope that I see you all again soon!'

Love Joe

I have always made a point of thanking my fellow musicians because it is their playing that allows me to perform the way I do. It's not often the sound and lighting gets much of a mention but once again it is an essential part of any show.

There is one other man I should thank too – Tony himself. Tony Arnold's studio was the first to specialise in an echo sound, which I understand is today called a 'stereo stack-tracking Ampex sound'. His engineers Bob Pearce and Les Payne did a great job for me. I had some excellent musicians with me on that recording too. As well as Chris Summerfield there was also Chris Rae on guitar.

Tony Arnold's studio saw many of the great names in popular music pass through it over the years, people like Van Morrison, Eurythmics and Dave Dee, Dozy, Beaky, Mick and Tich.

Ron Page's wife Traci wrote some very nice notes on the sleeve too.

'To quote a very famous song 'You've either got or you haven't got style' and after watching a Joe Longthorne concert there can be no doubt about it, the man has an abundance of style. His exciting and powerful voice, coupled with his dynamic personality, has added sparkle to the world of British showbiz. The professional and exacting qualities of his style of showmanship have gained him many admirers from all walks of life, and have earned him the supreme and coveted title of 'The Entertainers' Entertainer'.

I always liked Traci! I'm sure I must have thanked you at the time Traci, but if I didn't then please accept my thanks now.

There was another release from Arnie's Shack too, what used to be called an EP, with *Lido de France* – written by myself and Summerfield especially for Jersey; Abba's *Thank You For The Music*; and my own *Joe's Song* on the A side; and a collection of impressions on the B side including *Misty; It's Not Unusual; Till; Forever & Ever; The Wonder of You;* and *'My Way*.

It was a few years later in 1986 that I recorded my next LP called *The Singer* on Great Britain Records.

As you can see by the sleeve notes my management had by now changed over to Ron Page. Let me tell you how that came about.

I wasn't fed up with Bournemouth, it's a great town. That's still where we were living during the two years I spent touring the Pontin's sites up and down the country, and we had moved into the first ever property in my name – 138 Herbert Avenue, Upper Parkstone.

One of the good friends I had made at that time was John H Stracey, who was one of our fantastic British-born world boxing champions. He knew that I needed to move on professionally and proved a useful man to have on your side when you needed to convince someone about what you wanted to do! At that time I had a man called Ron Page who had started to manage me and believed I had potential to do well in the clubs around London.

Don (Jones) and a lady called Bridie Reid, who worked together as entertainment agents, and booked all the acts for Pontin's, wouldn't sign me off from my contract with the holiday resorts. This was to be my first-ever ending of a contract, giving notice. All I wanted was to be nearer the real action in the entertainment world and I'd had several approaches, particularly following my *Search for a Star* TV appearances. But Don wouldn't release me.

I had done a lot of gigs with Don but I knew it was time for me to move on. My *Search for a Star* appearances had meant there was a bigger audience just waiting for me and I didn't want to miss out on it. Maybe he wouldn't release me for a very good reason. Only Don will ever really know.

However, one day he wouldn't let me go, the next day he did. I don't know fully what was said but John (H. Stracey) told me later that he had rung Don and told him that he was stopping me from going where I wanted to go. He also told me there was no violence involved. I think he was joking. Anyhow, the next day I was under contract to Ron Page.

It was time to leave Bournemouth, the doves, stroppy dancers and the magician's new chicken! We moved to Maidenhead. Ron wanted me closer to London, and I went on to play many times in his really great club, The Silver Skillett. It was a very popular venue and he booked everyone from Lonnie Donegan to Bernard Manning to play there.

When we first moved from the coast we lived with Ron and his wonderful wife Traci before getting our own property.

I had been introduced to a man called Malcolm Vinecor who looked after me for a while as I moved over from Don to Ron. Malcolm was to be around for a few years yet and lived near to Jimmy Tarbuck at the time. He was also chairman of Crystal Palace FC and ran The Priory Clinic, the rehab centre.

You would be silly if you didn't like Maidenhead, it's beautiful and the Thames Valley area is gorgeous. I was very happy and felt very lucky to be there. Myself, Rita and the sound and lighting man, as well as Abdul most of the time, lived in Maidenhead through quite a bit of the 80s, at 14 Cranbrook Drive. I had some very happy times there and career-wise it became another real step up for me.

The biggest live dates of my career at that time were about to come my way. And I was ready for them.

Instead of playing holiday camps, and no disrespect to those, I was now playing the big well-known clubs like the String of Pearls in Wembley, where I played regularly and, in particular, I remember the time when I was booked to play at the legendary Talk of the Town in London. This is where all, and I mean all, of the world famous cabaret acts had played. Frank Sinatra, Sammy Davis Jr., Eartha Kitt, Stevie Wonder, Dusty Springfield, The Carpenters and of course Dame Shirley. She recorded a tremendous live album there in 1970.

I was actually the last headline artiste to play the Talk of the Town, which closed in 1982. Peter Stringfellow took it over. Funny thing is that it's now currently being transformed back into a cabaret venue, as well as a major casino and is back under its original name of The Hippodrome. I honestly believe variety and cabaret is on its way back and it could even be that we will see the return of The Talk of the Town one day.

I played there for a month, which was a real kick in the teeth to the reviewer on the *Evening Standard* in London. He had said something along the lines of 'who's this bleached blond guy from up north who has come to close our beloved Talk of the Town? Why him? Why not someone like Sammy Davis?' Well I got up there and gave him Sammy Davis and all the rest of the Rat Pack. We had four great weeks and the shows were all sell-outs. So much for the *Evening Standard's* reviewer!

My family also did a bit of business when the place closed down. My Uncle Joe – the same Uncle Joe that turned the trick for me with Jess Yates on *Junior Showtime* - bought all the curtains and by the time we had left for the after-show party he had also taken all the tables!

I remember seeing Roger Whitaker at the Talk of the Town. I have always loved his songs like *Durham Town*. The Bachelors were one of my mam's favourites and they appeared there too, so I already had a fondness for the venue before I played there. This wasn't my first time in London. I had played the big city during the 70s too, when I had come off Jersey to do a show or two.

But now, by being in and around London, basing myself close to the city and performing regularly in front of a lot of influential people, I was beginning to earn a reputation amongst the TV people who were based there.

What *Search for a Star* had done was to put me in front of millions of people and it had proved to be the launching pad for a decade of being 'on the box' in a number of entertainment shows, including my own series. Ron Page knew that and it was why he was so keen to sign me.

My first recordings for mainstream record labels were still a distance away but television was knocking even if 'Opportunity..' hadn't knocked.

I appeared on another TV show called *The Big Top Variety Show* with Michael Barrymore in 1981 and was well on my way to fame... and a fortune that came and went.

But first let's go to Scarborough, that beautiful jewel on the Yorkshire coast. I love Scarborough. I think every kid growing up in Yorkshire loves Scarborough. There's something about it that's still great today.

And no, you're not getting a break this time. Maybe after Scarborough!

SCARBOROUGH

I feel it coming together, people will see me and cry
Fame!

Joe Longthorne *Fame* released 1980

Tony Hardman and Mike Hughes get their first mention here. Tony is an agent and had seen me over on Jersey where I once appeared with Des O'Connor. I make fun of Des when I'm on stage but truthfully he is one of the nicest guys in the business.

Tony was always really good for me apart from introducing me to 'Stanley Kubrick'. I'll tell you more of him and that slightly embarrassing tale later.

Mike (Hughes) was the best manager and agent I ever had up until James. I've had some really good ones. Jean (Parkes) who I'll come to later was another. But Mike was a seriously great operator and was always so sincere. It was him who put me on for my first summer season in Scarborough, and it was Mike who was also the man who negotiated for me over my TV series.

Scarborough, in 1982, was to be my first time with a full live orchestra and just meeting the band was a big thing for me. I went into the orchestra pit with the band, Maurice Merry and his Merry Men. They played as Gene Pitney's UK band when he came over so you can imagine how I felt. I was there in the pit with them, all these great musicians. I was now 27 and had my own orchestra for a season. To me it was like being told you could have all the sweets from the shop!

I was up at the Floral Hall in Scarborough with The Krankies. They were the Number One family entertainment act at the time. They were doing shows like *Crackerjack* on the BBC and appearing in *Royal Variety* shows. They're still going strong now and what I really like about them is that they have kept their act as a family show, they haven't given in to smutty talk or sold out commercially.

I loved Jeanette and Ian (The Krankies) but soon there were to be changes to the billing in Scarborough. I was supposed to come on after Stu 'Crush a Grape' Francis had opened the show. He was then to come back on after me.

Now I'm not talking daft here but I knew that within 20 minutes of being there I was going to be top of the bill! Maybe I couldn't be top on the posters at that time because they were already up, but for the first time in my life I'm on stage with a wonderful orchestra backing me. It's exciting and I can't stop smiling. I'm a singer – Stu, Jeanette and Ian are comedians. This band is mine – all mine. It felt so good. This is what all those years in Hull, Sunderland and Jersey had been about. I am still smiling about it now as I write. Mine, all mine.

The TV stardom was great later on, and please believe me when I say that I really do want it all over again if that is possible, but there is nothing to compare with playing live with your own band. There is nothing I get a kick out of more.

When you give Joe Longthorne an orchestra all you have to do is stand back, because you've already lit the blue touchpaper. I had Maurice Merry on keyboards, Alan Savage on drums, one of the best in the business, but I could have gone through anyone in the band and there would have been the same reaction. These fellahs were quality players and I was going to use every one of them to the full.

I don't think anyone properly realised just what would happen if you put an orchestra behind me, probably not even my own family who always had belief in me anyway, but they all soon found out. I was going on in the first half of the show and the audience would be on its feet. They just couldn't get enough – and neither could I – but I never once did what Pancho had done to me. I came off on time, every time. And every single performance I stormed it – thanks to Maurice and his Merry Men.

In a short while I had ripped up the first set of the show. I didn't care what anyone else thought, I just knew that was the way to go. I told Mike (Hughes) that Stu wasn't coming back on again after me. Why would any promoter want to do that to a show once you had the audience on its feet giving a standing ovation? No disrespect at all, but Stu would have to do more than crush a grape to get that kind of reaction. The first half had to finish with me.

Jim Davidson once said that he would only ever go on before me, not afterwards. He knows the power I have in my voice and the way an audience reacts to it. Jim has always known what I've been capable of and the special relationship I have with those who come to my shows.

Back to Scarborough, I think Jeanette and Ian even started getting worried at the point when Stu was being dropped from doing his second spot. I heard rumours that they had tried to get Mike to pull me off their show, but they never mentioned anything and they were always very friendly.

I know I was a bit ruthless at times but I just knew this was how things were meant to be from then on. I just love having a big band behind me and this one was simply top dollar. I have immense respect for all those who have played alongside me over the years, because I know that their contribution to what I am singing is also why the audience applauds so much. It's a team effort on stage, not all me-me-me. Now where have you heard that before?

I'm not trying to get big headed here, just perhaps a little excited, but if you give a singer like me an orchestra you really can't go wrong. The show is going to be big. The songs are just going to be fantastic and everyone is going to go home happy that they have had a fabulous show. Once again I mean no disrespect to Stu (Francis) or Jim (Davidson) but how can you follow a fantastic orchestra and singer?

There's only one way and that's if you had another one to follow – like Mr Frank Sinatra. I would have loved that - me and the great man himself.

My good friend Bobby Ball, who produced my summer season show for me last year and did a great job, said to me recently, 'You know where me and Tommy went wrong Joe? We got rid of the band.' I told him that wasn't it at all. The pair of them are two of our greatest comics, an absolutely brilliant duo and have no real need for a band. But for me, as a singer, a band is everything. I also like my audience to see where the money goes when they are buying the tickets.

Mike Hughes took a calculated gamble on me with that first summer season. After all, I was untried in the big theatre venues at the time. I had played the Talk of the Town; I had played resorts, clubs and hotels, but nothing as big as that first season. There was no guarantee that I would be successful throughout the run, but I knew once I was there, even before I was there, that it was right for me. I will forever be grateful to Mike for getting me in there.

I have played Scarborough nearly every year since then, but in recent times only once or twice a year since my main summer season shifted to Blackpool. But it is still a very special place for me.

Like a lot of people who come from Hull, I have always loved Scarborough, the town, its people, the beach. Mam and dad didn't have a lot of spare money to be able to take us to many places when we were young but we would come here on the train like a lot of families did from all over the county. Actually dad wouldn't quite make it to Scarborough. He would 'come over all funny' he would say to mam and end up back in the peever in Hull.

I remember mam on the beach, her lovely big legs and a warm jug of tea! We usually ended the day singing back home at pubs like The Beresford or the White Lion.

There's a place for me,
Somewhere a place for me
Hold my hand and I'll take you there...

Joe Longthorne *Somewhere* released 2002
(lyrics altered here for artistic purposes!)

Like I said earlier, when I used to play truant from school I didn't just go to New Holland and into Lincolnshire. I would also come up to Scarborough, and that's how I found my favourite place in the world, just a few miles up the coast at Ravenscar. It has been called 'The Town That Never Was' and if you ever go there you will see why. It's four miles off the main coast road from Scarborough to Whitby, and the cliffs reach out into the sea. It is so isolated and I have always been at peace there.

Let me tell you more than I did before. The first time I found out just how much I loved Ravenscar was when I was about 13 years old and as soon as I saw it I knew there was a connection, that it was my type of place. I fell in love with it and I'm still in love with it today. It's the peace, the absolute tranquillity of it all. As a kid I can remember thinking 'I really love you'. You see I fall in love with places in the same way I fall in love with people, and I never forget any of them. I then had to walk the four miles back to the main road to get a bus back into Scarborough and then the train back to Hull.

George III lived there at one time at Raven Hall, which is now the Raven Hall Hotel. There was once a railway line which ran from Scarborough to Ravenscar but that had been closed down in 1965. Harold Wilson said he was going to keep it open, but it never happened. Years later I lived for a while in the old Station Master's house and stayed in it whilst I was doing a 12 week summer season just down the road. I used to love going across to Raven Hall. One of the houses at Ravenscar, and there aren't many, was owned by a man called Otto and his wife, who looked after children who had difficulty in learning, which is close to my heart for obvious reasons. I regularly used to go across and chat with them whilst I was there.

I still long for going back there whenever I can. I've been all around the world – Australia, the States, Thailand, right across Europe, Hong Kong, on cruises through Scandinavia and the Eastern Bloc – but there still isn't a single place that compares to Ravenscar. It is so remote and a real hidden gem. The view from Ravenscar to Robin Hood's Bay is fantastic.

I decided a long while ago that this is where I am going to be buried. I know that sounds a bit morbid, especially given what I've been going through for many years, but hopefully that's not going to take place for some time yet.

It can't happen just yet anyway because I'm back! It's been a long hard road at times but now I really am right at the top of my game. The engagements are coming and I'm as busy now as at any time in my career.

Back in 1982 I was just starting to hit the really big time too. Television had only come my way once or twice by then, but that was all set to change as the decade moved on. Thankfully I had some good people looking after me – and I'm pleased to say that's exactly what I've got today too.

CHAPTER TWELVE

CHICAGO

If the sun should tumble from the sky
If the sea should suddenly run dry
If you love me, really love me
Let it happen and I won't care

Joe Longthorne *If You Love Me* released 2003

The 80s and early 90s saw me combine regular live gigs with plenty of TV work, releasing albums, touring the States and winning my first Variety Club award. It was also the era that saw me with two Rollers and four Bentleys, a massive house with seven acres of land, a 500 foot frontage and its own swimming pool. But life isn't measured that way. I know it's far more precious than that as I was to find out right at the start of my TV career.

It was a great time, as you might expect, but truly I am just as happy now as I have ever been. When you can have all of that, lose it all, and yet still entertain people you realise what's important.

I loved my time when I was earning really big money from TV contracts, as anyone would, but it's not the be all and end all. I am still here and that's what counts to me.

Did I ever lose the plot? What do you think? How can a man who has suffered a nervous breakdown say he hasn't lost the plot? How can a man who has been bankrupt say he hasn't lost the plot? How can a man who has taken drugs quite extensively over the years say he hasn't lost the plot? And, although I'm not after the sympathy vote here how can a man go through what I have been through and not lose the plot? Yes, I have lost the plot along the way, several times.

But first let's just take a look at the good things that were happening. By 1982 I hadn't just appeared on *Search for a Star* and performed for a month at the Talk of the Town; I had also appeared in Scarborough for the first time in a summer season – and I had also made my debut at the Palladium.

The following year I was to pick up the Variety Club's award as Most Promising Newcomer. I also appeared on a TV special *Gala Evening* and was on the top-rated game show on TV at the time, Ted Rogers' *3-2-1*, which was filmed at Yorkshire Television, bringing me back full circle to where I started on TV with *Junior Showtime*.

I nearly had an embarrassing moment when I went to collect my Variety Club award though. I went to put on my suit and found out that I'd forgotten it. I cheekily went over to the Grumbleweeds, my good friends who I'd seen on Jersey, and asked whether I could borrow one of theirs. Fortunately it wasn't the little fat one's! I'm not naming names here. Things were always fun in those days and I've always tried to enjoy myself wherever I've been and whatever situation I've found myself.

I've always seen myself as just me, just Joe. I will talk with anyone. I would never want anyone to think I was in any way better as a person than anybody else. I'm a singer, that's it.

I recently bumped into a man who was an 'extra' at YTV at the time I appeared on *3-2-1*. He mentioned that I was one of the few 'stars' who would pass the time of day with him and his fellow extras. That's where I come from. All I've ever tried to be is who I am. Hopefully that has come across wherever I have been.

1983 saw me appear on two TV programmes – one was *Live from Her Majesty's* which I was to appear on several times over the years to come, but the other was more important for me because it was the first time I'd ever had my own TV show. It was part of a series on Channel 4 called *The Entertainers* – and mine was called, appropriately enough *The Joe Longthorne Show*.

It was a one-off and I wasn't to get my own TV series for another five years, but it was a start. It appeared on screen 13 October 1983.

David Bell had been instrumental in getting me the programme, but he didn't produce it and I wish he had. The producer had previously done *Opportunity Knocks*. Typical! I couldn't get on the thing years before and then when I had a show it was produced by someone from that background. Maybe that's why I felt it didn't work.

Four years later I had my next stab at a show, this time on ITV on 26 August 1987. David Bell managed to get me another break and *Joe Longthorne Entertains* featured my good friends in the business Kate Robbins, who was a great impressionist and had a hit single with *More Than In Love*, and Wayne Dobson, the magician who I still feel had the best slight of hand ever in this country. The show was meant to be a pilot for a series and it must have done OK because the following year I had my first ever six-week series with Wayne as my resident guest. Mike (Hughes) was pulling the strings in the background.

There were plenty of other shows too. I appeared on the late Marti Caine's series that was very popular at the time, and I was by now a regular on *Live at the Palladium* and *Live from Her Majesty's*. David Bell had looked after me by getting me on TV, whilst I had Mike Hughes looking

I spent my early years in Rifle Terrace, just off the famous Hessle Road in Hull. I had such a happy time there. There was always lots of hustle and bustle.

My two grannies - Annie & Lizzie - were the greatest of friends. They went to school together, they went out together.

This is Ravenscar Station. It's a picture that I have in my Blackpool home. Ravenscar is my favourite place in the world, on the North Yorkshire coast. Harold Wilson said he would keep Ravenscar Station open, but he didn't. I have many happy memories of this lovely isolated place.

Mam worked for a Beverley company called Armstrong Patents in the 60s. Here I am giving the thumbs-up to the photographer at the Children's Works' Christmas Party.

I appeared in a lot of different costumes during my time on Yorkshire Television's *Junior Showtime* programme from being 14 years old.

Here's me in another *Junior Showtime* appearance. I used to catch the train from Hull every Friday afternoon, go to the City Varieties Theatre in Leeds and come back on the Monday.

This was one of my first ever impressions - Albert Steptoe.

Here I am with my dad Fred. My dad was everything to me. He made sure that I was treated right when I started off in the clubs. He never lost an argument!

My mam, Teresa. It was mam who advised me to add the impressions. She had a great voice and calls herself a Vera Lynn singer.

This is an early booking slip from when I played Huntington Working Men's Club in York. In those days it was standing room only by 7pm. They could have at least got my name right couldn't they?

I've appeared with Jim (Davidson) a few times. Here's a picture of me, Jim and the Water Rats from the 70s. See if you can recognise anyone else in the picture!

Receiving my Most Promising Newcomer Award from the Variety Club in 1981, with Bernard Delfont looking on and Eric Morley handing over the award.

Back in Hull and outside the Hull City Hall where I won the Kingston upon Hull Parks Department Talent Contest when I was 13.

This is how I looked around the time of my *Search for a Star* TV appearances in 1981.

... and this is how I looked at the time of my TV shows in the 1980s and 1990s.

The publicity shot which was also used for the *Joe Longthorne Songbook* album.

Taking to the stage at The Starlight Rooms, Enfield, London in 1988.

Filming the TV promo for the *Joe Longthorne Songbook* at Caesar's Palace in London.

Chatting with HRH Prince Philip, the Duke of Edinburgh, following my appearance on the *Royal Variety Performance*.

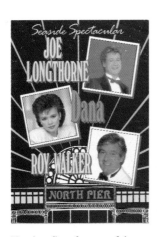

Here's a flyer for one of the *Seaside Spectaculars* that I did with the lovely Dana and the great Roy Walker. I was with them in Scarborough when I found out I had cancer.

In concert over in Belfast in 1992.

Arriving at the Opera House, Blackpool during my record-breaking run in 1993.

Mam and Dad were so happy the night I was honoured on *This is Your Life* in 1994. Michael Aspel presented the programme and surprised me in time-honoured fashion at the Manchester Apollo Theatre.

The night I appeared on stage in London for the legendary Bob Hope's charity show was amazing. Mr Hope invited me over to the States as a result of my performance.

The Wonderful Ernie
Dunstall - my musical
director and fellow
songwriter.

JOE LONGTHORNE FRIENDSHIP CLUB
EXCLUSIVE MEMBERS' PHOTO

One of the pictures which was originally exclusively for my fan club - the Joe Longthorne Friendship Club, which was run so well by Rita, and is now looked after superbly by Geraldine.

Forget the snooker... here I am with my Gold and Platinum discs. I ended up auctioning them all off for charity.

With the cast from another great summer season.

I don't wear any props and
costumes these days -
here's me as Elvis!

Here's Jamie. He was a 1-handicap golfer when I met him. He's now my partner and my manager. I've ruined his game though, because he now doesn't get enough time on the course!

The lovely Pat Mancini with me at Turpin's in Berkshire.

Time for an ice cream! At the funfair with James, Big Mick and Brian Hatt.

after me on stage and negotiating all the TV and stage deals.

Unfortunately, the way things worked out it wasn't always to be that way. I managed to hit a few self-destruct buttons as I went along. Maybe if David and Mike had been around then some of the things that happened after they were not around wouldn't have, but as Frank Sinatra would say 'That's Life'.

Mike always liked to lay out a five year plan for the people he managed, but I never wanted one. It just wasn't me. I know that tours have to be booked in advance and that TV programmes are planned well forward, but five years! I don't look at life that way. Maybe if I had then Mike would have stayed with me.

In actual fact I very nearly didn't have anything other than a possible jail sentence back in 1985. This was all before I landed my first TV series.

Following my initial successes on TV shows and around the country I had been signed up to play in the States. I was to play some fantastic theatre venues with the first being in Chicago. However, just before I signed up to go over to the States I had been back home in Hull and it nearly cost me my Philadelphia dates.

This next incident was nothing of my doing, I just happened to be in the wrong place at the wrong time, but it did create a lot of problems for me in the States – not that anyone there knew about me having to go home to appear in court!

What had happened was a pretty extreme fight in a pub, which led to one of my nephews being viciously attacked. Its aftermath saw me, and others, up on a charge of affray.

It had all been due to go to court, but I had to fly out to the States. These were to be my very first US gigs and I was looking forward to them, but I knew I had this case hanging over me. I was one of several due to appear.

The court case came up whilst we were in Philadelphia, which meant we had to fly back so that I could appear at Beverley Crown Court, a lovely market town just north of Hull.

Once again I made up some phoney excuse. We weren't about to tell those who had booked us why we were coming back. The idea was to get back by Wednesday having been in court on the Monday, otherwise the Stateside deal was off!

My barrister stopped me from representing myself in court by saying, 'You have your stage Mr Longthorne, this is mine'. He did a good job. All I wanted to do was get back across to open in Philadelphia. We had just finished the Chicago run.

The affray charge was dropped to a lesser charge of carrying an offensive weapon and we settled for that. The judge ordered me to pay a £2,000 fine and I was that bothered about getting back so soon that I just came out with, 'Can I pay you now, your honour?'

Within an hour we were back on our way to Heathrow Airport and to this day, until the publication of this book, very few people have ever known too much about it.

Ron Page had done everything to get me over to the States and he had made contact with a man called Al Anthony who had produced what were the famous *Superstars* shows in the US; and another man, an Italian called Tony De Santos.

It has always been my biggest dream to play in Vegas as you must realise by now, and although this wasn't that, it was a step in the right direction. I didn't see it as my big break in the US. It was all about getting experience. Maybe I've just about got enough experience now.

I was scheduled to play for five weeks at the Drury Lane Theatre in Chicago and they had already sold 2,000 tickets by the time I got there. I went down so well that I ended up playing for five months before Shelley Winters took over. It was here that I started rubbing shoulders with some of the greats in the business. I had lunch with Tony Bennett and another time had lunch with Sammy Davis Jr's manager.

Tony De Santos was great with us. He told us there was a car in his garage that we could use whilst we were there. When we opened up the garage it wasn't just a car, it was only a Rolls Royce Corniche! I can still remember seeing his face as our jaws dropped. I hadn't yet made it to the land of purchasing Rollers. I remember it was f***ing freezing at the time, something like minus 25 degrees with the windchill and white over with snow.

There was some problem with the side window but we managed to fix it easily. Tony showed us the bank and the fire station next. Why? That's because he owned them both.

'There's your bank account and there's your fire engines and there's your car' he said to us. He cared for us and looked after us splendidly throughout our year in the US.

Philadelphia, our next venue following my courtroom appearance, went even better than Chicago. I was appearing in two shows a day at the Encore Theatre. I was also invited on to *Jerry Lewis' Telethon*. It was such a great experience. Something new was happening every day. It has to be one of the favourite times in my life.

Before we went out to the US we had to get some backing tracks recorded, because there would be no band with us. I don't generally like backing tracks for a performance as I prefer everything 'live' but sometimes you have to use them. That way your energy can help all of the musicians and you can feed off theirs too. Obviously backing tracks are useful for rehearsing, but on this occasion it was something that just had to be done.

When we returned to the UK in 1986, after 12 months of being away, the regular guest spots on TV shows started again. I was back on screen with *Jimmy Tarbuck & Friends* almost immediately we got back, and I also appeared on *Live from Her Majesty's* and *Live at the Palladium*. Jimmy was compere on both shows too.

The Joe Longthorne Friendship Club started the same year, with Rita at its helm. And my second LP, *The Singer* was released. Many of the songs appearing on *The Singer* later appeared on *The Joe Longthorne Songbook* album that did so well and ended up going platinum.

By this time we had moved to Northern Heights in Bourne End. Dennis Waterman, who made his name in *Minder* with George Cole, lived in Bourne End too. Ours was a lovely house, but we weren't to stay there too long before moving to the biggest house I ever had.

The catalyst for the move came when I landed a regular support slot on the *Les Dennis Laughter Show*, which I was to appear on for four series. Mike Hughes was once again the man who sorted it out for me. He conducted all the negotiations. That's the time when I started spending some serious money. I was starting to live the celebrity life and I used to go to the recordings in my beautiful yellow banana of a Rolls Royce.

Although I like them, as anyone would, possessions have never meant that much to me that I get too carried away with them. And if you believe that you will believe anything!

I remember pulling into my driveway one day. There it is, worth 28 large ones and sat on my driveway. I'm admiring it when seconds later my housekeeper, Jean, is backing into it, crunching it and causing thousands of pounds worth of damage. I wasn't that bothered though. Things like that don't matter so long as no-one is hurt.

Not true. I went absolutely f***ing barmy. No sooner had it arrived then we were having to get it carted back to the garage!

The *Les Dennis Laughter Show* didn't just give me more money, it also gave me an opportunity to perform on television every week. I was very lucky that Mike (Hughes) had put me in and conducted all the negotiations, but he wasn't content with just that, he was already working fast on the next stage – my own TV series. I might not have wanted a five year plan, but he had already planned it out for me.

Wherever I was needed I joined in with Les' sketches but I wasn't involved with too many of them. I would have liked to have been included in more of them even though I still wouldn't have been very good with the scripts.

I had an ambition to act, in fact I would still like to act today. What I'd really enjoy would be to be given a part in a serious drama about social life, an upbeat style of programme.

Another *Live at the Palladium* followed in 1987 as well as regular appearances with Des (O'Connor) on his *Des O'Connor Tonight* show. On a couple of the shows were Whitney Houston and Dionne Warwick. I sang *We Are The World* with Dionne.

I was also in summer season on the North Pier, in Blackpool. Little did I know then that just a dozen years later this town was to become my home. In fact the North Pier itself was to become a temporary home as well, but that's not for a while yet and involves a few more funny tales.

The most important event of 1987 to me though was not a TV appearance or the summer season but the opportunity I had to help honour one of the greatest entertainers our country has ever seen.

One of my all-time favourite singers Matt Monro had passed away on 7 February 1985. As I mentioned in the 'favourite songs' chapter, I still sing the songs he made famous even today such as *Portait of My Love* and *Born Free*. *If I Never Sing Another Song* went on to become one of my most famous songs and was recorded by him in 1977. Matt died of liver cancer in his 50s, but strangely, for some reason, his life wasn't celebrated on screen in the way that other singers or entertainers who pass on have been over the years. When you see how some performers are honoured after they have passed on it is nothing short of criminal the way Matt was ignored by television.

Matt's daughter Michelle was hurt and angry that her father had been ignored by the television companies and decided she wanted to host her own tribute to him.

Michelle did everything. She organised the whole evening at Grosvenor House in London, Sunday 22 February – the room, the invitations, the menus, the toastmaster, the raising of funds for Cancer Research – and she was going to top the whole thing off with a 100-strong choir singing a medley of Matt's songs acapella with video footage of the great man himself. But she was short of one thing.

This is how Michelle thanked me afterwards, with a story which now appears on my website. It makes me feel so humble every time I read it – and also so pleased that I was able to help.

'.... But still I didn't have a star name, and then my white knight came along, Joe Longthorne, who was at the height of his career, had won every accolade, had his own television series and was at the top of his game. Joe rang me out of the blue.

He offered to be my escort at the top table for the evening and absolutely tore the room apart with his cabaret performance. He not only offered his services for free but also was there because he genuinely admired my father.

Not once did he throw a 'wobbler' because he wasn't closing the show, which is what every star would normally expect. He just asked what he could contribute and accepted his fate humbly. That is the mark of a true star.

Joe usually does a tribute in his stage shows to dad, which is a great honour in itself. He always talks highly of my father and his voice, but in fact Joe has the most amazing voice and a range that very few singers can compete with.

Joe is a very unassuming, gentle man. He did me and my family a great service that night and contributed in making the evening a resounding success. He has overcome adversity himself over the years and although he has won fights against his illness, he hasn't won the war.

I have only met Joe a handful of times and each time he has been more gracious than the last. Although I do not know him really well, he will always have a very special place in my heart. There are not many people who can make me see reason when I don't want to, but the one thing he did for me that evening, when he stepped on that stage at the Grosvenor House Hotel, was that he took away my anger at the world. He made me realise that you don't need corporations and television companies to acknowledge what a great talent the world has lost. You just need people – people who love and admire the legend that is Matt Monro – and the amazing legacy he left behind.

That's so nice isn't it? Thank you again Michelle, but really it was the least I could do in the circumstances.

I still love Matt's music very much today. He provided the world with a fantastic catalogue of wonderful numbers and is still sadly missed. In many ways he was never appreciated as much as some other singers in this country. Recently the TV producers have set the record straight and finally Matt has received the programmes his voice deserved.

Looking back I was somewhat luckier than Matt television-wise, and in 1988 the roof blew off my career. Everything was under way. I was now appearing in not one but two regular series – *Les Dennis' Laughter Show* on BBC1, as well as my own series on ITV. It was the start of a massive time for me, the time when I really was in my hey-day. It was a time when young girls wrote to me and everybody seemed to have time to devote to me. It was a time when everyone I saw swore they knew me. I think there's a song that goes a little bit like that isn't there?

Now before this all becomes a little too much of a list of TV programmes I have appeared in or hosted let's go to Turpin's. You've not heard of Turpin's yet? Well this is your time to find out. It's time to see how far I had come – and also how far I had to fall!

TURPIN'S

*...I'm not too smart,
I may be foolish
But I've got a heart
I love the flowers
And I love the sun...*

Joe Longthorne *Don't Laugh at Me* released 2003

Before we move on I must tell you that those wonderful lyrics at the start of this chapter were never sung better than by the great Norman Wisdom himself. Norman rang me once he'd heard my recording and said he'd really enjoyed my version. That meant so much.

So what is this 'fame' thing all about? To me it means a good laugh, good times and good prospects. I had all of those back in the 1980s and early 1990s. Thankfully I've now got them again.

Let me tell you what life is like being a celebrity, from my side. These are not complaints, just facts. I know I have had things that many will never have. I understand all that, but what does it all mean?

Firstly, you never really live anywhere for very long. By that I mean that you don't live somewhere that you can call home all the time either because you're touring or recording.

I know there are some who would say, 'Well you're a traveller Joe and you should be used to it'. They're wrong. Believe it or not all I ever sometimes want is quiet, peace, tranquillity. Sometimes a big house can give you that, if you can afford it, and I thought I could. My problem was that I thought I could afford anything.

I had gone from £6 a week on *Junior Showtime*, to £18 a night in Hull and Sunderland, followed by an increase to £25 a night if my dad had done the deal, in whichever fashion he chose!

I'd played Jersey and Pontin's for £100 a week. All of a sudden I'd had a few goes at television and the money was much bigger. For a lad who has come from Rifle Terrace in Hull I suppose I was always going to be in danger of a fall!

I guess it's all about going out and getting what you thought you could never have – and it did get out of hand. As James tells me today, I know nothing about money. I don't have the first idea of the value of money and if it's there I just spend it, or give it to others who say they need it to buy things they want. I never ever knew how much I had. I just thought that since I was earning a lot of money at the time I could say 'yes' to just about anything.

I would go out for a pint of milk and come back having bought another Bentley! I bought a car for my niece. There were always people around me who needed feeding, and I didn't begrudge one bit of it ever.

This was only 1988. I wasn't hitting the bottle any more than I had always done since I was 16. Yes, I was doing cocaine and generally enjoying the celebrity lifestyle.

Rita was with me and so was my sound and light man from Hull. Abdul was there, Anne came down to stay many times, but none of them were taking drugs. Everyone came to visit, quite a few stayed a while.

What was I saying about getting a little peace?

Maybe I would have been better just buying a place at Ravenscar, but that wasn't how my life was going at the time. I was flying – in more ways than one.

The big contract that Mike arranged for me to take on my own TV series had made me feel as though I could buy anything – and at that time when I wanted something I would buy it, after all I was doing well. That's all I knew.

I fell in love with a house by the side of the River Thames in Maidenhead. It was right next to where Rolf Harris lived at the time. Sheila Fergusson of the Three Degrees lived close by too. I had gone down to it in the big yellow banana, my bright yellow Rolls Royce, with my two Rottweilers. Typical of me at the time, I had only gone out to walk the dogs and I came back having bought a mansion! Or so I thought.

Let me take you through it as it happened:

I am stood on the bank of the river opposite this house and the agent is putting up the 'For Sale' notice. By the time he has put the notice up I'm calling him from the other side of the river. 'Look at the opposite bank,' I said. 'That's me with the big yellow banana on wheels. I'm buying that house. I'm putting the deposit in your bank account tomorrow and I'm having it.'

They say money can buy anything, but in my case money couldn't buy that house, at least not my money. I did get to look at it on the inside though. The table inside it must have been worth a fortune! It was like the table you would have expected King Arthur and his knights to sit around. It had a fabulous indoor swimming pool, moorings on the river. I just had to have it, but unfortunately, from what I can gather someone from arab royalty wanted it for their family.

I had been determined to get it but the agents kept telling me I was being gazumped. The house was originally priced around £380,000 – this was 1988 remember – then it went up by £20,000, then up to £430,000. And this was all happening when house prices were crashing everywhere else.

The agents also told me of the disadvantages of having a house that backed on to the Thames, especially if you're a celebrity. 'When you sit in the garden people will go by on the river and they'll all be watching you and pointing at you in your garden. So it's best you don't go there, Mr Longthorne.' That was their advice. It's not what you'd expect an agent to say.

I wasn't to be put off that easily. I had fallen in love with the house and I still desperately wanted it. I went back into the agents' office. They really were lovely people. What was going on wasn't their fault, but by now I was getting quite demonstrative.

'I'm having that house,' I told them in no uncertain terms. There may have been a few expletives thrown in at this point I grant you! All of the people who were in the branch started walking out, you could hear customers tutting as they went. Can you imagine that? It's a bit like a sketch all of its own, something out of Mr Bean. So the branch is now empty apart from me and the manager. That was when I found out that I was never going to live there.

He told me: 'Joe, it's impossible. You can't have that house. They don't want you there. He's (the King or Sheik or whoever) going to buy it for his niece so she can knock it down and have a bigger front garden.' (They already had the house next door.)

I'll say no more about it other than I was looked after with a brown envelope by way of compensation for all of my inconvenience. I'm afraid I can't tell you what was in it though.

After I'd finally realised the deal was never going to happen, no matter how much more I offered, I moved in to Turpin's – so called because, allegedly, Dick Turpin had once stayed where this house had been built. I tell you, if he'd had a house like this he'd never have bothered with his main job.

It was to become my home for the next 12 years, although the last four years were a difficult period for me.

Turpin's was my palace. It had everything I could ever have wanted and it cost about £480,000. It will probably be worth around £6m today. It had a 500 yard frontage, a swimming pool, sauna, snooker room, recording studio (built by my brother-in-law Mick), stables and plenty of grass in its seven acres of land for what was to become my very own smallholding including lots of animals.

All of the bedrooms had their own en-suite facilities. So much for peace and tranquillity – everyone came! I wouldn't have wanted it any other way.

The thing I learned though is that none of it is clever. Like I said earlier, life's not all about what you've got possessions-wise.

When I needed to go abroad to tour everyone would come in and house-sit for me. I have such a wonderful, adaptable family who are all so different and who all look after me today. Who better to look after your home for you?

The daft thing is that every time I would come back there had been something different done to the house.

One time I came back and the kitchen had been painted in corporation green. Corporation green I ask you! It was horrible – and I remember the fridge was always full of stuff I never ate as well!

Anyway, enough of that for now, let's get back to the fun times at Turpin's.

It's important for me to tell you that I wasn't ever trying to be flash or anything. Well maybe just a little. I know that Turpin's sounds a lot bigger than just something comfortable when you read what I had back then, but all I can say is it felt good at the time.

One of my favourite parts of the house was the beautiful recording studio that my brother-in-law Mick, Lizzie's husband, the one who used to take me to the gigs, built for me.

There's a saying that once a songwriter gets his own studio it f***s him up, and that was true for me. Whilst I had always sung other people's songs I had also written my own material as well. Once you're in a studio you're constantly fiddling with everything to make a recording better, or so you think, rather than writing new material. Every time there was a new bit of recording equipment on the market I'd buy it. Whether it was three grand here, four grand there, it didn't matter. Being full of cocaine didn't really help I guess, but I still loved it. Who wouldn't? A singer with his own studio, it's what every singer wants. There can't be many more perfect things than that can there? There was also a constant flow of musicians in the house as a result.

Turpin's also gave me time to look after my own animals too. I have always loved animals and at one time we had pigs, chickens, goats, horses and the Rottweilers.

My brother John was always at Turpin's and he would go to the local supermarket, where he had a deal going with the manager, to buy the left-over foods for the livestock.

There was nothing better than walking around with my dogs. I had my two Rottweilers – Bill and Ben, at 12 stone a piece you could hardly call them the Flowerpot Men! Then there was my Yorkshire terrier called Sparky, my Labrador Henry and Kizzie, my Jack Russell. All my other animals had names as well. You see this was my peace, my solitude, walking in my very own bit of land. It was to be my real solace when I was at home.

I'm looking at buying a few acres again now, not far from Blackpool, and starting again with some more animals. I've never lost my feeling for them.

It must have seemed slightly eccentric to some of the locals when John used to go off in a Bentley just to get the bales of hay for the horses. He'd just get them to bung them in the back. Seems a bit mad doesn't it, using a beautiful car for that? But it's not, that's just how we all are in my wonderful family. We just get on and do things. We don't worry about whether we're in a big expensive car or a Bedford truck, to us it's just a way of going from place to place.

If you have animals you have to spend time with them and make sure they are cared for when you're away, so before I'd leave for a tour I would always tell whoever was stopping to make sure the chickens were locked up on an evening.

Unfortunately there was one time when whoever was responsible hadn't remembered though, because all the chickens had gone by the time I got back. Maybe it was the Revenge of the Magician from Pontin's! Either that or they had all seen an early copy of the film *Chicken Run*.

I have more happy memories than I have bad ones of my time at Turpin's, but there was one day that will always stick in my memory – and it was one of the most distressing times in my life, to say nothing of my Aunt Rosie's. It still affects me when I think about it today.

Me, my mam, Aunt Peg and Aunt Rose had been for a wonderful day out at Windsor Zoo. We had videoed the whole day and everyone was in high spirits. It had been gorgeously sunny and really things couldn't have been better. We had come home ready to watch it, all feeling full of the joys of spring. It felt like the world really was a great place.

Then the phone rang.

It was a call to tell us that one of my cousins from Leeds had been killed. We watched my Aunt Rose drop like a stone. After such a wonderful, sensational day at the zoo, and so much laughter, the day ended in tears. It had suddenly become the worst moment ever in my life.

I cannot explain in any more detail how I felt that evening. I cry just thinking about what happened to my dear cousin. I have never experienced anything like it in my life, the change in mood that day. And I've been through some dramatic times since.

I can sense we need a break here. There's so much more to come, but after something like that maybe it's best if we lighten the proceedings up a bit. Come on now. I can see that your glass needs a refill. Stick with me here; hang on in. We're about to have a bit of fun as you find out more about my favourites.

FAVOURITES

Every moment spent with you
makes me more content with you
Just as you are, you are all I prayed for
And all that you are is what I wake up each day for…

Joe Longthorne *As I Love You* released 2003

We haven't even got to the first time I ever knew I had cancer yet, and I'm still a long way from being declared bankrupt.

I'm about to ride even higher on that wave of fame.

But first, what and who do I really like…here's an interesting and diverse list for you:

THE HUNCHBACK OF NOTRE DAME
RUFUS WAINWRIGHT
FRANK SINATRA
BORIS JOHNSON
TAKING CARE OF BUSINESS

Now I'll explain…

My favourite film of all time is the epic version of *THE HUNCHBACK OF NOTRE DAME*. Charles Laughton came from Scarborough and he was one of the greatest actors the world has ever seen. He was brilliant in this very moving film. It just shows you can have all the special effects in the world, but there is no substitute for talent, real talent.

RUFUS WAINWRIGHT is a brilliant young man and his song *Dinner At Eight* from his *Want One* CD is a really powerful song. He is a great singer songwriter, and he has such a unique vocal style. His re-recording of the whole of Judy Garland's 1961 *Live at Carnegie Hall* show was an amazing feat and it is a true masterpiece.

FRANK SINATRA. Do I need to say anything more? He was one of the greatest exponents of singing a lyric in his own way, his own style. I learned so much from the way he performed. We play his album *Live at The Sands* in Vegas regularly back at home. Mr Sinatra was a real man's man who stuck by his principles too and looked after his people. I hope the people who are around me feel the same way.

These names are not in any particular order so please don't think I'm putting Mr Sinatra below Rufus Wainwright in the pecking order.

BORIS JOHNSON will probably come as a bit of a surprise to some, but I do take an interest in politics. I have always listened to Radio 4. I am very concerned about how the world is today and the future for young people. Boris is a breath of fresh air because I think he takes politics away from the norm. He breaks boundaries between Conservative, Labour and everything else.

TAKING CARE OF BUSINESS was the 'live' album which saw Diana Ross and the Supremes join forces with The Temptations in 1968 on a TV special. It's always been a favourite of mine and includes the song I have sometimes closed my shows with *The Impossible Dream*.

Right! That's your very short break! I could have given you more of my favourites but let's get back to the story.

TELEVISION – THE START

Yesterday – I knew the games to play
I thought I knew the way – life was meant to be
And now there's you – my foolish games are through
Now at last I have found
Just what make this whole world turn around

Joe Longthorne *Love is All* released 1988

So I'm at Turpin's. The family's here and the breaks have kept on coming. There don't seem to be any clouds on the horizon.

How wrong was that? The cloud that was to come would be the darkest there could be. But it didn't concern me, or any of us at the time. I think we were all just enjoying the moment.

1988 was a massive year. My own TV series *The Joe Longthorne Show* saw us with 12 million viewers, as many as the *X Factor* gets today!

I was also still appearing with Les Dennis on his *Laughter Show* and there were even more TV appearances on other shows.

For the Les Dennis TV programmes we used to write six minutes of the show every week, but it wasn't like writing a script. What we did was decide what six minutes of music I would be singing. One week we would concentrate on country music, another week Latin and so on. We used to go in every Monday to organise what we were going to do.

Mike Hughes had even more good news for me. It was all happening now. He was putting me on with Roy Walker for the 1988 summer season at the Futurist Theatre in Scarborough. That's the one right on the seafront on the South Bay. Roy was a household name with his *Catchphrase* programme being one of ITV's top rated shows.

'I'm going to put Roy Walker with you,' he said. 'And Dana, but you're going to top the bill. You're not going to play the clubs any more.'

Layton Institute Club in Blackpool was my last main club gig. I did it because I'd already had it booked and as usual, I wasn't going to let anyone down.

Mike was always very straight with me. He always told it like it was. He has made millionaires out of several very talented people and even one or two who are not so talented. He is a very direct man too.

His first question of me, about the house when he visited Turpin's for the first time was: 'Do you like it?' I said yes and his next question was: 'Yes, but is it paid for?'

I said 'No, but isn't it lovely? We'll pay for it down the line.'

That answer probably told him all he needed to know, and was what he had perhaps expected anyway. I wasn't bothered whether it was paid for. I'm sure he knew that, but he also probably knew then that it would never be paid for.

In my head I thought I was earning enough at the time to pay for anything, so I never thought about the money. I thought that's what I thought you paid accountants to sort out.

I'm a performer, I'm more concerned about what goes on when I hit the stage rather than getting involved with finances. That's where I am very lucky today. James looks after all of that with the rest of my management and promoters. They keep me on the straight and narrow, but all I had then was an accountant – a man who shall remain nameless. I was thinking about saying more about him and what I felt he did to me, but like I mentioned earlier it is more important for me to name those who have helped me rather than those, like him, who didn't.

As I said, Mike always had his five-year plan for each artiste. He had them for Freddie Starr, Roy Walker, Les Dennis and Russ Abbott – and most of his acts were successful. He tended to stick more with comedians than singers. Like I've already said I don't do five-year plans.

There was one time when Mike and I had a big argument and it was after that when he said he didn't want to manage me any more.

I was on £64,000 a programme for my TV series, plus what I was on with Les' programme, plus everything else that was going on. Mike had sorted all of that for me. The first of my mainstream release UK albums on Telstar was out. An EMI contract was on its way a few years later. Things were going through the roof. I seemed to be in demand everywhere. No wonder I felt like I could buy anything.

Mike said that although he would no longer manage me he would continue to negotiate all my TV contracts and he earned me hundreds of thousands of pounds over a number of years. They really don't come any better than Mike in the business. He made me a household name through those TV show negotiations.

But if you are a performer and you are successful it means that you attract a number of people who might not be as straight with you as Mike was. That's what Abdul was trying to tell me at the time and I have to say that Abdul was right – as he was most of the time.

I'm not a 'money man' as you know by now, and I was about to start finding out what life is like when you suddenly seem as though you have such a lot.

We'll get one thing straight from the start here. No-one ever stole anything from me, not that I'm aware of. No-one could ever be found guilty of ripping me off along the way. You know why? The reason is that I should have looked after what was happening better than I did. I'm not saying I should have suddenly become a figures man. I just should have looked after the money better myself. I should have got someone in who I could trust. It's always easier looking back after the event isn't it? But that's what I should have done, so I won't name names, because I cannot prove things.

What I really do feel though is that, without swearing, there are some who probably took more than their fair f***ing share! Oh, I did swear after all. Well with good reason I think you will find.

But there was far worse to come than accountants and others with over-inflated bills, people with lesser principles than Mike.

My first ever TV series was about to hit the screens in September 1988 when the wheels came off! My world stopped. You might need a stiff drink and to grab your Kleenex for the next chapter!

CANCER

Why does the sun go on shining?
Why does the sea rush to the shore?
Don't they know it's the end of the world...

Joe Longthorne *The End of the World* released 1988

'I'm going to do the best for you that I can.'

They are the words I see in his eyes. He hasn't spoken them, but I know what his eyes are saying to me. I am sat in front of Doctor Anthony Childs in his house in Leeds. The year is still 1988 but it could 2088, or even 3088 so far as I'm concerned. I have nearly completed my summer season with Dana and Roy Walker in Scarborough.

I am one step away from the biggest TV event of my life – my first ever TV series. There is a 32-piece orchestra waiting to back me in Nottingham.

Nigel Lythgoe, later to become Nasty Nigel in the *Pop Idol TV* shows and then a worldwide TV star in his own right, is my producer and director. My first album for Telstar *The Joe Longthorne Songbook* is set to hit the charts for Christmas.

The whole of my future, my bright and shiny future, is ahead of me. But is it? Or am I about to die tomorrow?

These are just some of the thoughts that go through your head when you are faced with what I found out.

I had been losing weight. I thought it was great at the time. At 33 years old you want to look good, particularly when you're on stage. You don't want the audience staring at you saying, 'he's getting on a bit isn't he?' At least not at that age! It's not a thought that enters your mind when you're in your teens or 20s, but when you're in your 30s that's different. When you're in your 50s as I am now it is not quite as important as it was then, but this was a big time for me. So I wasn't concerned about my loss of weight at first. It was Dana who noticed that I was losing probably more weight than I should have been.

The next thing that happened was that I started getting a stiff neck. I thought I'd got it because as I had been driving back from Scarborough to Ravenscar after the show with the window not going down properly. I just thought it was a muscle thing and thought nothing more about it.

My loss of weight accelerated. I lost getting on for two stones. I had never been fat, but I was now starting to look more like Stan Laurel.

Darryl James, who was my PA at the time and was a sweet guy, told me I had to get myself checked out. He knew there was something wrong, something that needed sorting out. So I went for a blood test and saw Doctor Baxter in Scarborough. As soon as I saw him I asked him whether I'd got AIDS. That's what everyone was talking about at the time. He didn't beat around the bush and told me I had to go to Leeds as soon as I could.

His actual words were that if I didn't go I would be in a 'wooden overcoat' by Christmas. It was some shock I can tell you and I felt as though I had to scrape myself off the floor!

I still had three weeks to go of our eight week run at Scarborough. I was a few weeks away from my TV series.

It was the worst kind of feeling I'd ever had. I was depressed. Was it AIDS or cancer? The next thought was daft I know, but I thought if it's cancer it's alright, I can cope with that, but I don't think I can if it's AIDS. That's how frightened I was at the time. I carried on with the show for a few more weeks before I finally decided something had to be done.

Darryl took me to Leeds where I met Dr Childs at his home in Roundhay Park. His home was so peaceful. He had a big fat grandfather clock ticking in the hallway. I could see wellington boots out in the porch area. There wasn't a TV to be heard. I had to wait half an hour for him. We went through to his study. That's when his eyes told me how serious this was. Then he told me for real.

'I'm going to stay up all night to look through what we think we've got here. First I'll have to take you for a biopsy. We have to get you in as soon as we can.'

The following day I was under his knife.

I only ever thought I was definitely going to die when I saw the brown soap in the bath! I had to take one before my operation. The bath water was six inches deep with cold, tepid water. It was Dickensian. I honestly felt that at that moment Oliver Twist had a better life than me ahead of him.

I thought 'brown soap, tepid water, I'm used to far better than this'. I know I'm National Health but this is f***ing serious. All I felt was that I would be dying in the next six months. I thought about my mam and my sisters and John. I didn't want to go before my mam, because of what it would do to her, losing another of her children. My world was literally turning upside down just at the time when I should have been on top of it.

The results were confirmed by the end of the summer season. I had cancer. My mam, who's not usually very outgoing sang me the song *Good Luck, Good Health and God Bless You*. It meant so much to me.

As I mentioned at the start of this book, what I have is called CLL –

Chronic Lymphocytic Lymphoma – it's a particular strain of leukaemia/blood cancer, a lymphoma. That's what I had, so now I knew.

Soon everyone knew. I was still in Scarborough when my story hit the headlines. There it was emblazoned over *The Sun* and *News of the World*. 'Star dying of AIDS!'

But there's always a funny side to everything you know – even cancer!

Whilst I was in the Brotherton wing of Leeds General Infirmary for the biopsy my family were still there for me, but they were also proving a bit of a handful it seemed.

My nephew Keith has been with me ever since he started touring with me when he was 15. He has played a major part in looking after me over the past 25 years as my minder, my driver, my one-time manager and as simply a great man. I was one of the first people to hold him in my arms after he was born. He, his brother Derek and Keeley, my niece, were in a big camper van parked outside the hospital. They were all there for me.

It just so happened that the camper van was opposite the nurse's quarter.

There I am half dead in hospital and the ward sister asks me whether I can go and see some people in the car park and tell them to quieten down. They were watching the nurses all the time. You couldn't make this up could you? It was only youthful behaviour and they were looking out for me as we travellers do. In their mind I was the first thing, that's what I like to think, although Keith and Derek were probably having a few testosterone-charged moments too. I wouldn't begrudge them that. It certainly helped me to get some perspective on life.

Cancer is such a powerful yet meek word, because you can beat it. Not everyone can, I know, but you can have a go. I've been having a go ever since and there have been lots of times when I've had to get myself back up again after another setback. I guess it's what life's all about. I've even thought I'd beaten it sometimes and found it has come back.

Like I say in my concerts, we've all got something wrong with us at some time or other, and in my case I wouldn't say it's sad, because it just happens.

CONSTANT FEAR

The leaves of brown came tumbling down remember
that September in the rain
The sun went out just like a dying ember
that September in the rain

Joe Longthorne *September in the Rain* released 2008

They had found out what it was at Leeds General Infirmary and my treatment started. CLL is a disease of remission and relapse. That means it keeps coming back. When you're in remission there is no sign of it. When you're in relapse it's back. When it comes back you have more treatment. It's a nightmare. You never know whether you've beaten it or not.

I was immediately put on to a drug called Chlorambucil, which a lot of people who've followed others with CLL will know is the first thing they put you on. It's a tablet you can take which is reputed to have very few side effects. I've taken it now for over 20 years.

Dr Childs told me: 'Look Joe, nothing's going to happen tomorrow. The cancer isn't going to march up on you.'

He also told me that I would need to be in hospital for quite a while and not to go to work, but I was out within the week and I went straight back to performing. You see it's all I know.

I had everything still to live for. My own TV series, my first nationally released album on a major label, more TV appearances scheduled – there was no way I was missing out on anything. I felt great now as I looked in the mirror. At least I now knew what I had and there were things in place to help me. And I had Dr Childs on my side. I knew, looking into his eyes that he wasn't going to let me go.

This was also the time when my charity work really started. I had always done charity gigs but this was when I started doing some serious big bucks work for others. I have continued raising money ever since. There must be some way we can find to beat these awful diseases in the end.

The thing with CLL is that you don't feel like you've got anything sometimes, then other days it's the worst thing ever. People who haven't got it cannot possibly fully understand what it is like to live with that constant fear that every time it comes back you might be given only months to live.

Cancer was also the last thing I expected when everything else in my career had been going so well. I had felt invincible and suddenly, out of the blue, I felt so helpless. I had two choices – to give in or to fight. I chose the latter. I did what every other performer has done before me, I dusted myself down and I got on with the show.

CHAPTER EIGHTEEN

TELEVISION – THE SERIES

The colours of the rainbow so pretty in the sky
Are also on the faces of people passing by
I see friends shaking hands saying how do you do
They're really saying I love you.

Joe Longthorne *What a Wonderful World* released 2006

Throughout my first TV series of *The Joe Longthorne Show* I was undergoing chemotherapy, and I've undergone 'chemo' many times since.

But despite having to have the treatment this was still a fantastic time for me. You see, I was probably luckier than most again, because if I hadn't had the programme coming up I may have been very depressed, but what actually happened was that it was a great success and it made me into a real household name. I won't deny that it was also a very trying time though, because of what I was going through.

Where I was very fortunate was to have Nigel Lythgoe as producer and director. He gave me great direction. Terry Wogan had his own show on the BBC at the time. He was interviewing people like Madonna and yet we were pulling in more viewers. On the show I had the lovely Lisa Maxwell and of course my favourite illusionist Wayne Dobson, who deservedly also ended up getting his own TV series.

I'll admit I wasn't the easiest guy to accept direction, as Nigel will tell you. I've never moved too much on stage. It's usually a case of just give me the microphone and I will entertain you.

There was far more to it than that at Central TV studios where we recorded all three series.

I remember feeling that having my own programme was actually quite frightening at first. It's always nice to be on someone else's show and get off after you've done your six minutes, but here I was with the whole programme to myself, plus my guests.

The set they used at Central was radically different to any other TV show at the time. It featured me coming into the show from out of a tunnel with the band all around me, playing in the wings on a circular-style set. It was filmed using an all-around camera. We had a 32-piece orchestra and all the musicians came up from London for every show. Every one of them was excellent and we had five musical directors within it. That's how good these players were. The core of them were the 'A' team, Alan Ainsworth's at the Palladium, and I was exceptionally fortunate to also have them tour with me.

We were on at 8.30pm on a Saturday night, the prime time viewing slot. I was singing as myself and doing impressions every week.

In the first ever show from the series I did Barry Manilow, Elton John, Stevie Wonder and Al Jolson. In the last show of the six week run I impersonated most of the singers who took part in the Famine Relief recording of Michael Jackson's *We Are The World*.

It should have been the absolute high point in my career as a singer, and I'm sure to many who had followed me up until then it was, but it was a tremendously tiring and trying time for me. I'm not trying to make it sound like anything it wasn't. Of course I was happy with the show. Who wouldn't be? Prime-time, *The Joe Longthorne Show*! It's surely what every performer wants isn't it, a programme of their own.

Life at Turpin's was great, my new album was about to be released – but the cancer was making life difficult in a lot of ways. I had to make regular visits to hospital for chemo.

In retrospect it also probably gave one or two people a chance to make more money than they had a right to out of me at the time, catching me at weak moments.

That doesn't mean I wasn't being looked after though. I was being protected at the same time.

Because of the treatment I was undergoing whilst the TV shows were being made, there were occasions when the people who were managing me would have to say, 'Sorry, Joe just can't do it today'.

When you have a 32-piece band ready to record a show and they're costing the production company £70,000 a day that can cause quite few headaches for the company that is committed to putting on the show.

I was having chemotherapy and shows were getting cancelled, rehearsals were getting cancelled. All the programmes ended up being made, and I appeared in every one, but not without a lot of hassle for the programme makers along the way.

I knew that there were some who were starting to say 'Don't touch Joe' or 'Joe's a no-show' - and for me that also included the Michael Parkinson show.

I had been booked to appear on the show. Mr Parkinson had even asked for me to be on, or so I believe. Like a lot of people I always thought Parky's interviews were the best, but I just couldn't make it when I was supposed to be on and I never got the chance again. I really wasn't very well. Maybe Mr Parkinson never got to hear anything more than an apology that I couldn't get there. All I know was that the opportunity to appear on his show didn't come up again.

When I sang at Don Black's 70th birthday show in 2008, which was broadcast on BBC Radio 2, Michael Parkinson was there introducing all the acts. I sang to close the first half of the show and Mr Parkinson just said 'There is no way we can follow that, so ladies and gentlemen that is the end of the first half.' He also said to me 'Long time, no see.' That was the closest I have ever come to being interviewed by him.

During the series, which ran in 1988, 1989 and 1991 including a one-hour special in 1990, I also sang some of my own songs. It was great to be able to perform them on TV but after a short while Tony Wolfe the executive director said he didn't want them.

He wanted me to sing the songs that people knew, and do the impressions that the viewers wanted. He didn't see me as a singer-songwriter and I can understand that. That's not the reason I had been given the show. We were in a prime time slot and people wanted to hear what they already felt familiar with. I had been fortunate, I suppose, that I had the opportunity to at least try some of them out on a TV audience before Tony's decision.

I never really wanted to come out of a tunnel on to a stage. I was never really a dancer either, although if you watch any of the old programmes back then you will see that I could move – a bit.

I have always been the man with the microphone. I can sing all that needs to be sung just like that. Just put one camera on me and I will interpret the song that will make you cry or smile. For me it's not about a lot of jumping about. It's all about giving me the microphone, the orchestra and the audience. I can do the rest – either as me, or whoever you want.

We made some really good TV shows. Nigel (Lythgoe) certainly made them colourful and fun and we never dropped below 11 million viewers throughout the run over the four years.

One of the really great things about making TV programmes is that they are great opportunities for buying new clothes. I have always enjoyed clothes, right from trying on all of my granny's second hand stuff from her shop, and when we were preparing for each series we would go off to Oxford Street. But I wasn't one of those who always wanted to get dressed up in different costumes every five minutes. I just wanted nice stuff. Armani, Boss, that kind of thing.

Of all of my TV programmes I particularly enjoyed the one-hour special in 1990. I didn't do a series that year. I think you can do so much more with a longer time. When you're putting together a half-hour show for ITV you've only really got twelve and a half minutes for each half either side of the commercial break. There's no real chance to build much momentum into the programme. The special, which was broadcast on 25 April, 1990 featured Grace Kennedy who had just had a disco hit with *Take It Or Leave It* and I was really happy with the programme. It gave everything more room to breathe.

I really loved the recording of every one of my TV programmes and would dearly love to be back recording a show like they do now such as *An Audience With ...* We could really do something with that – and all of my friends in the business including everyone from Barbara Windsor, Robbie Williams, Barry Gibb, Jimmy White, Ronnie Wood, Chris Evans, Jeffrey Archer, Engelbert Humperdink, Phil 'The Power' Taylor, Liz Dawn and many more of them would be great to have there. I'd definitely have Chubby (Roy 'Chubby' Brown) there too, although I don't think they would let him do a 'turn'.

The Joe Longthorne Songbook was released for the Christmas market in December 1988 and reached No.16. It stayed on the Top 40 for 12 weeks, which is still my longest lasting album in the charts. It featured some of the songs I still sing today – *To All The Girls I've Loved Before, Hurt, Danny Boy* and *When Your Old Wedding Ring Was New* and I was backed by some of the best in the business: Dave Arch on grand piano and keyboards, Brett Morgan and Mike Morris on drums; Chris Rae and Lewis Osborne on guitar; Trevor Barry on bass. These guys had all played in the 32-piece band with me on the TV show. I have nothing against the musicians in the Midlands, where we filmed the show, but these fellers who came up from London were the ones for me. They never played a single note out of place in any of my TV shows.

Two more Telstar-releases came out the following year with *Especially For You* released in July 1989, at the start of my second TV series. It spent 10 weeks on the charts and reached No.22. *The Joe Longthorne Christmas Album* followed later that year. They both went 'gold' for me.

My last TV series in 1991 featured Kelly Monteith and the late Marti Caine. Unfortunately dear Marti wasn't as lucky as I have turned out to be. She had lymphatic cancer and died in 1995. Here I am still going strong over 20 years after having been diagnosed with it and Marti has been gone for 15 years. Marti was a fabulously talented lady. I can't believe that she's been gone that long. She had also worked hard in the northern clubland scene before making it big.

I suppose the years of 1988-1991 could be described as my main TV years, but I was still playing live throughout that time too, and there were several really big shows that meant so much to me.

Through my Friendship Club I held my first ever Charity Gala Show to raise funds for the Leeds General Infirmary in 1989. It had suddenly become so important to me and I have maintained the fund-raising ever since.

The biggest show in my TV life came in 1989 as well, when I appeared on the *Royal Variety Performance* at the Palladium. Even my mam was impressed! Her Royal Highness The Queen attended with the Duke of Edinburgh. I was on the bill with Tina Turner, Freddie Starr, Michael Ball, Jerry Lewis, David Essex and the cast of *Coronation Street*. There I was, just a cabaret act from Hull. You see I've never forgotten my roots.

AUSTRALIA

I told you once before – and I won't tell you no more
So get down, get down, get down…

Joe Longthorne *Get Down* recorded 1975
(never released – early session)

Even though I was waging a personal and constant battle with cancer in the early 90s I was still riding on the crest of a wave. The TV shows were hits, the albums, whilst not being massive chart hits were selling very well and eventually they all went either gold or platinum, or both, each making over 300,000 sales.

If I had been bothered about the money I would be telling you now that I had lots of it and just how much I had, but truthfully I never really knew what I had. All I knew was that I was earning big fees wherever I went.

You might think that I was silly really, but I think we've already established that I'm not a money person haven't we?

What I really needed around me was the team, the people I have around me today – James, Keith, John, John Boy, Mike and Fran. But just at the time I needed it the main people who had looked after me and guided me along the way were either going or gone.

I know a lot of people who have made it in show business will probably agree with me here, that the bigger a celebrity you become the more you seem to become surrounded by people who may only be looking to you as income for themselves. It is at times like these when you need people around you who you can confide in and are willing to help.

Abdul, who was always a steadying influence, had always warned me about what would happen along the way. He'd say. 'Joe, watch out because these people are only after one thing. Your money.'

Although my sound and lighting man who had been with me since those clubland days hadn't left just yet, and Rita was still there too, they were both to have moved out of my life by the year 2000. The sound and light man was to leave in the early 90s, Rita later. I still miss all three of them – Abdul, Rita and him very much indeed. They would always tell me what they felt, without any thought of money at all.

Mike (Hughes) had given up as my manager by now and his business partner Tony Cartwright had taken his place. Tony was to land some good stuff for me, but looking back I think I would have preferred Mike to still be around.

Anyhow, with all of the media exposure I was getting and the money that was coming in there still didn't seem to be too much of a problem.

Within four years my career had spiralled and it still didn't look too bad for a few years yet, but what I hadn't realised was that the seeds had been sown for my financial downfall. Of course I didn't see it at the time. I'm a singer, an entertainer. I didn't have a crystal ball, contrary to what you might think about my Romany heritage.

I didn't know that in the coming years I was about to lose some of the good people I had known, loved and respected, people who had been with me every step of the way. I also didn't know that some of the people who were to be around me would not end up looking after me as I had been looked after so far.

I was to find out the hard way.

Much as I would like to I cannot name all the names here for legal reasons, but they know who they are – the people who I believe took more than their fair share. They know they did. Cars were bought in my name and given to wives and girlfriends of those working for me; my 'signature' was being written on so many cheques, but not by me. I even saw what I was told later was £10,000 in 'walk-up' money (the cash generated on the night of a performance, rather than the advance ticket sales) on the bed of someone who was working with me at the time! There were far more stories like this, but because everything seemed to be going so well I let things pass.

The thing is that with all the money I was supposed to have earned from the TV contracts, the album sales, and touring I still didn't know how much I had. Little did I know that most of it I would never see, or be able to spend because of the size of inflated bills coming in all the time. I really didn't know what was coming!

We'll come back to all that later, because right now we're heading for Australia. We're hopping about a bit here but we're now in 1991 and we have come to New Zealand first and then on to Australia on the good ship Canberra.

By now my fame, from appearing on the Royal Variety a year and a half before, had obviously spread to Australia because I was signing autographs as we were getting off the ship. It was my first time 'down under' and I've been back many times since.

We had managed to get an appearance on the *Ray Martin Show*, which at the time was Australia's biggest daytime TV show. My appearance, so I was told, had brought about the largest ever phone-in from viewers. They were so excited about it that they invited me back the next day. I ended up appearing on the programme four times that week. I've had a love affair with Australian audiences ever since.

The first time I ever saw the Sydney Opera House I knew I had to sing there. Call it another notch on a singer's bedpost if you like but to me it was just somewhere I had to play. Ronnie Corbett and a lot of other big names from the UK were touring over there at the time. Everyone wanted to play this beautiful place.

When we visited the Opera House I didn't have any of my own management or booking agents with me. I simply went to see the manager there and asked how much it was to book it. I was told that it would cost 6,000 Australian dollars so I said, 'Here's £3,000 as a deposit. I'll be performing here one year from today.'

Apparently it caused quite a stir at the time. They were planning on having the Bolshoi Ballet and apparently I'd gazumped them. I was told afterwards that there was all sorts of fuss going on with people saying 'Who's booked him in? Who's promoting it?' They made all kinds of objections but there was nothing they could do.

So we booked the Sydney Opera House, just us and just by walking in and asking. That kind of thing just doesn't happen does it? It will probably never happen again either, but we did it!

I had taken a big chance on booking it and now, for one night, the Opera House was mine. It was a bit like going up to the owner of the big wheel at a funfair and saying we'll book the lot for 50 quid!

The following year we went there and sold it out, all 2,600 seats. I took my band across with me and we tore the place apart. It was a gamble worth every penny.

But even then I had another problem that needing sorting out. I was still battling cancer, but this time it was my hearing that needed surgery. This is how *The Sun* reported it whilst I was in Australia: 'I'm finished as mimic if ear op fails, by Joe – Exclusive from Amanda Cable in Sydney, Australia – Comic singer Joe Longthorne last night admitted that his showbiz career will be ruined unless surgeons are third time lucky in finding a cure for painful deafness in his left ear. Two operations to save his hearing have already failed. Joe, 35, who nearly dies two years ago from a rare blood cancer said: 'My livelihood relies on listening to other singers and copying them to perfection. If I can't hear them properly or rely on my own impressions my career will be finished. I've always been slightly deaf in my left ear but the cancer made things worse. While I was weak a tiny hole in my eardrum grew bigger. By January this year I was totally deaf in that ear. The only sound I could hear was air rushing in as I breathed.' The top mimic who impersonates 88 stars began slurring his speech, the first sign of deafness. Friends accused him of being drunk or snubbing them in public. Joe, whose one man show is a hit at the Sydney Opera House, had surgery just before his sell-out summer season in Torquay. In a two-hour operation surgeons covered the hole in his eardrum with a minute graft. They ordered Joe to rest for a month – but he refused to disappoint his fans and went on stage. But his newly-repaired eardrum ruptured during an impression of Luciano Pavarotti on his opening night. 'I felt an agonising pain in my ear. The graft had ripped apart.' An emergency operation repaired his shattered ear. But now the doctors say only a third operation will work. Joe said: 'The deafness makes me afraid. I dread radio interviews because I can't hear the questions. I guess at the answers and pray that I'm not making a fool of myself.'

My sound and lighting man and I were finally to part company in 1992 after 17 years of Jersey, the clubs, Pontin's, Chicago, Philadelphia, Scarborough, Sydney and the TV series. I tried to get him to stay a number of times. We had done so much together, but the time had come for him to move on. He was always like family to me, but now he is family for real because he married my niece and together they have a lovely family of their own.

But 1992 was also to bring about the most bizarre approach I have ever had.

STANLEY KUBRICK

People see us everywhere – they think you really care
But myself I can't deceive
I know it's only make believe...

Joe Longthorne *It's Only Make Believe* released 2003

Summer season in 1992 saw me playing both Paignton and Bournemouth. I was back on the south coast appearing with Roy Walker, Wayne Sleep and the Nolan Sisters. It was another big show and we were doing really well.

Now there are many famous names that have come to my shows over the years – stars of stage and screen, TV and film, sports people, politicians, famous people from London mobs (which we will come to later) – so I didn't think there was any real surprise in learning that another famous name had been to my show at Bournemouth International Centre, another lovely place to perform.

Stanley Kubrick, I had been told, not only liked my show, he also believed I would be ideal for movies. Of course, when someone comes to you and you're already an established performer with TV credits to your name you do get approaches from time to time. So I was happy to meet him and talk about what we might do together.

Tony Hardman introduced Stanley Kubrick to me through that wonderful actress Dora Bryan.

This man was one of the most successful moviemakers of all time – he'd made *2001 A Space Oddysey*, *A Clockwork Orange*, *Spartacus*. And he was to go on to make *Full Metal Jacket* and *Eyes Wide Shut*. I'd just finished my TV series run. I was available.

So why was this American film director watching me in Bournemouth? Surely it didn't all add up?

Well, Mr Kubrick lived in the UK for 40 years, until he died in 1999. All I knew was that I had a film director, one of the most famous film directors in the world, telling me that he could do great things with my career. I had to be interested – who wouldn't be?

Only he wasn't Stanley Kubrick at all!

I didn't know, but the real Stanley Kubrick was a bit of a recluse. So who was the man I had not only met, but whom I had also laid on one of my cars to ferry him about and who I had ended up arranging hotel accommodation for? I'd also bought him clothes too. He conned me by saying things like he just didn't have any cash with him and could I help out.

He was a very clever man called Alan Conway who ended up as an alcoholic, but who *The Guardian* dubbed 'The Counterfeit Kubrick'.

He would act as though he was on the phone with stars like Tom Cruise when he was in company with me. He persuaded not just me but several other influential people, some of them sports stars and one even a film critic in the US, that he was the man himself. I understand from a press report around the same time that Julie Walters was deceived too, but I'm not sure whether she had the same approach as me.

I went for a meal with him at a Chinese restaurant in London, which is where we found out that he wasn't who he said he was. I'd taken my lawyer Russell Roberts from the solicitors Sheridan's with me and Zeb White, my tour manager by then, came too. Russell looked after me well.

When it came to the end of the meal I said that I would pay the bill but 'The Counterfeit Kubrick' said he would pay. He paid by credit card. As we left the restaurant, Russell went back to ask whether he could have a look at the bill. What he saw on the credit card receipt was the name Alan Conway, so that's when we knew something was wrong.

Russell then contacted Warner Brothers, who the real Stanley Kubrick was involved with, and they confirmed that Mr Kubrick had not been in the vicinity of Bournemouth during the time that I had been visited by Alan Conway.

So I'd been conned.

We found out whilst we were on the train back to the south coast. It was like something out of an Agatha Christie story, which was quite appropriate because that summer season we happened to be stopping in the Agatha Christie suite in the hotel. Once we received confirmation of his real identity the people around me took our own action. This didn't involve my solicitors by the way.

We chucked Counterfeit Kubrick into the sea at Paignton!

THIS IS YOUR LIFE

Tonight I'm going to a concert
To see a very special man
He's tall, he's blond and handsome
Joe Longthorne is his name

I'm getting in a right old tizz
Deciding what to wear
What dress? What jewellery? What shoes? What bag?
And, oh my God, my hair!
Now does my bag match the shoes?
Does the perfume smell too strong?
Oh my God, look at the time
The taxi won't be long

I gather things together
To put into my bag
My keys, my purse and of course the ticket
Then get into the cab

Soon enough we're at the theatre
The driver gets his fare
I go into the 'Ladies'
To readjust my hair

I dash into the concert hall
And settle in my seat
To sit and enjoy, and swoon at Joe
The guy I'd love to meet!

Maggie Prickett of Rushden *I'm Going to a Joe Longthorne Concert*

Firstly, before we move on, thank you Maggie for such a lovely poem!

In 1993, there were still so many good things going on in my life. My first ever show in the Royal Albert Hall on Sunday 22 November 1992 had been a marvellous experience. It was yet another high point in my career.

I received an excellent write-up in *The Stage*: 'ROYAL ALBERT HALL – Joe Longthorne - It is now over 21 years since Joe Longthorne first appeared on television as a 14 year old in *Junior Showtime*. Since then he has made remarkable progress to become one of the world's greatest vocal impressionists and built up a tremendous following that includes a 3000-strong fan club, many of whom – mainly female – were at this concert in force armed with flowers, balloons and even a banner inscribed 'Hello Joe, Simply the Best.' Joe Longthorne certainly believes in giving value for money. Opening with *Somewhere* it was an hour and three quarters later before he finally left the stage, his arms filled with flowers and the audience on their feet after his sensational Elvis Presley finish. All his big show stoppers were there: Tom Jones' *It's Not Unusual*; Neil Diamond's *Sweet Caroline*; Sammy Davis Jr's *What Kind of Fool Am I?;* Bassey; Sinatra; a moving tribute to the late Matt Monro; even Des O'Connor; and half the cast of Coronation Street; he also played piano for Jerry Lee Lewis' *Great Balls of Fire*. Longthorne not only has an incredibly large number of impressions to draw on – they seem to include nearly every major star of show business – but his main strength is the uncanny, consistent accuracy with which they are all performed. The musical backing, under the direction of pianist Ernie Dunstall was superb.'

Thank you to Michael Dynan who wrote such a glowing report. There was a relative newcomer appearing as support act for me that night you might just have heard about. His name? Bradley Walsh. I wonder where he ever ended up?

I was later to release both an album and a video of the show. It was amongst the first of many 'live' albums, videos, CDs and DVDs that have been released since and the CD was the first ever mainstream release to feature me doing my impressions of other singers.

I toured Australia for a third time. We were selling out everywhere and despite the fact that I was still suffering through the cancer, my world hadn't come crashing down at all – not yet anyhow.

My fans have a lot to do with keeping my spirits up whenever I have looked like flagging. They have always helped me through, whether by coming to the concerts or sending me letters.

I was also to spend one-third of 1993 in the town that has since become my home. Our 16-week run at Blackpool's Opera House broke all box office records and remains the biggest earning show that has ever played there. The takings were £1.7 million. It was a fantastic run and I enjoyed every moment apart from what I found out once it was over.

I topped the bill and Little & Large appeared with me. It was a fantastic show.

At the end of a run like that you might have anticipated that I'd at least get around half of the overall monies, after the theatre and the band had been paid, but all I ended up with was just £16,000 – from a run that had grossed £1.7 million. I was starting to get the idea that things weren't working out on the money front. I asked a lot of people where all of the money had gone but no-one could tell me.

I'd even been presented with a special award on stage from First Leisure to mark the box office receipts record and yet this was all I had to my name at the end of it all. Where had it all gone?

The show had been tremendous and everyone had loved it. Some of my fans had been several times and I was feeling great. For any of those TV bosses who by now thought I might not complete another TV series because of my fight against cancer they should have come and seen me. I'm told that was their main reason for not giving me another series or even another one-off one hour special, because of my cancer. And yet I was at my absolute peak at that time.

I find even an empty theatre fabulous. When you're in there on your own you can just feel the spirits of those greats who have played there before you. It's magical. It's my home. Later in the year my name was added to the Winter Gardens Roll of Honour of headline acts, which had also included Dana, Marti Webb and Paul Nicholas.

The team around me at the time now included Tony Cartwright as my manager, Zeb White, my tour manager and sound and lighting man, and Darryl James, along with the family, as always. My nephews John Boy, Keith and Derek, and my niece Keeley were all around.

So how did I not have much at the end of the run?

Well, I suppose it was partly because I had people for this, people for that. But that doesn't explain everything. I don't think I will ever know, apart from that feeling I have of some taking more than their fair share. I know those who I felt did, but I won't name them, like I said before.

At one time when we were on tour we had around 60 people involved and we were using a big tour bus. Turpin's was costing £2,000 a week and the bus was costing £400 a day. In retrospect you could probably see what was happening. Everything costs money. But I wasn't on television any longer, and I didn't have the same big contracts I once had, yet I was still living as though I had them.

My TV shows had brought about the three Telstar albums in 1988-1989 and there were also three best selling videos to come – *The Singer, The Very Best Of Joe Longthorne* and *The Ultimate Collection* during the 90s.

But my TV series, after four glorious years of great viewing figures, were over and I haven't had my own show since then.

Although television was no longer to come knocking this wasn't to be the end of my on-screen career as 1993 also saw not only the release of my new album in November, but also the production and subsequent release (in 1994) of my record-breaking show at Blackpool on video.

My new studio album *I Wish You Love* pleased me for several reasons. Firstly, I was now signed to EMI, the UK's biggest record label at the time, which Tony Cartwright had negotiated for me. Secondly, of the album's 14 songs nearly half were collaborations, written by myself and Ernie Dunstall my musical director. Ernie was one of the industry's best musical directors and wrote songs with Dorothy Squires. Together we penned six songs. Ernie was a man who really cared about his craft. We released two singles from the album – *Lady Blue*, one of the songs written by Ernie and me; and *Young Girl*, the song originally made famous by Gary Puckett and the Union Gap in the 1960s. *Young Girl*, in particular, was a fantastic production.

We had been recording the album during 1992 and 1993 at Chris Rea's studio in Cookham, Marlow (I also played with Chris Rae, who was a lead guitarist, but this was Chris Rea of *The Road to Hell* fame) and Cranbourne in Dorset. Zeb White had been the project coordinator for the album and my ex-sound and light man was the production consultant. The album also featured four songs that have remained a regular part of my shows to this day: *So Deep Is The Night; If I Only Had Time; Mary In The Morning* and *Say It With Flowers*.

I might not have been beamed on to people's television sets any longer, but I was getting loaded on to them through their video players via the Telstar videos.

At the tail end of my record-breaking run at the Opera House 1993 I was approached by what now seems like one of the most bizarre of sources to make a video of one of my live shows.

A man from Yorkshire introduced himself to Zeb White after seeing one of my performances, but his only previous experience in the world of filming had been with birds! And we're not talking anything smutty here, because his experience was with the feathered variety. This Barnsley man was apparently one of the leading names in the pigeon racing game and until he approached Zeb he had never made a video of anything other than these birds. He had become a fan after bringing his wife to see the show.

He said he wanted to produce a video of the last in the run of my shows at the Opera House. I remember being slightly apprehensive about allowing him to do it. After all, he had no track record in live entertainment, but he had said that if I didn't like what he filmed and how he recorded the show then he would just bin it.

To be fair to this man who is now no longer involved with me hence no name, he produced a fantastic video of the very last night of my summer season and sold in massive quantities. He went on to produce several videos and DVDs of my live shows over the years.

The *Live In Concert* video, filmed at Blackpool in 1993, was eventually released by EMI in 1994 and reached Number One in the video charts where it stayed for six weeks, my first chart-topper, and it was on the charts for 81 weeks. We knocked Take That off the top! We followed this up with the *Live at the Royal Albert Hall* video the following year, which reached Number Two. I then reached Number One again in 1996 with *A Man & His Music*.

There were still so many good things happening for me recording-wise and concert-wise. 1994 didn't just see my first Number One video; it also saw my *I Wish You Love* UK tour with a huge tour bus announcing JOE LONGTHORNE IN TOWN, ON TOUR all over the side; and then came another very special moment for me – I was, in time-honoured tradition, surprised by Michael Aspel with his big red book, at the Manchester Apollo, announcing 'JOE LONGTHORNE – *THIS IS YOUR LIFE*' which was aired on ITV on March 20.

It was one of the proudest moments of my life when Michael stepped out on stage at the end of my concert. I was amazed. I can honestly say I did not have a clue about what was going to happen. The whole occasion was like a dream and what had happened didn't really sink in until I saw the TV recording of the show several weeks later. The evening itself was very moving and emotional – to walk out and see all my family and friends together was wonderful, and to share it with 3,000 people who had come to see me was just brilliant. Most of all it was fantastic to be able to share the evening with mam and dad. I really feel it was as much their night as mine.

Roy Walker, Little & Large, Liz Dawn and Bill Tarmey were all on the show, along with Norman Collier, Bobby Bennett, Danny La Rue and Dr Childs. Those who couldn't make it but sent their best wishes on video were Les Dennis, Marti Caine and Jim Davidson. Ray Martin, from Australia, even appeared with all of the audience from his show that day.

Danny (La Rue) and I were good friends and everyone should know that not only was he a great performer, he was also a marvellously warm and generous man. He really was in a class of his own. When he passed away in May 2009 it was another sad loss to the UK entertainment world. There really was nobody like him and probably never will be again.

Jim (Davidson) and I were mates long before we ever hit television and he has been very good to me over the years.

The producers had also dug up a clip of me from *Junior Showtime* as a barrow boy, and ran a clip from my appearance as Dick Whittington in *Noel's House Party* Pantomime. They also played part of the video of myself and Marti singing *I'll Never Love This Way Again*.

I auctioned off the big red book for charity, on the *Richard & Judy Show*, and it raised a lot of money for Leukaemia research. I think it raised something like £7,000.

To see mam's face radiating joy and happiness throughout the night was better than anything else. Don't get me wrong, it really was a wonderful evening and I thoroughly enjoyed every minute, but it is mam's face that sticks in my mind even now. I know dad enjoyed it very much too.

Dad even cracked a gag when Michael Aspel said he played the piano by ear. He said, 'Yes, I use my fingers sometimes as well.' They were both as proud as punch - and for mam I think it then made it official that I was a star.

Even then, there was still much more to come in 1994. I had returned to headline another successful summer season at The Futurist Theatre in Scarborough and I had also recorded with two of the leading ladies in Britain's biggest soap operas. I sang a duet with Liz Dawn (Vera Duckworth from *Coronation Street*), who came along and said some really nice things about me at a Variety Club award I received a few years ago.

We sang *Passing Strangers*, which was released as a single and made the charts. We had a few other possible songs and nearly recorded *These Boots Are Made For Walking*, but Dawn had already done *Passing Strangers* previously so she was familiar with that one.

Then I received a call from Barbara Windsor (Peggy Mitchell in *Eastenders*) who asked me if I would sing a duet with her too. We sang *They Can't Take That Away From Me* on Barbara's *You've Got A Friend* album. Both of these songs were recently featured in my *40th Anniversary Collection* album released in 2009.

And still that wasn't all. Although I no longer had my own TV series I was hardly being neglected as I also appeared on Cilla Black's top-rated *Surprise Surprise* TV programme.

Even without my own TV show I was busier than I ever had been! In fact, thinking about it now, it would have been difficult to have fitted in the TV schedule with everything else that had been going on. Barbara also made an appearance, by video, at my Variety Club awards evening on the same night as Liz.

Then, right at the end of the year I also sold out the Royal Albert Hall once again.

But 1994, for all the touring and recording, plus the big red book surprise, was the year when it started becoming clearer the kind of mess I was in money-wise. I still had no real idea, but others around me could see it.

At that stage I still didn't know that I was going to be declared bankrupt,

I didn't think about it going that far. All I knew was that I was working hard and when you work hard and you can see lots of people coming to your concerts you don't worry about the money. I was also signed to a merchandising company called Sanctuary. Everything seemed to be going all right. But I had found out where some of the money was going.

I have to say here that my family has never been responsible for any of the financial mess I was in. They have always looked after me and I have always looked after them. If you come along to any of my concerts today you will see just how well we all work together. James tells people that we're like a jigsaw, if one of us is missing then the whole thing doesn't look right. But at this time we had a lot of wrong jigsaw pieces I guess.

The first time I truly realised that things were not good was when I found that I was getting overcharged. Over the years I have since found that people don't do it to you in one big lump, they take it from you bit by bit, say through a tour or two. The accountant was one of those who I feel did it to me. He was charging me hundreds of pounds an hour.

I did not let one date down in 1994, despite still living constantly with CLL and enduring more treatment. I wasn't in remission, so I was still living with the fact that I had cancer and yet I was managing to fulfil every engagement.

Serious money was still coming in but the problem was that it was going out just as quickly and bills were becoming bigger than they should have been.

I will be the first to admit that I had bought a big house that still needed paying for. I'd bought the Rolls Royces and the Bentleys, we were taking a massive bus all around the UK with an entourage of around 60 people – riggers, caterers, drivers, the band – and I was no longer getting the TV fees which I had been used to for the past four or five years.

But that was still no excuse for people shafting me upside down. I felt that I was being conned, robbed by any number of those who thought they could get something out of me easily. And what's more I felt I was being conned by some of the people who had been very close to me.

James always tells me that I was never robbed. He tells me that all people did was to overcharge me and that I have no concept of money, as I keep saying, and he's probably right. But that still doesn't stop me from thinking that I had been 'done'.

There was one man, someone who is now pretty well-known in TV, who I have no respect for. I went to his office one day with Big Mick Johnson to have it out with him. Mick stands 6 ft 7 inches tall. He's handy having around when you need someone who just by his sure size can intimidate. This TV man had three or four Page Three girls there, all with their tits hanging out, but there was no sign of him.

I knew he had been there as soon as I stepped into his room. There was a warm cup of coffee and a half eaten apple on his desk, and a jacket on his chair. He owed me money. I'm sure he was on the f***ing roof. He wasn't even man enough to see me face to face! Come to think of it maybe he is one of the reasons why I'm not on TV that much.

We made a visit to the accountant straight after that.

There were still a great deal of good things going on in my life at this time, but my world was soon to go through yet another calamitous period. It was as though my life had turned into one of those rollercoaster rides that are so famous at Blackpool Pleasure Beach.

In the period of 1996-1997 I was to be hit with three hammer blows – bankruptcy, the return of cancer and a nervous breakdown. I think we need a break before we tackle all of that don't we?

Drugs & Fights

Along with the sunshine,
There's gotta be a little rain sometime.
When you take, you gotta give, so live and let live…

Joe Longthorne *Rose Garden* released 2008

Let's turn to drugs, stealing and fighting. And let's also throw in a few shotguns too – not mine, in case you're starting to get concerned. But before we get into it too much let me say that no, some of this does not make me very proud, but if someone attacks any of my family I will not just stand around and watch things happen.

I said I'd tell you everything here didn't I? Apart from one or two names and allegations that cannot be printed for legal reasons I'm not about to pull any punches either.

Yes, I have done lots of drugs. I have gambled. I have been in fights. I have and do still smoke, and I have always liked a drink or three.

Frank Sinatra once said, about smoking, 'You die your way, I'll die mine'. Actually I've never been a great smoker, I've always dragged a bit behind!

Performance-wise, let me get one thing straight as well. I never have a drink before I go on to do a show. I might have done years ago, but I never do that now. When I get to a theatre I like to arrive fresh and ready to get on that stage.

That's one of the reasons why I don't usually arrive at a venue until 20 minutes before I'm due to go on. I know there are some of my fans that still get worried when I haven't arrived and yet the interval is already under way, but I make sure that I am fit and ready, and that I look good when I go on to that stage. After all the people who have come to see me have been home, had a shower and made themselves look good to come out for the night. So drinking is out of order until after the show.

But what about those other things? What about the drugs?

I've been on drugs since 1988 when I was first diagnosed with CLL, but in all honesty I had been dabbling with all sorts of drugs for years, mainly marijuana, ever since I was in my teens like many people of my age. I was 'tripping' on LSD when I was 17 in a local pub. I was doing two bottles of cider a night at 16. And I was driving home each night as well. I'm not advocating drugs anywhere, or drinking and driving, I'm just telling you what happened to me.

When I was living in Cranbrook Drive some 'friends' gave me Speed, they put it in my tea and I became hooked on it for a while. It was like jumping powder to me. I was off the rails every other night. I took it to keep me up. Keep me going. I was doing cocaine and experimenting with lots more in the 80s too.

You know, there's no drug in the world, or alcohol, or nicotine that can take the place of audience applause and the love and warmth I receive from everyone, but as soon as I come off that stage it's different. For a number of years I needed something to help keep me up on that adrenalin high for longer than just finishing a show.

When I was at my most busy in years gone by I started taking more and more silly stuff.

I was doing Temazepam and things like that. It's now a Class 1 drug and you can only use it if it has been prescribed. It's a killer otherwise. It is now banned from general usage. All of these drugs have been produced for very good reasons in the first place and Temazepam is meant to help those with insomnia, or those who are feeling over-anxious, for short periods.

I would come off the stage having played to 2,000 people all standing and cheering, and there in the wings would be one of the people looking after me at the time with what they used to call 'wobbly eggs'. Each one contained 20 milligrams in liquid form and the idea was I would take them to calm me down, because coming crashing down from the high of the applause, the standing ovation, to nothing once I'd finished was too much for me. I'd come off, insist that I had them, go back on for the encore and then half way through the last song I was gone. They were all prescription drugs, nothing was purchased on the black market.

All I do these days is I smoke a little marijuana and have a beer at the end of each performance, because it relaxes me.

I did an interview on the radio recently and said that I'd taken drugs purely for their medicinal purposes, but you know that was really just an excuse, it really was.

So what about my fighting?

Yes, I got into fights at school, like quite a few kids do. And yes, I did sort out Pancho when he messed up my act in Jersey – and yes, I was involved with the affray that saw me fly back from the States to appear in court. But I've had a few more hairy moments than just those.

There was one occasion when I didn't exactly fight, but I really thought I was going to land myself in deep trouble. I was 17 at the time and should have known better.

I've never thieved at all, apart from one time when I took a torch from a shop as a kid – and mam knew straight away anyway. Mams do don't they? Actually it might have had something to do with me having left it switched on underneath my jacket as well. Not very bright - although the torch was. Too bloody bright in my case!

But I came very close to being branded as a thief for a long time on one occasion when I was 17. A mate of mine at the time said, 'Come on Joe, we're going to go shopping.'

We went to one of Hull's big department stores. What I didn't realise was that he wasn't talking about buying anything. I found out later that my mate was what we call in cant, a chorer (Romany for thief) but honestly, on my life I didn't know what was going on. It was only when I was asked to be a 'look out' that I realised something wasn't right. By this time they were on with the 'hoisting'. I decided I had to get out of there as I didn't want to be arrested for something I hadn't meant to be involved with.

I panicked and ended up throwing a guy out of the way as I made my way out of the store. I'd never been involved in anything like that. When I was out on the cart with my dad I'd never taken anything for scrap that people didn't want taking from their homes, and I didn't intend getting caught up in what I now knew was happening in the department store.

The man I'd thrown out of my way fell down the stairs and although I didn't give much of a thought to him at the time I hope he turned out okay, but really all I wanted to do was get out of there. I didn't get out of it altogether though. I had been spotted.

I know this next bit sounds a bit daft, but because I felt like I was on the run I dyed my hair from blond to black so I wouldn't be recognised. It didn't make any difference. I was still arrested and it was as though I was admitting that I was guilty because I'd dyed it. The case ended up getting kicked out of court. It did frighten me though.

If I hadn't been frightened enough about possibly being sent down when I went to court, the incident that took place down in London, which I'll tell you about next really did frighten me.

I was doing a gig in a pub I believe was called The Feathers somewhere in London. I'm on stage singing *Danny Boy* when all of a sudden these cars go past and shoot all of the windows out. I just carried on singing. The landlord gave the band another £150 that night and we carried on for a while longer. And you think that kind of thing only ever happens in films!

That's the shooting over – now back to the fighting! Although this is more comical than anything else.

I was back over to Hull last year. There was a lovely karaoke session going on in this pub and I got up to do *Strangers in the Night*. Then there was a bit of pushing and shoving. I thought nothing more of it.

I went outside to have a smoke and the next thing I know there is this woman coming out of the pub and all I see is a load of flailing black hair coming towards me, and she's built like a f***ing Chieftain tank. I weigh 10st 8lbs. I can't say what happened next. Well I could, but it's probably better that I don't.

I love going back to Hull, to Hessle Road, to the pubs I used to sing in. I have a very loving family that all want me round at their houses, but I won't stop going into those pubs, it doesn't matter what happens. I love Hull, it's my home town and it's wonderful how it has come on in recent years.

That's pretty much my fight history by the way – a few knockouts, no defeats, a few near misses. Well, I should say that's all, apart from one, the big one that really did see me end up in court. We'll leave that for now and come back to it later in real detail.

CHAPTER TWENTY THREE

BANKRUPTCY

We were on life's roller coaster
Holding on each new twist and turn
Finding out how far the road would go
How many bridges we could burn
Never caring for tomorrow
And the danger lying round the bend

Joe Longthorne *Never Say Never* released 1993

It's funny you know, but nervous breakdowns creep up on you. They certainly did with me. It's not just one thing, a lot of things all come on top of each other. For me it was bankruptcy, chemotherapy, drugs, money troubles and also a car crash. They're a pretty unhealthy cocktail to start with.

1995 had seen me really busy touring as usual. There was the release of the *Live At The Royal Albert Hall* video and in September I took part in a Gala Tribute to Lord Delfont in aid of the Entertainment Artistes Benevolent Fund, along with Aled Jones, The Grumbleweeds and Cannon and Ball.

I was also to meet one of the entertainment world's all-time greats.

It was yet another fabulous moment in my career when I performed for and met the legendary iconic comedian Bob Hope backstage at a special night in his honour at the Palladium. Danny La Rue and Roger Whitaker were also on the bill that night. It was on behalf of one of Mr Hope's big golf charity nights. Afterwards he told me how much he had enjoyed my performance and even invited me over to his home in Palm Springs. I never took him up on his offer, but I did have a photograph taken of Mr Hope and me together which still takes pride of place in mam's house. I was so proud to have been invited to perform in front of one of the biggest names ever in showbiz.

During all of this time and ever since I was first diagnosed with CLL I had been raising funds for Leeds General Infirmary in order to help those with cancer.

Little was I to know how hard CLL would come back to haunt me in the coming years. The disease really is a f***ing nightmare.

First though, it was my financial troubles that were increasing.

Back in 1995 I had a house that I still hadn't paid for and that was now costing me a great deal to keep up with the payments, I had massive expenses to pay out for a number of people who were overcharging me, and the money that was now coming in, without the fat cheques from TV contracts, was never going to be enough to pay all of the bills. And it was starting to make me ill.

I still didn't realise I was heading for bankruptcy. I was too busy taking drugs to calm me, drugs to keep me up, drugs for my cancer, drinking and smoking. I was putting so much up my nose at the time that it's not to be sniffed at you know!

When I did realise that bankruptcy was on the way, and that I couldn't spend anything because I didn't have anything it was bloody awful. It made me feel ruddy awful. I was falling apart at the seams. So much for sex and drugs and rock 'n' roll!

Earlier I talked about whether I'd ever lost the plot. This was the time.

But just at the time I was starting to feel really bad, things were about to get a whole lot worse than they had ever been.

The years of inflated costs and buying expensive items like cars and the house had now caught up with me.

It still didn't stop me from just popping in to Harley Street one day though, as you do! The next bit is pretty comical.

I had some bags under my eyes, or felt I did, and decided I wanted them sorting out. I also had my teeth sorted out around the same time. Anyway let's talk about the eyes!

I'd been told that an operation to get my eyes fixed, to remove a bit of fat, would cost £1,500 and I took the money with me. They were putting me under the anaesthetic, but just before I went to sleep they told me they needed another £1,500. It was £1,500 per eye! Jokingly, I said I thought you did a two-for-the-price-of one in an afternoon. But they weren't joking. So I had to get on to 'Snowy', my man with the money at the time, who sent someone on a bike and got there with the rest of the money in 10 minutes.

I was still touring all around the UK in 1996. I made an appearance on the TV show *This Morning* as well.

However, just five years on from my last TV series, only three years on from creating box office record takings at the Blackpool Opera House, several gold and platinum selling albums, two Number One videos, and with one of them at the top of the charts at the time, I was now bankrupt!

But even that wasn't all of it. I had further to fall just yet. Isn't it stupid? Here I was, still performing to audiences in their thousands, doing what I do. The next year 1997 was to see everything else getting far worse than where I had already fallen.

CHAPTER TWENTY FOUR

NERVOUS BREAKDOWN

Many times I've been alone
And many times I've cried
Anyway you'll never know
The many times I've tried
And still they lead me back...

Joe Longthorne *The Long & Winding Road* released 2006

I was told that my total debt at the meeting of the creditors was £1.4 million and that with interest it was going up day by day. The meeting had been arranged by Segal and Co. to try and arrange a VCA (Voluntary Creditors Agreement). The receivers wanted something like £15-£20,000 themselves before we even started on the rest. The Bentleys and Rolls Royces had to go.

Darryl James was claiming; so was Bridie Reid; Sheridan's; there were quite a few more at the meeting. I couldn't believe how much was being claimed, but then again I hadn't ever realised just how bad things were. I knew now. I guess it was another case of me not knowing what was going on.

The taxman was the biggest one of the lot. Apparently I owed £400,000 to the Inland Revenue.

I didn't want to sit in front of all these people, all looking at me, a lad from Rifle Terrace and Woodcock Street in Hull, and seeing what had come of all my hard work. I walked through the room. I wasn't going to stay. Andrew Segal, the official receiver, said, 'Joe, you've got to meet them all face to face.' But all I could think about was it would be a bit like going into the lion's den. So I didn't stop. I just couldn't.

Rita was still at Turpin's and she offered great advice. My friends were still with me after all. And so was my family. The only thing they can ever be guilty of is sometimes going maybe a bit too far in order to look after me, like my dad used to do in my early days around the working men's clubs.

Big Mick was there too. Big Mick Johnson is another of my relations and has been around for me many times over the years. I introduced him earlier when I visited the TV producer who I cannot name, the one who left his half eaten apple on the table and scarpered to the roof. Mick's a traveller, lives in the south of England and has a heart of gold. He took the horses when we finally left Turpin's a few years later.

Although I'm not too attached to possessions I must admit I was starting to think that the house – Turpin's – would have to go. I wasn't bothered about the swimming pool or the recording studio, or anything like that, but I was worried for the animals. That was the most upsetting part. I felt I had let down my animals, particularly my horse 'Lady Blue' and a trotter I had at the time, but the pigs, the chickens and the dogs too.

Walking around, seeing some of the wildlife like the badgers, and being on my own was my only real solace at Turpin's like I said earlier, and now that all looked like it was going.

That's when it all dawned on me. It wasn't about losing the house, or how big the house was that I was in danger of losing. That's when my tears fell. To see my horses have to walk out and go somewhere else was soul destroying.

I really didn't understand what was going on and it was messing with my head, to say nothing of the drugs. I knew that if I lost Turpin's I would miss my animals, my walks around the land, my Vietnamese deer. I thought about the pond, how beautiful it was. So it wasn't the possessions that were bothering me, it was the nature. This was my place, where I could relax. It was my retreat, where I could get away from everyone else. It was all going to have to go.

Turpin's was once featured on David Frost's *Through The Keyhole* programme. The late Richard Whiteley got it in 28 seconds bless him. He knew it was my place straightaway. I got the key that they used to give out. Now I thought I might have to give the key to the house away for real.

But Turpin's was saved for a while when another good friend from North London, Fred Nash, who was a member of a powerful business organisation, and who is a very cool operator, said he would buy Turpin's when he needed to and let me stay there. 'Just keep up with your monthly payments Joe,' is what he told me.

We kept the payments going for a while. Turpin's was costing me £6,000 a month. And how did I do it? I carried on playing the concerts. I carried on touring. It's all I know and it's what I do. I've never really changed over the years. All I've probably done is matured, as a singer and a person. I've tried to make a few shillings, singing songs. To me it's still like it was when I started. I'm still singing for those fish and chips for me, mam and dad, John, Lizzie and Anne.

At that time though it wasn't so easy to just keep going, there was so much going on in my head either with the drugs that were helping me when I came off-stage or those that were keeping me alive.

I now didn't have any money, or at least what I was bringing in was only enough to keep paying what was outstanding already.

Bankruptcy or even the sniff of it also gives the newspapers another opportunity to write about you, and of course they did, that's their job.

My fans were always there for me, as they have always been. You're going to hear that a few times more just yet. They have always helped me so much, it doesn't matter what I have gone through. I had one group of fans who, at the time, were going to club together and get me out of bankruptcy. I am sure they would have done too, but that would have killed me. They did send me money. I had to get them to stop. I really appreciated their words and gestures, but it's not what I'm here for, to be bailed out by the people I sing for – although I don't mind the odd M&S voucher!

I went broke and that's it. Willie Nelson went broke too, lots of other singers have gone through bankruptcy. I wasn't the first and I don't suppose I'll be the last.

Some took what they could from me that's my feeling – more than their fair share, but they couldn't take my voice and they never took my grand piano! It was a good job they didn't too, because that's where we'd hidden the money – in the piano legs! That's a joke by the way if the taxman's looking at this book.

Sure, I went broke, but it didn't change me, the person that I am.

Looking back, with the benefit of hindsight, there is of course no wonder that bankruptcy was going to come up. You cannot spend the way I was spending, or having the expenses I was carrying with the band, the tour bus and everything else that comes with it unless you know that your earnings are going to be massive every year.

I was down, seriously depressed. It was as though I was banging my head against a brick wall. It seemed as though everything I was doing, everything I had done, counted for nothing. Apart from my family and Rita there was no-one I could trust, no-one who was really looking after me.

Over a period of time I had now become really ill and I couldn't afford to even pay household bills, let alone afford luxuries.

That brought about a time when I just didn't want to go out. It was a time when, for the first time in my life I didn't want to be in front of lots of people. My depression got worse and for quite some time I couldn't move and just stared into space all day. I was like a zombie. My fans knew that I was going through a bad time and they continued backing me. I did get bags of fan mail but I couldn't even bear to read any of it. I appreciated it though, everyone was meaning well, but by then I just wasn't right. I was too far down the road.

I overdosed.

I woke up in High Wycombe Hospital not knowing how I'd got there. I only spent two nights in the hospital, but that wasn't the end of my downward spiral.

Back at Turpin's – and with me staring into space, my sister Anne was well aware I still wasn't right. I couldn't perform and I was in a terrible state, but my family looked after me thank God, because right at that time for the first time in my life I just did not want to live. It was Anne who started dragging me out of it.

My GP paid me a call. I think Anne or Rita must have called for him to come, and he told me of his psychiatrist friend who flew planes. He tried to persuade me to let him refer me to the Cardinal Clinic in Windsor where his psychiatrist practised.

I was as low as I could go. All I remember is that at one point I took some pills to help me sleep and three days later I woke up in the clinic. Apparently I had to be put in there forcibly, but I cannot remember a thing, only what I have been told since.

The Cardinal Clinic in Windsor is a bit like the Priory is today. I was now officially having my nervous breakdown.

Finally the pressure of what I had been going through, starting probably as far back as 1988 when I had first found out about having CLL, had got to me. But I'm a fighter. I do fight my way out of situations and with the help of the wonderful people at Cardinal I was able to do just that.

They started getting me back right again. I tried running out at first, but then I started to come round. I was only in four days but in that time they helped me considerably. They made me start thinking for myself again, telling me that if I fell out of bed during the night they weren't going to pick me up. It was up to me. It was good psychology and set me back on the right road.

Michael Barrymore got to hear about the rough time I was going through and invited me on to his show. He said 'Come on mate, I want you on my show'. I told him that I didn't know whether I could make it because I was nearly dead. You can tell how bad I must have been can't you?

At that time I was in a wheelchair, and I was in that bad a state that Keith had to push me around. When I got to the studio and they saw how I looked I think they were shocked. I don't think they could believe what they were seeing.

Fortunately for me it was Nigel Lythgoe who was producing Michael's show at the time and I believe it was Nigel who said 'Look at him. It's not Joe.' If it had been anyone who hadn't known me I don't think they would have even allowed me to go on.

I just looked at them and said, 'Put me on a stool and I'll sing whoever you want me to sing. I did Johnny Mathis, Shirley Bassey. Then I sang one song as me which was *How Do You Keep The Music Playing?* Honestly, I don't think I have ever sung it better in my life, I put so much into it.

When it came to being put out as the show itself they put me at the bottom of the bill, which was absolutely right. I really wasn't fit enough to do a complete act. They didn't use the impressions, but they did use me singing as me – and I still got my seven large (£7,000) appearance money. I needed every penny. That was a month's rent sorted.

Michael and Nigel were great doing that for me and so was Keith for encouraging me. God bless Michael for giving me the chance and God bless Nigel for paying me top money. It really boosted my confidence. Getting me back in front of a TV audience was just the thing I needed to get me back going again. I am really an eternal optimist and they both helped in getting me back to normal. Thanks again Michael and Nigel wherever you are and whatever you are doing.

I have never been short of offers to sing, it doesn't matter whether I have been bankrupt, at death's door or whatever. And at the same time as I was going bankrupt I was paid £64,000 to play the Caesar's Palace, unfortunately not in Vegas, but in Luton. Once again I didn't think about the money too much even though it was good and welcome, I just like the audiences. It was for four nights and I only sang for 40 minutes each night.

My receivers even offered me £2,500 just to do a show on a boat in the Thames.

There was some good news as well though. In 1997 I was given the all-clear from cancer. After having come through the Cardinal Clinic as well it meant I was clean both in my head and in my body. I played a Summer Season at the North Pier in Blackpool with George Marshall and Wayne Dobson. But how wrong can one man get? You'll find out.

Let's have another of those breaks shall we? I know I could do with a drink after all of that. Bet you could too.

CHAPTER TWENTY FIVE

IMPRESSIONS

I can feel a new expression on my face
I can feel a glowing sensation taking place..

Joe Longthorne *Walk In The Room* released 1993

I live for singing in front of people. I always have. It's where I come alive and everything else is just a prelude to that. You can see the change in me once I'm there – under the lights. Performing live on stage in front of an audience is the greatest experience I can ever get. I live to perform. Sure, I live to make CDs, DVDs, appear on television, but there's nothing on earth that matches the feeling I get when I walk out on stage. To be with an audience is something else. There is an unbelievable rush of adrenalin, a buzz of energy.

To me it's like a love affair, the audience and me, together as one. It's all about love and communication – and this is where I communicate.

I'm really still doing what I have always done, right from singing on my mam's knee or for all the children at play school, outside the fish and chip shops, on tables in pubs or on a fold-down stage from a trailer in East Park in Hull.

My singing has given me everything I've ever had. Forget about the bad times, they've been and gone. I've had far more wonderful and exciting moments than I have ever had bad, even though I've had my fair share of those.

There are times, and I'm sure most live entertainers would say this, where the audience sends you into another gear, something you hadn't realised would happen. That's still so exciting today, as much as it ever has been, whether it's the reaction to my hands being spread and my eyes rolling around in my head when I do Shirley, or whether it's the gyration of my hips when I go into Tom.

Which quite neatly I think, brings me back to the impressions and how wonderful they have been to me. Without them I wouldn't have come this far in show business. They have been my passport to success wherever I have gone and they are still doing the same for me today.

In the time I have been writing this book I have had several approaches from the States to go back over to Vegas and by the time you read this I will have been over to play a week at the New Orleans Hotel & Casino Resort.

My ticket for being offered this new opportunity? My impressions. It's always been that way, and that's why I will be forever grateful to mam for setting me on the right course when I was a little boy. My impressions have been what gets my foot through the door – and once I've done that the audience then gets to hear what I'm really like as a singer in my own right. The impressions are like my Trojan horse for getting me in anywhere, and then I storm their castle with the rest of my act. It's beautiful when it happens that way and I really believe it will happen that way for me once again back over here on television as variety comes full circle.

Sometimes when I'm in a theatre, like I said previously, I can really feel the spirits of those performers who have played there in years gone by. The world famous London Palladium is steeped in show business history and when I step on to that stage I can feel the spirits of those legendary entertainers – Frank Sinatra, Danny Kaye, Judy Garland, Sammy Davis Jr, Ella Fitzgerald, Johnnie Ray. It celebrates its centenary this year (2010). I've had some amazing nights there – and none more so than when I appeared there in 2006.

I often think that if I'd taken up purely singing straight, rather than performing the impressions, I would have been more disciplined as a singer. That's because with impressions you can always mess about a bit and make people laugh and I've always enjoyed the freedom of that.

I've got you, under my skin
Yes I've got you, deep in the heart of me
So deep in my heart, that you're really a part of me...

Joe Longthorne *I've Got You Under My Skin* released 2002

I love doing Shirley.

What I mean is that I have always loved her music and my performance I hope is also seen as a tribute to her. She has just brought out her first all-new studio album, the first one for years, and I congratulate her on that. Let's correct what I feel about her, I don't just love her, I adore her. When I'm on stage doing my impression of her I believe I turn into her. My feeling is that you have to feel that way to get the impression right. To me Dame Shirley always has been, and still is just absolutely sensational.

There was a time when I understand that Shirley, and I really do hope she said it this way because it would mean so much to me, said: 'He does me better than I do myself.' I really do hope she said that, because my impression, whilst it does also get some laughs in the way I exaggerate some of her mannerisms, is always meant with real, unbounded affection.

Dame Shirley is by far the greatest female singer we have ever had in the UK and you can hear some of her singing style in quite a number of the songs I perform as myself. I don't get to talk to her very often, but we have spoken in the past. I don't think there will ever be a time when I feel there isn't a part of Shirley in the way I perform. That first Shirley Bassey LP I bought back in 1968, was what started it all for me in terms of my real stage impressions.

Frank Sinatra came to me at around the same time. *Strangers In The Night* had just become a big hit for him and I could do his voice too. I ended up doing the whole of the main three in the Rat Pack – Sammy, Deano and Frank.

Sammy Davis Jr is probably the most complete entertainer there ever has been. He was so special. He could do impressions, sing fantastically well as himself, could play instruments and he could dance. The only one of those that I can't really do is dance. I've never really been able to properly.

One of my fans contacted me recently to say they recall having a conversation with my dad who told them of a funny story about me. Apparently dad had told them he once dropped me off for a dancing lesson but I didn't want to go, so I went in, then climbed out of a toilet window and went straight back home.

What actually happened was that Jess Yates (*Junior Showtime*) had mentioned to my mam that I could do with some dancing lessons, so she had taken me. Jess used to always send telegrams. She says that I lasted five minutes before coming out of the back door of the dance class and telling her I didn't want to be in there. I was no Billy Elliott. That was something Jean Pearce had known all along.

I might not have taken to dancing, but I have always thrown myself totally into all of my impressions and those who come to my concerts will know just how many I have done over the years. They do run into the hundreds, not just singers but anyone. I've done snooker players, like Alex 'Hurricane' Higgins, Frank Spencer from S*ome Mothers Do 'Ave 'Em,* Rigsby from *Rising Damp*.

My *Steptoe & Son* routine has always remained a favourite, but I particularly enjoyed the snooker routine I used to do a few years ago. I've always enjoyed putting lots of different personalities together in my routines and in recent years I launched a brand new routine revolving around David Dickinson's *Real Deal* TV programme. I won't tell you all about it here, you'll have to come and see it.

Keeping up with current trends and what's happening in the entertainment scene is important and I'm doing that, but people also want what they know and what they've liked for years.

I have been told recently that Robbie Williams likes what I do and I admire his work too. He's been through some similar things to me with his career but he's coming back again now. He has his own unique style so maybe I'll add him to my repertoire of 'special guests' in my shows. I really enjoy the work he has done too.

David Gest told an audience at a show I was in a couple of years ago that he and Michael Jackson had also watched some of my shows on DVD together.

As I've already mentioned earlier I got rid of the props a while ago. Occasionally I've brought them back over the years, but I don't use them at all now. I just found that sometimes they were getting in the way of the impressions. I prefer to put myself fully into the character and I find I can do that, immersing myself into the person I am doing for two minutes, rather than fiddling around for props.

What I can tell you though is that, props or no props, I would not have had the success I've had without my impressions. I will forever be in the debt of Shirley, Tom, Frank, Deano, Sammy, Judy Garland, Tony Bennett, Neil Diamond, Barry White, Johnny Mathis, Barry Manilow and all of the rest of my 'guest stars' in my shows.

Right – after bankruptcy and a nervous breakdown it's time for some good news in my story do you think? Let's see…

JAMES & PAT

When I was very young and life was new
My world was always full of dreams
Growing old was far away
When tomorrow's just today
Nothing is the way it seems
But I knew that one day I would fall in love
The way that people always do
How could I know what lay ahead
Life played games with me instead

Joe Longthorne *Only Once* released 1980

Life has certainly played some funny games with me along the way and surely, after the bankruptcy meeting or at least trying to avert what seemed inevitable, and the nervous breakdown there had to be some good news on the horizon?

1998 proved to be a year of fresh starts for me, a time when several new people entered my life, and two in particular who I have every reason to be thankful for – my partner James and my very good and close friend Pat Mancini MBE who sadly passed away between this and the first edition of this book.

But you're not getting away with it that easy, because it wasn't a year without incident either!

During the time of my nervous breakdown, both before and after the four days I spent in the Cardinal Clinic, I must have gone at least six months without performing, except for the appearance on Michael Barrymore's show. I just couldn't. Life was really that bad for me. But in 1998 I got back under way. I played a series of sell-out concerts at the legendary Green Room in the Café Royale in Regent Street; appeared on the *Sunday Night at the Palladium* TV show once again, also produced by Nigel (Lythgoe).

I seem to recall that Nigel said to me at the time 'Joe, for once will you do it my way?' I thought he'd meant sing *My Way* so that's what I did.

One very famous name saw me for the first time when I played the Café Royale. Although I didn't know it at the time he was to pay me the biggest of compliments many years later. Intrigued? Well, you'll just have to wait.

It was also the year when Garry Bushell, the TV pundit, started bashing away with stories to get me back on television. He was also highly complimentary and even suggested where I should fit into any TV schedule. He reckoned I'd be great at around 10pm. He said 'Who other than a TV executive could wilfully ignore someone like Joe Longthorne? The greatest singing impressionist England has ever produced, and a seriously world class singer and funny too, in favour of yet another programme with people who just read from autocues.'

Garry did mention some names at this point but I didn't think it was fair on them to include their names here. Garry has since become a great friend and he is still telling everyone that I should be back on screen with my own programme. Who knows? Maybe this book will do some good?

You know, deals for things can be done in some strange places.

Have you ever done a deal on a roundabout? I have. Well, it was actually on the revolving stage at the Palladium. I've never done one on a roundabout since, but it feels as though I've been on quite a few roundabouts in my life.

Another great friend of mine is funny man Johnnie Casson. He's an absolutely superb comedian and we were both on this revolving stage. We were appearing as part of Bruce Forsyth's 70th birthday show. On the bill with us were M People, Danni Minogue and the star of the show – Miss Diana Ross. It was Sunday 15 March 1998.

As the stage was moving around Johnnie and I were talking and I asked him whether he fancied doing the next summer season with me in Blackpool. I didn't know Johnnie particularly well at that time, although I had met him years before when he was drummer with The Diamond Boys at Keighley Variety Club. He had made his name on TV's *The Comedians* show, but he had also played with another very popular band called The Crestas, who once opened for The Beatles.

We did the deal there and then, whilst the wheel was going around! Johnnie is now another of my best pals. He really is a diamond himself and such a generous and unassuming man. He can make me laugh at the slightest thing.

I was still living at Turpin's. Rita was still around too, but we were nearing the end of our time together. It seemed like she had always been around, helping me out of situations, offering advice. She was always there to come back home to.

I had enjoyed living in this fabulous house in Berkshire, but I hadn't enjoyed some of the paparazzi or some of the people who just wanted to see where I lived. I'll always try my best to have a nice chat with someone but my privacy was constantly being invaded.

More and more people were coming to Turpin's to have a look at where I lived, often using a neighbour's garden to get a closer look. In the end I had the view into my land from his blocked off. The neighbour concerned became a bit stroppy and told me I'd spoilt his view. I just told him that he needed to understand that every time I went out for a walk there were camera flashes going off. 'I can't have it.' I told him and I went on to say that I reserved the right to put up a fence.

He had been a flight bomber, some sort of squadron leader and gave me that 'Do you realise who I am?' routine. I just told him straight, no airs and graces. 'No sir, but I know I'm proud to be a traveller.' I felt sorry that I'd rowed with him. He'd been decorated for his services during WWII like my dad. However, he still went to the newspapers about the fence. He also went to Esther Rantzen and her TV programme *That's Life*.

That was hardly the big incident though. That's still to come.

When I came up to Blackpool that year I had no money. All I had once again was pretty much the clothes I stood up in and whatever I would earn during the season. And most of that was paying the monthly rent at Turpin's.

I stayed in Great Eccleston, at digs just about six miles away from where I was appearing. I stayed on a farm with a great man who also became a really good friend, 'Tatie Alan' (Alan Thomasson). He helped me out through those times when I had nothing. Alan provides potatoes to most of the fish and chip shops in Blackpool, so I suppose that was another thing that had come full circle. I was back with the fish and chip shop people I'd started with when I was little.

Although I now live in Blackpool, I hadn't originally wanted to stay in the town where I was performing, that's why I ended up in Great Eccleston. In a way it's a little bit like putting on the show in Scarborough, but staying up the coast at Ravenscar. It allowed me that space.

I managed the season okay but I was starting to get worse again, health-wise. I didn't feel particularly good. The money situation was still not good either. I also hadn't quite come clear from the nervous breakdown at that time, but I had got back to putting on my show and I was at least able to pay for things.

After such a bad time the year before, the nervous breakdown and the bankruptcy meeting, my life was suddenly to get a lot better – although typically not without incident, we're getting close to it now!

I was at a 'Stage night' - one of those nights where all of the entertainers who are in town doing summer seasons all get together. It was sponsored by *The Stage* newspaper. I was still ill, but making a recovery. I was chatting with Chubby (Roy 'Chubby' Brown) near to the bar when James walked by. You can call it whatever you like, but I was drawn like a magnet towards him. I asked him where he was going and I thought he'd said he was going to have a dance with his wife.

We didn't get together there and then on that night. What happened was he came to see me, where I was appearing, on the North Pier. He'd given up his ticket to go and see *Cats* to come and see me. He gave me a little peck on the cheek and we've never looked back. We clicked; it's remained that way.

He couldn't drive when we left Blackpool and Great Eccleston behind to return to Turpin's so I tried to teach him, but we weren't very successful. Put it this way, the big oak tree that had been there for hundreds of years didn't last that long with James at the wheel and me as the instructor.

I suppose we became, how do you call it these days, suited and booted. We are an item and I'm happy to say that we've now been together for 14 years. James has been with me all the way, through everything that has been thrown at us, and I love him dearly. He is my lover, my best friend and my very official partner.

James and I are a bit like chalk and cheese. When I first met him he was 20 years of age and the first thing I wanted to know was what he liked doing. He said golf – he was a 1 handicap golfer at one time, a left hander, one of the best in the area – and I just thought 'bingo', at least we wouldn't be in each other's pockets because I can't stand someone around me every second of the day. I said that we'd look for the best courses for him to play, but the way it's turned out I've screwed up his game as he looks after me so much that he can hardly fit in even a single round now.

No-one else, apart from my mam, has cared for me quite as tenderly as James. He's there every time I need him, every moment when I am really low or tired. He doesn't do it to win any prizes or to show others. He does it all just for me. There are plenty of times when he has had to put me to bed, tend to me when I have been in those desperately low periods and make sure that I am looked after properly. I have a wonderful family that also does that, but James is so very special to me. He's there for me every inch of the way. I think I'm going to cry after writing that!

It's at this point I should really mention Fran properly. Fran (Frances Cunningham) is one of the nicest, kindest, most warm-hearted ladies I have ever known. Fran and I have gone through so much together. Like James, Fran has bathed me, cared for me, looked after me and is always around for me at home. She started by coming to my concerts, but Fran is now one of the most important people in my life. If I told you about all of the horrible jobs she has had to do in looking after me when I have been through my worst moments you would really understand why I think so much of her, but I really don't want you to feel sick by telling you them in full detail.

Very soon when James and I had got together I asked him to also be my manager. He was reluctant at first, which was only to be expected because he hadn't been involved in the entertainment business. But he has a beautiful mind and is a very astute businessman. I could see he had that in him at only 20. He is also good at buying and selling anything, and can very quickly tell you what most antiques are worth.

He's shrewd – not a yes-man. He will say 'no' to people, and to me, which is important. Sometimes people will only tell you what they think you want to hear, but not James. He does it all nicely with me though. I've never had that kind of management in my life until he walked in.

What that has enabled me to do is to get on with what I do, to perform and entertain with even more confidence. I think we've already established at how rubbish I am with things like finances.

James resisted managing me at first because he had never done it before, so he watched how others did it for a while to learn the trade. He worked with those who were managing me to get things sorted out in his own mind, but he now handles it all with the team we have around us. He tells me it took him five years to get used to the environment, that it was like an apprenticeship for him, but he's now not just my manager but a very well respected young man in the entertainment world. He managed all of the merchandising, including the sales team and the printing of the brochure for David Gest on his UK tour in 2010.

We have had some good people who have helped me too – people like Jean Parkes and her husband Mal Ford. All of the help I have received since 1998, when James came into my life, has brought me to the feeling today that my finances are now being looked after correctly. Whether it's working with other promoters, booking theatre dates, talking with the Variety Club, setting up deals or talking with Mr Sinatra's manager, with a view to playing in Vegas or even down to making my supper, James does it all.

What James saw straightaway was that I was not always getting the monies I was entitled to. As James puts it, if I was doing a concert where it had been a sell-out and £25,000 had been taken on ticket sales, I would be getting only a very small proportion of it. He's the one who always tells me that no-one was robbing me at any time, they were just taking what was there and if no-one questioned them they would continue taking what they could.

James and I lived together at Turpin's for around three years.

After nearly 25 years Rita finally moved out of my life not long before James arrived. I'd told James that I had a relationship with this girl called Rita and that we had been together for a long time.

Looking back I don't think I really handled the situation very well. Rita always was a wonderful woman. She never swore, even in the most passionate moments, and I still love her. It's one of those horrible modern day things where we are all frowned upon for saying we love more than one person at a time. There was a song called *Torn Between Two Lovers*. That's exactly where I was coming from. Whilst I just said James had cared for me more tenderly than any other it would be wrong to say that Rita hadn't cared for me less.

Getting together with James; and Rita leaving, were still not THE INCIDENT of 1998. What happened with both of them was very important but THE INCIDENT was something else, involving blue flashing lights, blood, fighting and THAT court case!

I guess you're ready for it now.

It happened on the night James and I were officially an item for the first time, and what happened that night saw me up in court at Preston Crown Court nearly two years later on a charge of assaulting two punks after a five-hour drinking session. That's how it was put on the BBC News website. I don't deny the drinking by the way.

What happened was this. We had just finished a charity show for Lord Delfont at the Opera House, within the Winter Gardens complex in Blackpool. It was more of a comedy night than anything else, but I had my band on with me and was headlining. There was a young man called Dave Spikey on the bill, who went on to achieve great success with Peter Kay in *Phoenix Nights* as well as packing theatres throughout the UK with his own one-man shows.

I'd come out in my dinner suit, with James and with Keeley, my niece, and a few of the others from the crew. By the time I had finished signing autographs and meeting and greeting people we couldn't get a drink at the theatre bar, so we went outside to a local bar where we could get served. It wasn't a particularly upmarket place, the Regent, not at that time anyway, but I wasn't bothered. It was somewhere to drink.

The main bar was packed so Frank, who ran the Regent, opened the other bar for us.

So, I'm sat there in this bar in my dinner suit, all done up to the nines, looking like a penguin.

We were there a while and I had drunk quite a bit, but I still knew what I was doing. These punk rockers were there. I know you can't always judge a book by its cover but you could on this occasion. They were taking the *iss out of me, probably because of the way I was dressed, but also, so they ended up saying in court, because they said I was 'bragging about my wealth'. Their words not mine.

If only they had read the newspapers they would have known how wrong they were in thinking that. I might still have been living at Turpin's but none of it was really mine anymore. I remember mentioning a swimming pool in some way, not to them but they obviously heard, and they started having a go at me about it.

How it all kicked off was that Keeley went to the Ladies and when she came back we were outside. She had scratches all over her. The gold crucifix had come off its chain and she had clearly been assaulted. There was blood on her neck from where they had obviously attacked her. Like I've said all along, if anyone does anything to any member of my family we do something about it. That's how the fight started.

The punks said they hadn't done anything to Keeley but I knew it was them. How else could it have happened?

My niece has always been able to handle herself, like the rest of the family. She knows a thing or two about protection. It was quite a bit of a fight with fists and kicks flying everywhere, and then the police and an ambulance arrived.

Because we had blood on ourselves we were bundled into the ambulance. Keeley and I just sat there for a few minutes getting our breath back and 'manging' in cant (speaking in Romany).

All of a sudden the doors of the ambulance flew open and we were dragged out to be put in the black maria. We swapped with the punks, with their bright orange and purple hair. They went in the ambulance. It was unbelievable. All we had wanted to do was go for a quiet drink after the show and we ended up making a visit to the cop shop.

Keeley and I were locked in a cell, over in Bonny Street nick, in Blackpool. Very quickly the word got around to all of my fans who were in the area at the time. They all came down to the police station where I was being held and demanded that I be let out. If ever there was a case of 'fan power' for me this really was it.

Inside I was screaming, 'Get me out of this ****ing jail!' Whilst outside all the girls were screaming 'We want Joe! We want our Joe!' I don't think Bonny Street had ever heard anything like it. Not for a singer anyway.

It was Jean (Parkes) who got me out that night. Jean was working for International Artistes at the time, who had booked me for the summer season in Blackpool on the North Pier. She paid the bail and got both me and Keeley out. Keeley had broken her arm during all that had happened so she should really have been in the ambulance after all!

Keeley ran the merchandise side of my concerts for a number of years. She doesn't now – that's where Michael, one of my nephews, has taken over in recent years. Keeley now has a very loving, adorable family. She still comes along to some of my concerts when she can.

You may by now be wondering whatever happened to James that night. All I can tell you is that the prosecution alleged there was a mystery 'third man' who was also involved with the fight that took place. I can't tell you who that person was because it all happened so quickly, but whoever it was they really helped out.

The next day the national and local media was full of TV COMIC IN PUNCH UP stories. I hated to be labelled as a comic. I'm a singer, an artiste, performer, an impressionist, but not a comic.

As I mentioned earlier, the court case didn't take place until around 20 months later, which meant I had it hanging over me for all that time.

But we've a bit more ground to cover before we get to that – and it's pretty important because this is where the lovely, magnificent, sexy and beautiful Pat Mancini MBE makes her regal entrance in my story.

> *Can it be I stayed away too long?*
> *Did I leave your mind when I was gone?*
> *It's not my thing trying to get back*
> *But this time let me tell you where I'm at*
> *You don't have to worry 'cause I'm coming*
> *Back to where I should have always stayed*
> *And now I've heard the meaning to your story*
> *And it's enough love for me to stay*

Joe Longthorne *I Want To Be Where You Are* released 2003

I was first introduced to Patricia when Johnnie (Casson) and I were appearing at the North Pier in 1999. It was the early part of the year and it was another great friend of mine, James and Johnnie's, the lovely Ann Marie (Slack) who brought Pat and myself together.

Pat was the proprietor of the extremely well-liked and well-known Queens Hotel on the seafront in Blackpool, and had recently lost her husband, Rudi, when we met. She was still in mourning for him and had been struggling to come to terms with things, but we had an immediate connection. She reminded me a lot of my sister Lizzie.

We had just finished on the Pier that night and went back to the Queens. We were in the cocktail bar, which is really nice and secluded. It was Ann Marie's idea, she thought us being there might help Pat.

In her own book Pat tells it like this:

'... they persuaded me to go downstairs and have a chat with them. I was all in black and desperately down. I'd never met Joe before but I'd enjoyed his show very much and I thought, being in show business, he might like champagne. He looked at me and he said I reminded him of his sister. We

got chatting and it was like the endless feeling of grief was lifted off me. I can't describe the feeling exactly because it was a bit unreal. My emotions were all over the place at the time but something in Joe's personality rang a bell with me. Something happened that I can't really explain. We just talked and gradually I felt a little bit easier about myself for the first time in months. After he went I felt quite different. As I walked back up the corridor to my flat in the hotel I started to sing for the first time since Rudi had died. I sang 'I Wanna Be Where You Are' (one of Joe's). It's one of my favourite songs.'

Pat's book is called *Queen of Blackpool* and that's exactly what she will always be to me despite her passing. You can buy copies of her book direct from the hotel. It's a great read and tells of how she came from nothing to running this famous hotel on Blackpool's seafront.

We had a fantastic night and Pat came along to one or two of my shows after that, but little did James and I know just how much of a part Patricia was to play in our lives. I hold her close to my heart today. Along with James she's been my best pal.

We were still on our uppers in 1999.

We hadn't been thrown out of Turpin's, but we just couldn't afford to live there anymore. We needed to be nearer to where the action was in terms of summer seasons, but we also didn't have enough money to pay for accommodation.

In desperation we turned up one day at the Queens Hotel, but Pat wasn't there. Ironically it was she who was in Las Vegas – not me!

James and I didn't have anywhere to go.

One of Pat's staff managed to get a message to her in the States and she rang back saying, 'Tell them they can have anything they want and can stop as long as they like'. It was so kind of her, such a marvellous gesture. But it didn't end there. Pat had also recently purchased a house on the seafront. It had been intended for her and Rudi to live in and was empty at the time. We stayed in the hotel for about three or four weeks, then moved back out to Great Eccleston for a short while, before moving down to the seafront house for two years until we were back on our feet. Ann Marie also came to our rescue during that time too. She let us stay in her apartment with her.

By now Pat knew what I had been going through. She knew about the cancer, the nervous breakdown, my impending court case and the bankruptcy. She knew all of that. She didn't have to help us the way she did, but I am so grateful for her kindness, love and friendship.

So let's just take stock here.

In the past year I had been locked up for an affray, was due up before a judge in court again, still couldn't afford to pay off all my debts that had been lingering on since the creditors' arrangement in 1997, no longer had TV contracts to fall back on, I was still not completely clear of how my nervous breakdown had affected me and was getting closer to saying a final goodbye to my lovely home in Berkshire.

> *I've had my share – of life's ups and downs*
> *But fate's been kind – and the downs have been few*
> *And I guess you could say – that I've been lucky*
> *I guess you could say – that it's all because of you*

Joe Longthorne *You're The Best Thing* ... released 2003

You would think it would be a sad time wouldn't you? But you know it really wasn't. I had James with me. I had wonderful new friendships with people like Pat, Ann Marie and Johnnie. And I had others too who were to help me incredibly - in many ways it was like coming on to the next chapter.

Now there's a good link, because that's the end of this one. We won't take a break this time – unless you want one, if you do then let's just charge our glasses this time – because I'm on a roll now.

Happier times! This was taken just before I was diagnosed with lymphoma whilst performing at the Futurist Theatre, Scarborough.

These are just some of the girls who looked after me - the wonderful Macmillan nurses.

The Estate of **Sammy Davis Jr**

Joe Longthorne

c/o Variety Club
4th Floor
St James' Buildings
79 Oxford Street
Manchester
M1 6FQ

31 May, 2007

Dear Joe,

Wishing you all the success this evening on this much deserved tribute.

You are a true showman following in the steps of all who have been honored with this accolade and I know I speak for the Sinatra and Martin families when I say you are singlehandedly keeping variety alive and well over there in the UK.

I only wish you had been around in Las Vegas in the 1960's at those legendary performances the boys gave at The Sands. Had they known about you, they all could have had a night off together and let you perform the entire show!

Enjoy the evening and I know that Sammy would have been so proud of you.

God bless.

Altovise Davis.

Altovise Davis, widow of Sammy Davis Jr, sent me this fantastic letter. How I wish I could have done what she says. This means a lot.

The legendary Rat Pack themselves - Dean, Sammy and Frank. This is another of my favourite pictures.

Just before being presented with the big red book on This is Your Life - I was performing at the Apollo Theatre, Manchester.

Ricky Tomlinson - who said some really fabulous things about me at a previous Variety Club Award.

Jeffrey Archer - first saw me down in London many years ago. He spoke so well, as you'd expect, when he attended my Variety Club Award in 2007.

Attending a charity night - watch out Beadle's about here - can you tell where he is?

All Hands on Deck! With the Duchess, my mum.

Filming for *The Joe Longthorne Show* on ITV - I'm the one waving the hat!

At the Variety Club Lifetime
Achievement Award in 2007.

Me the Philosopher!

And off we go... another show over!

Here's a clip with HRH Princess Royal (that's Princess Anne to you and me) and Iris Williams when we performed for a Save the Children Gala.

As President of The Save the Children Fund, I am delighted to have this opportunity to welcome everyone here this evening to this 75th birthday concert and to thank Mr Joe Longthorne for giving this performance.

In 1919 a remarkable woman, named Eglantyne Jebb, founded The Save the Children Fund, recognising that children were always the first to suffer in any conflict or disaster. Sadly, 75 years later, millions of children around the world still face hardship, poverty and famine. Save the Children reaches more than 5 million such children, working in partnership with their families and the communities in which they live to provide healthcare, education and rural development in 50 countries worldwide. In the UK alone, over 100 projects, including a number in Newcastle and other parts of the North East, aim to tackle the disadvantages faced by many children and young people in our own society as their parents grapple with the dual effects of poverty and unemployment.

All the money raised from this evening's concert, made possible by the Berwick on Tweed branch, will make a valuable contribution to Save the Children's work in the UK and overseas, providing both immediate relief where suffering is greatest and in support of long-term sustainable projects aiming to ensure that tomorrow's children benefit as well as today's.

Although I am unable to be with you tonight, I thank you for your generous support for Save the Children and send you all my best wishes for a most enjoyable evening's entertainment.

Anne

The letter we received from Buckingham Palace after a Save The Children Gala.

With two of my great pals, Bobby & Tommy, at their special Variety Club award in 2009.

Freddie Starr is overcome with emotion!

Yet another great honour for me was to be invited to sing at the Bee Gees' Variety Club Silver Heart Award in 2009. When I sang *I Started A Joke* Robin stood and sang with me.

PP Arnold was another of the singers to appear at the Bee Gees' Silver Heart award.

Chris (the Greek!), John-Boy, me, Keith and Michael.

Me with one of my younger fans
Kelly Earnshaw of Castleford

On tour in 2009 at Royal
Leamington Spa.

Me with Ernie Dunstall, fantastic musical
director.

Summer Spectacular with
someone called Bradley - I
wonder what happened to him.

Myself and James at home. We've always enjoyed just being together.

On tour in Australia 1991 -
back there this year.

In full flow at The Grand Theatre,
Blackpool in 2009.

Top Left: Me with the Joe Longthorne Orchestra at Grand Theatre, Leeds, in 2010.
Left: Giving it my all and another big finish!
Above: At the piano, playing as my dad taught me!

Myself and James with great musical director Colin Hadley.

With two of my wonderful fans Sandy and Mona.

With my good friend and marvellous comedian Johnnie Casson. We have worked together so many times and I love him dearly.

Geraldine presenting me with an award from my fans through the Friendship Club in 2009 - to mark my 40 years in show business.

Happy times in the 90s.

One of my proudest moments in 2010 - me holding Pat Mancini's book and Pat holding mine in Waterstones.

Me with Jamie and the wonderful Pat Mancini.

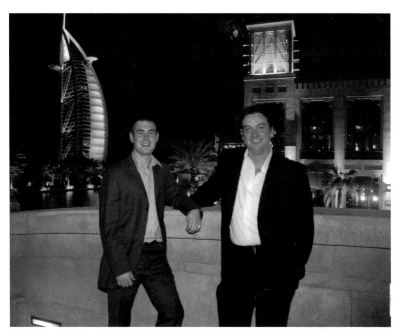

We performed two sell-out shows in Dubai in 2008. Here are Michael and James.

This is Jimmy the Suit (Jim Berry) with James' Aunt Madeleine.

Back in Hull, with my sister Lizzie.

Fort Lauderdale 2012 - myself, Jamie, Andy (Mudd), Leye (D. Johns) and our good friends in the States.

Roy Walker and me, together at The Grand Theatre, Blackpool in Summer Season 2012.

Me with Chris (The Book) Berry and ITV presenters Christine Talbot and Duncan Wood.

Enjoying my book signing in my home city of Kingston upon Hull.

Saying it with flowers... from my good friends every one!

CHAPTER TWENTY SEVEN

PRESTON CROWN COURT

I still love you, with a love that's true
I still love you, with all of my heart

Joe Longthorne *I Still Love You* released 2006

I'm not one for looking back and regretting things that have happened. You move on – and that's what I was doing in 1999 and 2000.

Funnily enough though, my first studio album since 1993, which was released in 1999, was titled *Reflections*. It was another release from Telstar, the last of my four studio albums with the company. There were 12 tracks in all including *Mack The Knife, We Don't Cry Out Loud* and *I Will Drink The Wine*. Quite appropriate if we've all just recharged our glasses!

It didn't make an impression on the albums chart but it has still sold well over the years. It was released in May.

I was back on television again in 1999 and I appeared on a programme called *The Big Stage* on Channel 5. But one of my favourite TV appearances of that time was when Chris Evans' team contacted me to appear on *TFI Friday*. You know the rest from what you read earlier!

If this all sounds to you like things were picking up a bit then you would be right. I was feeling far better. I was with James, had a great new friend in Pat, a new album out and I was back on television. Things were looking up. I was also back on the North Pier for the summer with Johnnie.

International Artistes were the agency who booked me on to the Pier at the time. I was getting some work through them and Tony Clayman was promoting me.

Of course there were two major problems on the horizon. Actually there were two that I knew about and also one that I didn't! We're now into the year 2000.

There was the bankruptcy, the official one this time. I have only been bankrupt once, contrary to what some may have reported in the press over the years; and there was the court case at Preston Crown Court for the affray outside the Regent Hotel.

But even before all of the three major problems, there was another! Myself and John, my brother, were questioned by the Thames Valley Police over an alleged incident. We were getting closer and closer to the official declaration that I was bankrupt and a local garage owner came to Turpin's.

He had come to take back the slate grey Mercedes S280 I had at the time, but things got out of hand and both John and I ended up being questioned at Maidenhead Police Station.

The official bankruptcy was only a matter of months away, and so was the 'affray' court case. It seemed as though I was going to be in court more than Andy Murray or Roger Federer!

In the end it was the court appearance that came first, followed hot on its heels by the declaration of bankruptcy.

But that wasn't the end of my problems either.

If bankruptcy, a voluntary creditors' agreement, charge for affray and a nervous breakdown hadn't already been enough for me to cope with there was even more still to come. I told you earlier that the problem with CLL, or non-Hodgkins' lymphoma, as it is sometimes referred, is that it isn't there one minute but is definitely back on the scene the next.

I think you can pretty much guess what happened next then can't you?

That's right – it had returned – 12 years on from when I'd first found out I'd got it, and just three years after I'd proudly announced in concert that I was living proof that cancer could be beaten, there it was again. This time it was far worse than before. I needed more chemotherapy. It was March 2000.

I had thought it had gone, but with this disease you do have periods when you feel perfectly alright. Somewhere in my head I had let myself believe it had gone when it hadn't. I was a week into my UK tour when I realised I wasn't feeling right. I went to my local doctor who referred me straight back to Dr Anthony Childs. I think because I was seeing doctors less and less I had felt that everything was okay. I had been feeling so good.

I died inside for a short while when I found out. I thought I'd licked the cancer and I hadn't. Coming on right after all I had gone through it was almost too much. When I left hospital I cried my eyes out. 'Here we go again' was all I could think.

That evening I cried on the way to my show at The Grand in Blackpool, but somehow I managed to block off all of those bad feelings. I'd fought it once before, I would fight it again – and go on fighting, no matter what it took. I have always loved what I do and I will do it to the best of my ability for as long as I can. There would be no nervous breakdown this time. I think after you've had one of those you do see the danger signs in future.

I now had good people around me, people who cared for me, people I could trust. Sure, I had a few of them around me when I was going through my nervous breakdown, but this time it was different. I felt better able to cope.

I had started the treatment again that same day. I undertook six months of intensive treatment that year, whilst also fulfilling all my engagements here and abroad. There were times when I felt as though I'd been to hell and back. Sometimes I felt as though I'd done 15 rounds with Mike Tyson and then started all over again. I would take the pills that I'd been given and 10 minutes later I'd be seeing double and would have to go to bed because I was feeling lousy.

From the resumption of my treatment and a UK tour I then went straight to court.

If ever I was to realise just how much my fans thought of me it had been when they all turned up en-masse outside Bonny Street police station two years earlier, but they topped that with what they did throughout my court case at Preston Crown Court!

There was nothing anyone could do about my illness, CLL, but the fans really felt that there was something they could do about my being in court. Some fans were there, in court, every day, including Fran. Others took spells at it. I'm not sure how they managed to wangle all the time off work that they may have had to, but their constant appearance was a great comfort to me. Every day there was a queue to go into the courtroom.

Pat, lovely Pat, made sure that I looked my best in court. She took me to Marks & Spencer's just before I was due to go in for my first appearance and I came out looking and feeling a million dollars. She had told me I couldn't go to court in the way I was dressed at first.

We arrived at Marks & Spencer's at 9 o'clock that morning and Pat gave me £300 to kit myself out. I came out wearing a navy blue pin-striped suit, pink shirt and shades. Pat says it was like someone going through the smoke they used to use for the *Stars in Your Eyes* programme and the same person you have just seen in his normal clothes looking great as he comes through it.

The trial was supposed to last just three days, but it went to six, and over into two weeks.

My barrister cost me nine grand to fight the case. He told me that he wanted the money before he went in. I think he knew that I was going to be declared bankrupt, since it had been reported in *The Lawyer* magazine, and understandably wanted to make sure he was going to get paid. So I rang Tony Clayman my promoter at the time. I told him that unless I got the nine large ones for my barrister he wasn't going into that court – wig or no wig. We got the money, and we were under way!

In court the prosecution asked me, 'Mr Longthorne? Did you kick my client in the head repeatedly?' I asked the jury what 'repeatedly kicked' actually meant. I said that there was no way anyone could have gone from our fracas with just a bleeding nose and be in the newspapers the next morning if I had 'repeatedly kicked' him. If I had done that then his head would have caved in. I asked the judge: 'Your honour, can I demonstrate a 'repeated kick'?'

It had been devastating for me to see what had happened to Keeley and I really didn't think we had a case to answer, we had only protected ourselves from these people who were intent on making trouble, but it had seemed as though we had no chance. We had only been in the Regent because I couldn't get a drink at the Winter Gardens. We hadn't gone looking for trouble.

I took over the courtroom for a matter of seconds.

'Here's what a repeated kicking is your honour. Listen to this. Imagine if I'd kicked him like it has just been said,' and I almost kicked the witness box out. I really showed them what a repeated kicking would be like. Then I turned back to the jury.

'Ladies and gentlemen, he would be dead. He wouldn't have been able to sell his story to the front page of the *Daily Star*.'

Although I was confident that Keeley and I had done the right thing I was still very relieved when the verdicts were read out and we were cleared of assaulting the two punks. The jury took two and a half hours to return the not guilty verdicts and they were two and a half of the longest hours of my life.

The solicitors, Budds, had done their homework and they had found a taxi driver who had witnessed what happened that night. In his statement the taxi driver had said that the person who was doing any kicking was someone in white trousers. That couldn't have been me as I was in my tux and suit, all black. I was in the clear.

All of my fans were clapping. Pat had organised the champagne again and when the jury came out I asked whether they wanted a drink.

So in May 2000 myself and Keeley were finally clear of all charges. We were not guilty! The incident had been hanging over us for 20 months.

Next up was the bankruptcy.

I had told *HELLO!* magazine in an interview that appeared later that year, a few months after I had been declared officially bankrupt, that I had tried my best to stave off going bust. It was eventually my creditors that had demanded it.

Once again I couldn't believe some of the bills. We had one from the accountant who I owed £50,000. Bridie Reid's bill was still there, and the Inland Revenue bill was £500,000. I know that others might say I should have looked after my finances better, but you know the drill by now. It's not what I do.

Andrew Segal, the supervisor of the official bankruptcy petition that I had avoided earlier by entering into the voluntary agreement, was the man who arranged for it to take place properly this time. Tony (Clayman), my promoter, told Segal's that I had tried to meet the terms of the voluntary agreement, but that I had been unable to keep up with the payments that were required. They were just too much for me.

No matter how much I had scrimped and saved, struggling to pay off my debts I just couldn't clear them. I was paying back £7,000 a month, by performing as regularly as I could, but it wasn't really making any impact on the million or so that I owed. I had kept Turpin's during the past four years but now was the time we just had to sell. I sold it for £500,000 and since the buyer had no reason to be in straight away James and I were able to carry on staying there for a little while longer.

The bailiffs had come to the house to claim what they could but by the time they arrived everything had gone apart from the piano. Like I said earlier, they should have looked in the legs!

I also told *HELLO!* that I would be breaking open a bottle of champagne on July 15, 2000, which was the date when I finally became clear of debt. At last! I'd got two monkeys off my back – the financial ruin and the court case. Maybe now I could return to a normal life – or as normal as my life gets.

But no. That wasn't all. Within hours I was back taking on yet more gruelling sessions of chemotherapy as I continued my personal battle with lymphoma.

I was feeling good about getting back on my feet financially and getting cleared of any charges in Preston Crown Court, so that helped me cope with the chemo and the return of cancer. That, as well as all of the help I was now getting from everyone now around me, as well as my wonderful fans, was probably the reason why I was able to cope better this time around.

In the space of six months right at the start of the new millennium I had been through more dramatic events than some might go through for years, but at least now I was able to deal with it. When you've come back from really dark moments like I'd had with the nervous breakdown maybe it makes you stronger inside. At least that's how it felt for me.

I invited Pat to come on tour with us for the rest of the UK dates and she did! We had a great time and we went all over the country together. Pat, James, me and the band. It was to be the start of some funny and amazing stories as we travelled around the world together.

When we were on the UK tour in 2000 we had a couple of days off down on the south coast. I got it into my head that we should hire a boat, one of those with a proper radar on so that we wouldn't get lost. I thought about us going to Jersey, as you do, just for the day!

Did we have any sailing knowledge between us? No, but surely if a boat has a radar everything would be all right wouldn't it?

I had been told that all you had to do was point the boat's radar to Jersey, press a few buttons and we'd get there! Simple really. It sounded so easy. I thought we had organised a boat and so the next day we arrived at the harbour armed full of stuff for a great day out. You know the kind of thing for sailing, essentials like champagne! When we got there we couldn't believe the boat we'd got! One was being painted, one was in, and all the rest were booked out.

We quickly forgot about anything to do with a radar. Pat describes the boat we saw as being like Popeye's boat, from the cartoon series, with a blue funnel. This was just an old fishing boat.

Ever the eternal optimist, I still fancied a go. It was just like having an old caravan to me. Needless to say we never got to Jersey. I think we made it about 200 yards outside of the harbour before we turned back. Not exactly the world's greatest voyage.

But I was to become a captain in another way that year.

My summer season saw me on the North Pier again. Johnnie was back too. He'd had a tough time of it the previous year because he'd needed a heart bypass operation during the run. This time he was fine. We also put together a charity show called *All Hands On Deck* which featured me as the Captain and Johnnie as the ship's cat. I would dress up in my captain's hat and outfit and go on to the pier shaking hands with people who were coming to the concerts. I really felt like the Pier was my own personal liner. I was a bit like Alec Guinness in the film *Barnacle Bill* where he tries to make sure a dilapidated pier is saved from being demolished when he registers it as a foreign cruise ship.

Sometimes, when the sea was a bit choppy it felt like we were sailing across to the Isle of Man.

I was not feeling too clever at times during the season, as I was still fighting the lymphoma and when I came off stage I was so tired. All I wanted to do was relax and it was a long walk off the pier on a night after we'd finished, so I started setting myself up for the night in the dressing room. I stayed there quite a few nights and I turned it into my home during the run, but the company that ran the Pier decided I couldn't stay on there each night. I think it was something to do with the insurances only running up until midnight.

It was quite enjoyable really, living on the pier. I could have carried on doing it. I would pop downstairs every morning to see the milkman. He would always come on board my 'ship' to deliver to me. I'd also hang out my washing on the pier.

Jean (Parkes) and I struck up a friendship during that time which has remained to this day. Jean was working with International Artistes and when the company who had the North Pier wanted me to get off they sent for her.

I didn't see why I had to leave the pier each night. I was tired, I wasn't going to do any harm to the place, but apparently I had to go. Why would I want to move?

Jean's visits became a nightly ritual. I wouldn't move from there until she came, then Jean would be sent for and she would have to come and get me at about three in the morning. We would walk off the pier together. Jean tells me she ended up just staying in her tracksuit until she got the phone call. I thank Jean now for what she did because, bless her, she was putting herself out to do it.

One afternoon when I was on the pier, Michael Grade came up and had a long chat. He owned it at the time but told me he was moving into television. He'd been interested in what I thought about him letting go of it. His uncle, Bernard Delfont, would have done a back-flip in his grave if he'd known. The company ended up selling it to First Leisure.

Later that same year saw me heading back to Australia – my first time since 1993. We played Perth, Brisbane, Twin Towns, Sydney, Melbourne and Adelaide in theatre and concert venues. All of the troubles I'd had in the past few years were gone and we all had a fantastic time. There was me, James, Pat and the band. We went to Thailand for a week first and then on to Australia for five weeks. Pat had said she was only coming for the first two weeks but she stayed for the lot.

Patricia and I went up to the top of the Harbour Bridge in Sydney. I told her I'd only gone there because I didn't think she'd do it, but we both did. It was a marvellous experience. When we got to the top Pat asked where the shops were.

I have always loved Australia, both the country and its people. My fans over there follow me everywhere when I'm on tour, a bit like they do here in the UK. They're so supportive.

When we arrived in Sydney I was asked to do a breakfast TV programme. I had to be up by 7 o'clock, but I'd only been to bed for an hour. I have to admit I felt a bit jetlagged, but I wasn't going to turn it down. They wanted to record it 'live' under the Sydney Harbour Bridge and they wanted me to do not just any impression but Pavarotti, as well as Dame Shirley. Pavarotti at seven in the morning?

Did they not know my lifestyle, or how much it takes to warm up to that kind of performance. I would never start a show with an impression of Pavarotti, but I did the impressions – no music, no backing, nothing. Pat was amazed, she was sure I'd fall on my arse with it.

But isn't it funny how small the world really is? I know everyone says it, especially with things like the internet these days, but it was brought home to me on one of our visits to Australia. And it wasn't in the most pleasant of ways.

Do you remember me telling you that my sister Anne was incarcerated in Rampton for a while? Well we were in Fremantle one day. We were all sitting together – me, the band, James, Pat. We were drinking champagne – again. Well, someone has to drink it you know.

Anyway, this woman on the next table, that was full of more mature ladies, had heard us talking and told me that they were all from Nottingham.

She went on to tell me that they all now lived over there. There was no problem with any of this conversation at this point. I get a lot of people coming up to me to ask for an autograph or just to chat so I thought nothing more of it. Then I heard one of them mention Rampton.

That was it. My ears were well and truly up. I looked around to them and asked whether what I'd heard them say was true.

'Did you say Rampton? The hospital for the criminally insane, a mental institution?'

When they nodded I told them that my sister had spent a bit of time in there. I mentioned her by name, to see if there was any reaction, to see if any of them knew her. Anne had told me she wasn't very happy with the way she had been treated at times. What I suddenly wanted to know right there and then was if they knew anything. I was hungry for information.

Maybe they didn't know, maybe they hadn't all worked at Rampton, anyone who works there has to sign the Official Secrets Act, but if I had known that one of them was responsible for anything out of order I would have blown up right there and then. Who would have thought it? I'd come thousands of miles to be sat with these people who were probably very decent and honest. Just the mere mention of the name Rampton had been enough to make me think this way. The world really is getting smaller.

My interview with *HELLO!* magazine had taken place during the time around the court case but the story didn't appear until later that year. Pat had come with James and me back to Maidenhead, to Turpin's. I took her breakfast in bed.

I think she was a bit shocked when she went into one of the rooms the next day and she found a big room with nothing in it but floorboards and a sliding window. She says she was even more shocked to see a big Welsh Cob, a goat and my dog, Henry, all inside it!

My Welsh cob, Rosie, appeared in *HELLO!*, looking in the house through the window. I had three horses all together, including a thoroughbred called Sugar and another called Lady Blue.

HELLO! also used a picture of Pat and me.

Pat stayed at Turpin's for nearly a month, it was to be the last couple of weeks myself and James spent there. I remember Pat saying to me at the time: 'Joe, don't you ever go out.'

I told her that when I was at home I generally didn't go anywhere, and that's true. When I'm on the road as much as I am I just like to stay at home when I can. I don't go out unless there's something special. I'm the same today.

But I did have 'something special' lined up for Pat whilst she was there! Yes I did, I took her to see Dame Shirley at the Festival Hall in London. We went in a Rolls Royce, not mine of course, and had a fabulous evening. I wasn't particularly well that night but we still had a great time. Well who wouldn't when you are going to see such an incredible woman, especially when you're with an incredible woman as well!

Considering the year had included a court case, my bankruptcy, the return of lymphoma and even more treatment it still hadn't been a bad one. I'd come through the court case unscathed, free of all costs; I was now free of debt and thanks to Pat was living in her house up the coast in Blackpool; and I was coping manfully with my illness. I'd done a UK tour, a summer season and an Australian tour.

Maybe not everything was well with my world, but it wasn't at all bad. I'd got James, I had a wonderful friendship with Pat, and Jean had looked after me really well on the North Pier.

In fact Jean had looked after me so well that I wanted her to manage me and eventually she did.

I first asked Jean at a Christmas function in 2000. She told me that she was reluctant to take me on because she didn't want it to spoil the friendship we had developed. I respected her for that, and I also respected her because once again, like James, she wouldn't just tell me what she thought I wanted to hear.

She told me things straight. It did lead to a few problems along the way, as she had thought it might, but we are still friends today, and her husband Mal is a superb, straight-as-a-die man as well as a fine musician. They are both very professional and that's exactly what I needed around me.

Around this time I also had Chimes International as my booking agents with Robert Pratt looking after my tour dates. Everything and everyone was now in place better than it had been for years!

THE MUSIC HALL TAVERN

Now my life's just like a symphony
When I'm with you and you're holding me
And the music's there to accompany me wherever I go

Joe Longthorne *My Life's Just Like A Symphony* recorded 1975

I was back on track. Not only did I have some great friends and business-minded people around me, who thought more of me than to 'take more than their fair share', they also liked and respected me.

James and I were building some proper friendships with people who cared about us, friendships that have more than stood the test of time. We had also been royally looked after by Pat and at last we were no longer on our uppers.

2001 was a great year for me. I was signed to a new record company Ritz Music Group and in the early part of the year we produced a fantastic 'live' recording of one of the concerts up in Aberdeen simply called *Joe Longthorne Live In Concert*. Peter Faint was my musical director at this time and he produced the CD with me. I mixed the album and some of the players on that tour were amongst the best I've ever had the pleasure of working with. There was Lewis Osborne on lead guitar, Peter Brent on bass guitar and Stephen Power on keyboards. The rest of the band was brilliant too. The album contains one of the best mixes of me singing as myself, as well as quite a few impressions. Of all my CD releases I think it's also the only one that includes my version of *He Ain't Heavy, He's My Brother*.

There was also my first ever DVD-only release. All of the previous films of me in concert had originally been released on video and then transferred to DVD. This was called *The Genius Of Joe Longthorne*. I was concerned about the title. I mean, what right have I to release something proclaiming myself as a genius? But the others around me liked it.

The recordings had taken place during my shows at the Grand Theatre in Blackpool the previous summer.

Jean was now managing me. She got the Friendship Club back up and running again. Geraldine Vine, who runs it today, has now run it for a number of years. Today my official website has over 38,000 registered users and a regular newsletter is sent out to all Friendship Club members.

Whilst Robert Pratt and Dave Halford of Chimes International were looking after most of my engagements Jean had picked up some work for me back on the cruise ships. This brought about a series of adventures – and of course a few misadventures along the way.

In 2001 we played on the QE2. We joined the ship in Singapore and got off in India, but that certainly didn't pass without incident either! Before we go any further I wasn't involved in what happened. Not personally anyway.

What happened was that I couldn't take the band, just Andy Mudd my musical director. Andy is great and he's been with me for nearly 10 years now. It's his studio that I use a lot of the time for recording. Andy is a great friend too, another of my great group of friends.

We had done okay on the ship but Andy didn't think much to the standard of the musicians backing me. I didn't either.

The band on-board the QE2 had its own musical director and Andy told him what he thought of his band. The other MD didn't like it. When Colin Handley had been my MD on previous cruises and he didn't think one of the musicians was up to the job he would just tell them they weren't needed the next night, but that's not Andy's way. What followed developed into a bit of a fight. But this wasn't me this time and this wasn't a Joe Longthorne affray.

The next morning I was summonsed to the Captain's office to hear what had happened.

We were getting off in India anyway, which was the next stop, and so did the ship's musical director.

We even caused a bit of a stir in India as well. Again not me! Jean was with us on the cruise and had forgotten about covering up. She was wearing a strappy top when we got out of our car at the airport, I told her to cover her tits up! I ended up throwing my coat over her.

Then they wouldn't let me through customs wearing my hat. I couldn't see why I had to take my hat off when all of these Indians could go through wearing their turbans – and I said so. We were all frisked as a result of it.

Back on home soil it was time for me to bring my own version of variety to Blackpool, in the form of my own club.

I have never been frightened to try new things and 2001 saw the launch of Joe Longthorne's Music Hall Tavern with its official opening the following year. It was something I wanted to make a go of, my own venue, but even some of my best friends were telling me not to bother. They would say, 'Why do you want to sell beer, Joe, when you can entertain like you do?' I just thought it would be a good idea and that I would enjoy it.

Pat told me not to get involved, she had told me it wasn't big enough to make money from. James saw it the same way, but do I ever think of the money? All I ever think about is whether it will be good fun or not. I think we established that quite some time ago, did we not?

The building had a curved entrance on the corner of Church Street and had previously been the Gas Board showroom. I would play there every Thursday evening with a five-piece band led by Andy. We had live music on every night and Mal (Ford), who is an accomplished keyboard player and played in several Midlands bands as well as being a band leader in his own right, performed on a Saturday evening. Every night's entertainment was free entry except for the night we performed, when we charged £20 on the door.

We had some good nights whilst it lasted but unfortunately it didn't last long. It just took up too much time and Pat was right, it wasn't going to work financially. Whilst it was great to have our own venue the problem was that people expected me to be there all the time. But I was still also working hard on tour. The tavern had been a really nice idea and is another part of my life that was particularly special for me.

It also brought, as you might expect with me, a few laughs, and gaffs along the way.

There is a feeling in the entertainment world that the bigger you get, the bigger the light show. I think we just might have taken that a bit too far in the Tavern.

One of the funniest moments ever was when Patricia and I went to Manchester on a mission to kit out the Tavern. I was after some chandeliers, fantastic lighting for the tavern that would give us the 'wow' factor. We got to the lighting store and started checking out the lighting on display. But I didn't know how they would really look back at the Tavern, so Pat said we should get down on the floor.

So there we are, me and Pat laid together in the centre of this store head-to-head, and there are people walking around us and over our bodies. Pat just said, 'There you are, that's what it will look like' and we just stayed there laughing for what seemed like ages. It still makes me laugh thinking about it now.

We ended up buying three of them. Two the same size that we had just seen and a bigger one that the manager said we could have for a lot less than its original price. We didn't see the bigger one on display and that was probably for a very good reason as we were to find out when it arrived in Blackpool.

You have never seen anything like it! You couldn't even get it through the doors! It was in this huge big box. The salesman had said it was bigger than the others on display, but hadn't told us just how big it was!

We just figured that the box would probably contain a reasonable amount of packaging. It couldn't be as big as the box it was delivered in, surely?

Wrong. It was massive. I might have wanted to create an impression with the lighting but this was way beyond all of that. If we had put it up then customers wouldn't have been able to even walk under it – and with its size I'm pretty sure it would have brought the ceiling down. Now it's one thing 'bringing the house down' when you're performing, but not doing it for real! This would have done exactly that. It was the kind of size you might expect in a cathedral.

There was another problem as well. Because I had been declared bankrupt in 2000 I couldn't be the licensee. When breweries saw that the place was to be called Joe Longthorne's Music Hall Tavern they didn't want to supply us. It was all to do with the bankruptcy, so we were in danger of being a bit like that Irish song *The Pub With No Beer*. Jean came to the rescue and ran it for me with Mal. She'd been a licensee in the past so she knew her way around and managed the whole building, with Fran working behind the bar.

I don't regret the idea one bit. I would have liked to see it carry on, but it just wasn't possible. One good thing it did was to give others a chance to perform, but what I found is that when your name is attached to something like that the people who come inside really want to see the man whose name is outside.

On a Monday night we had Jubilee Music Hall Night with Eric Hamilton, Maureen Nolan (Senior) and Connie Hall. Tuesday was Cabaret night with different singers every week. Wednesday was Cabaret Showtime with Pete Oliver and the Choir Girls. It was me on Thursday, then Friday saw a Summer Star Search Talent Contest where we gave cash prizes every week. We had some great talent that came through including Lady Elvis. Saturday Night Live! It was Mal, along with pianist Andy Knight, and they hosted an open mic spot. Sundays featured the vivacious Vicky le Plume. Something for everyone, every single day!

I'd still like to have another go at my own venue one day but as Bobby Ball said to me recently: 'Joe, what do you want to run a club for? That's for entertainers who are finished. You're in the prime of life right now. Why do you want to bother with drinks at £2 or £3 when you can be selling out theatres and arenas?' Pat said something of the same.

It's probably best I have people telling me, the way I have now. Jean and Mal have been great friends in that way too.

By now they were running Personality Artistes. Mal had been looking after bands like The Platters for a long time. Between them they were not only managing me as a performer, they were also making sure that I wasn't going to go bankrupt again and had set about rebuilding my reputation.

Understandably my career had suffered quite a bit during the various traumas I had been going through, so there was a bit of work to do, but Jean was a great help to James and me as he began taking more of a management role, and together with Mal they really helped me get back on my feet.

Of course in managing me the way they did there were one or two moments when those who had found it easy to bill me 'more than their fair share' also found that was no longer possible. Jean tells me that some of these people made their lives hell at the time, but they came through it.

'We only pay on quotes,' is what Jean used to say to me. 'We don't pay any extras.' Apparently certain people would turn up months after a concert had been played demanding additional payments. What Jean always said to them was that they should have put it in their original quote. I don't pretend to understand any of it really. All I knew was that Jean and Mal were looking after me and that the pair of them were and still are true friends.

By 2002 the Tavern was open and then closed. We had put on music every night but it just wasn't working. We'd had a gala opening night in the June of that year and I had played there every Thursday with Andy and the rest of the band, but we had to come out of it. Actually we received an award for it too. We came second in the Blackpool Tourism awards in 2002 for what we had achieved.

That same year we played an October season at the Opera House in the Winter Gardens complex once again. We broke more box office records, this time for the top selling show of the year.

It was also the year when my songs started reappearing on a variety of 'new' compilation albums. There were three released that year: *Love & Reflection* through the Demon Music Group on Music Club; *You're My World* through Snapper Music issued under licence from Telstar; and *Christmas Time Is Here* through Delta Music. It looks like I had more record labels than anyone in the industry that year without ever having to go near a studio.

Spencer Leigh, one of BBC Radio Merseyside's presenters, wrote some lovely words in the sleeve notes of the *You're My World* CD. He wrote: 'Joe was once appearing at the Floral Pavilion in New Brighton. When he arrived, the compere, Billy Butler, asked him if he could do John Lennon. Joe had never sung *Imagine* before, but that night he did a perfect copy as a tribute to the late Beatle in his home town.'

I might not have been recording new albums, but it seemed as though I was getting pretty good at re-releases.

Jean and Mal even helped James and I move house. She says that's just what they do, her and Mal. Just like when she used to come on the pier to take me home, Jean has always gone beyond the call of duty for me.

One of the proudest moments in my life was when Jean asked me to give her away, when she married Mal in 2003. She had come with us when we toured Australia again in November and December 2002. This time there was me, James, Jean, Andy Mudd and Zeb. It was another wonderful time, with sell-out concerts wherever we went. We played right across the country from Perth to Sydney, including Adelaide, Melbourne and Canberra. It was a six-week tour playing two concerts a week.

The tour also allowed me to once again make the most of this beautiful country. But our next destination was one that I had been aiming at ever since Chicago.

Our next stop was Vegas!

As I think I've drilled into you by now this is the place I regard as the pinnacle of my area of show business, in particular cabaret entertainment. Any top tennis player wants to play at Wimbledon; any top boxer wants to fight at Madison Square Gardens; any footballer wants to play at Wembley; any jockey wants to ride in the Epsom Derby; any golfer wants to play at St Andrews; and any snooker player wants to play at The Crucible. For me Vegas is the place to play.

Jean and Mal had got me there. Their contacts had got me close to 'the strip' even though it wasn't what I had imagined. It might not have been the best known of Vegas' clubs but it was Vegas.

Unfortunately I wasn't feeling too good around the time of my engagements but they still went well and I received quite a bit of TV and radio exposure. I think it was CBS, one of the US' biggest networks, who interviewed me.

Jean and Mal were married at the wedding chapel in the Little Church of the West in Las Vegas. Jean looked fantastic and it was a very real honour to be able to give her away. As well as Jean, Mal, myself and James there was also 'Tatie' Alan, his wife Sylvia and quite a few from the Friendship Club.

We would have stayed in the States for longer. Jean and Mal had also organised a lovely house for James and me in a really great place called Spanish Trails, but I really wasn't too good at the time so we decided to come back not long after the wedding. I was full of flu at the time and I also needed more treatment.

That wasn't everything though. As Pat always says, things just happen when I'm around. This time it was another crash, but it wasn't financial.

I'd decided to hire a car. The one I took was a green one. Now Mal is a pretty superstitious man and apparently as soon as he saw it he said that green was a bad colour. He could have told me!

I drove it from the hire company driveway and that was it. Bang! A truck wiped me out! It hit me, we spun, I had 'Tatie' Alan and Sylv with me in the back, Jamie in the front. I swerved to get out of the way because I'd seen it coming, but it was coming far too fast. In the end it only clipped us, but its speed was enough to make the green car a write-off.

And as if that wasn't enough we also had a near miss with another plane on our flight back from Vegas. We were coming in to land at Heathrow on a foggy, blustery day. I looked out of the window and there, right in my vision, was another huge plane. I saw the tail end of the plane veer away.

It wasn't a happy way to end our time we had in the States – next time I know one thing for sure. I won't be hiring a green car!

CHAPTER TWENTY NINE

THAILAND

You're my world, you're my night and day
You're my world, you're every breath I pray
If our love ceases to be
Then it's the end of my world for me

Joe Longthorne *You're My World* released 2006

James and I were on the move again when we came back from the States.

The beautiful house Pat had bought as a place for her and Rudi to live, away from the Queens, had been purchased just before Rudi passed away. Pat had no interest in living there after that. It was up for sale before we moved in. We were lucky that it hadn't sold at the time as it became our home for several years. It's a lovely place just up the coast to the north side of Blackpool.

Thanks to all of the people who were now working with me our financial situation was a good deal better. We were now able to afford to buy again, and we bought a house away from the seafront in Blackpool.

I was also back on another UK tour and was due to start my summer season, this time back at the North Pier in July.

Tours of Australia, appearances in Vegas albeit not on The Strip, successive years of UK tours and Blackpool summer seasons had seen me in work throughout the period when Jean and Mal, as well as Dave Halford, by now running Artistes Direct, were looking after me. Everything appeared to be on the right track.

But trouble was lurking just around the corner for me once again.

This cancer thing is such a killer, but it's not just that, it's also such a lingering illness. It has affected and continues to affect millions of people throughout the world. It affects everyone – those who have it, their loved ones, their family and friends. Everyone knows someone who has it. That's one of the reasons why I continue to help to raise funds to beat it every year. I'm lucky, I'm still here and I've come through, but many, like the lovely and very talented Marti Caine have not.

May 2003 saw the next stage of my lymphoma (non Hodgkin's Lymphoma) develop into full-blown leukaemia.

I'd lived with the prospect of my death since 1988, but now there had been an acceleration in my illness. My treatment was stepped up once again.

It was also around now that I stopped driving. I'd had my latest bout of chemotherapy and was out in the car. I clipped a wing mirror. It was enough for me to begin to realise that I was now a liability on the road, nothing to do with drink driving, nothing to do with being irresponsible. I just felt it might be better if I didn't drive anymore.

I got through the UK tour and the summer season, but it was becoming an effort to cope once again. I was feeling more and more tired. The chemo was slowing me down.

That's when James and I took ourselves off to Thailand.

It's another of my favourite places and I've been there a few times over the years. We went elephant trekking and saw some wonderful shows. I felt so relaxed, which was the general idea of going there in the first place. I was taking my medication and enjoying the break. But disaster was to strike as we were about to fly home.

I lost James.

I hadn't misplaced him. We hadn't fallen out. I just didn't know where he had got to. I wasn't concerned at first. He had packed our cases and gone for a drink. I'd stayed at the hotel because I wasn't very well. I was changed and looking forward to going home, watching *Die Hard* on the hotel's in-house movie channel. This next part is so heart-rending.

After James had been gone around an hour or so I started to get worried. Where had he got to? I watched *Die Hard* again, still no James. He'd now been gone for hours and I'd had no contact with him at all. *Die Hard* started up again for its next showing. I started panicking. Our flight had been booked for 2.30am and we were already going to be running late. I wasn't bothered about missing the flight; I was bothered about James. Where was he? I'm dying inside now, not just from the leukaemia but my heart is beginning to break.

In desperation I rang the Bangkok Hospital. Thank God he wasn't there. I got someone to take me on the back of a motorbike, checking out all of the bars that we had been to since we'd been there. I looked in every one of them that I could, but it was now about six in the morning and many were closed.

In the end I asked the man on the bike to take me to the nick. It was now nine in the morning. I was just starting to think about what I could tell his dad and his brother. I really was that worried.

When I went through the gates I saluted. It was the king's official birthday! I asked whether they had anyone who had been locked up during the night and that I was looking for my friend. Thank the Lord he was there.

It turned out James had gone to a so-called Irish bar for half a Guinness and his drink had been spiked. He says all he can remember about that night was seeing me. He asked me why I was crying when I saw him. I just said it was because I was so happy to see him.

He was in a pretty bad state and looked as though he'd had a kicking. It also looked as though he'd been bitten as well.

Finding him was one thing but getting him out was another. At first I thought the man in charge of the clink was asking me whether I was trying to bribe him, but I wasn't. It turned out he was asking for a bribe. Eventually James and I left – thankfully together.

Why is it that whenever we leave anywhere there is always drama? India, the States and now Thailand, but there was far more drama to come in the coming year and a half.

Now you're probably thinking that you haven't had another of those breaks for ages now. I think it's about time we had one don't you? Then we can tackle the period that led to the biggest challenge of my life. It's the story of how I came back from the dead. Drink anyone? This time you'd better charge your glasses because we're entering tear-jerker territory once again. I did tell you this was a rollercoaster ride didn't I? We're about to fall off right now. But first here are some of the people who a singer cannot do without.

MUSICIANS

How do you keep the music playing
How do you make it last
How do you stop the song from fading
Too fast ...
And since you know we're always changing
How can it be the same

Joe Longthorne *How Do You Keep The Music Playing?* released 2009

I told you earlier that the first time I was backed by Maurice Merry and his Merry Men in Scarborough I knew that the show was mine. But that's not trying to be clever about it. I just understand the value of having good musicians.

You can have bands with lots of musicians, but if they're not on the money you can tell the difference. I can hear when someone's not up to scratch, or if someone is playing a wrong note instantly.

I've played with the best. It's hard to mention everyone here, so for those who have played with me and not received a mention I hope you won't be offended.

My current musical director is Andy Mudd, who I've already mentioned once or twice. It's just the two of us on stage at the moment as I've gone for a more stripped-down approach in the past 18 months titled 'An Intimate Evening with Joe Longthorne'. It's something different, a change from what I had been doing and it's working well.

Up until the end of 2010 my musical director was the excellent Steve 'Stretch' Price. Steve is such an outstanding pianist and he marshalled the band brilliantly. If you're reading this having never seen him before there is a good reason why he's called Stretch. He's a really, seriously tall bloke!

The rest of the band was Paul Smith, Simon Goulding and Alan Wormald; and along with 'Stretch' and Andy they are all fantastic musicians. Paul is a brilliant drummer and has had a great career. He was also Matt Monro's drummer. There was a point in some of our shows where I would bring Paul to the front of the stage to stand alongside 'Stretch'. They both entered into the spirit of it, because where 'Stretch' is remarkably tall, Paul isn't – if you see what I mean! You would have done at a concert I assure you. Si (Simon) is an absolute gem on bass. When he's wearing his shades he sometimes gets called Roy Orbison.

Si is one of those guys who can pick up any song really quickly. He only needs a few bars; then he's got it. I always think it's marvellous how some of the truly great musicians can anticipate where a song goes without ever having heard it before. Si is in the Trevor Barry mould who played alongside me many years ago. Alan is a brilliant guitarist.

As for Andy (Mudd), well you've already heard a few of the stories involving him. He's a great professional who has stood by me just as much as I've stood by him. We have both had good times and bad. He's like family. He comes from Halifax originally and Roy Walker became like a dad to him when he first started in show business. Musically we have done everything together in the past decade and are still doing that right now. I am proud to call him one of my closest friends and look on him like a son. He's my musical associate. He makes sure that within two seconds of me hitting that stage the sound is perfect.

But what of all those others I've played with?

From my TV show days I would have to mention Ernie Dunstall once again, one of the greatest musical directors and with whom I wrote a number of songs. Colin Hadley was also another of my all-time favourite MDs. He has also sadly passed away. As well as Ernie and Colin I really need to give a mention to all of these: Alan Rogers, Trevor Brown, Alan Ainsworth (once again), Steve Sidwell, Dave Arch and the great Don Lusher one of the world's finest trombonists. There's also the fabulous Derek Watkins who played trumpet.

Lewis Osborne played on the *Live in Concert* CD recorded on Ritz. He was an amazing young lead guitarist who made it all the way from a little village near Bristol to the London stage. He started with me when he was 16 years old. Chris Rae played guitar on so many of my recordings. One of my other favourite lead guitarists would have to be Ian Aitken who played for me on *Always Something There To Remind Me*.

As well as Paul (Smith) I have been well blessed with fabulous drummers. Brett Morgan played for me in the 80s; and there's Graham Ward who went on to work with Tom Jones and George Michael. Graham has to be amongst my favourites. He developed one of the oddest of obsessions. On tour he became addicted to bingo. We used to play it on the tour bus to win the boxes of chocolate that fans had brought for us. Graham was just mad for it. And then there's Welsh drummer Harold Fisher – another great musician.

There have been so many great players. I count myself extremely fortunate to have been backed by such gifted performers and I never ever take for granted the hours of hard work they put in whilst I am not there.

Nor do I take for granted the work put in by my sound and lighting crew, particularly the man who was with me for many years from being in Hull. Zeb (White) also put so much time in for me. Today it's Arran Culpan and Paul Philips who are at the helm and they do such a terrific job. Then there are the always amazing backing singers who have been such an important part of my shows too. Everyone is important to me. It's a real team effort.

They all spend hours sound-checking and rehearsing so that we can achieve the standard of playing and performing that we all strive for when we're on stage together. It is a very real pleasure to work with each and every one of them.

Right, that's your latest break over! Are you ready for the onslaught that comes next as I hurtle towards that moment when all looks lost for me? Good! Then I shall resume. I have to say that you might be ready for this next part, but I'm still not. This is the part that really hurts, even now, no matter how many times I think of it.

DONOR TIME

The way you saved my life girl,
Oh they can't take that away from me

Joe Longthorne & Barbara Windsor
They Can't Take That Away From Me released 1994

Whilst 2003 had seen me diagnosed with leukaemia it wasn't until July 2004 that it was confirmed I needed to find a donor fast. That's when Dr Kelsey told me that a bone marrow transplant was my only hope of survival. He'd said the chemotherapy and the drugs would keep things at bay in the short term, but it was the bone marrow transplant that was the key. In fact if a suitable donor could be found the really great news then might be that I would probably make a full recovery, and that I would not have to live with this thing hanging around my neck 24 hours a day, as I had for years.

Wishing and hoping is one thing. Finding a donor, and then a match, is another. But then we found out about a wonderful charity, one that I now help in any way I can.

But before we get to the drama there was still plenty of other things going on. I had shows to perform, DVDs to release and money to raise for charity.

On the performance and merchandise front we were back on the DVD trail in 2004 with the release of *A Year In His Life*, which was split into three parts and featured rehearsal and concert footage from the Sheffield City Hall concert; part of the concert at Leeds City Varieties (where I had performed in my *Junior Showtime* days); and the Friendship Club party at the Hilton (it used to be called the Dragonara) in Leeds. There was also rehearsal and concert footage of my summer season at Blackpool Opera House and several interviews with Granada and Yorkshire Television recording my on-going battle against this horrible disease.

We released both *A Year In His Life* and the DVD of the Charity Gala Concert on behalf of the Sheffield Children's Hospital and Jane Tomlinson's appeal at Sheffield City Hall which was titled *Joe Longthorne .. With Love*. I wasn't too happy about all of the footage on the Sheffield concert because of the size of my glands at the time, but my fans thought it was just great to have another memento of me in concert. In my heart of hearts I knew there would be better concerts to come, if only I could pull through what was happening to my body now.

But people tell me the best production of all was the DVD which also appeared on The Biography Channel on the Sky network – *If I Never Sing Another Song* – made by the Vegas Films production company which was written and produced by the wonderful Paul Iacovou.

Little did the TV company know at the time that my life was to undergo such a rollercoaster ride in the months they were filming. It is a beautifully shot programme that I believe captures the real me more so than any other.

Our spring tour took in 37 shows in just 50 days. We travelled over 7,000 miles on that tour alone mainly because the treatment I was receiving at Blackpool meant that I needed to be there three times a week, and each session took around eight hours. It was the kind of logistical nightmare that makes some just shake their heads in despair, but James sorted it all out. It really was a Herculean task at times.

I was determined that we would get through all of the dates on what was a sell-out tour. There was one night when we'd finished in Southend, drove back to Blackpool that same night, went to Victoria Hospital in the morning, took a flight from Blackpool to Biggin Hill, then drove around the M25 to Dartford.

Zeb was tour manager, and he was to remain a close friend throughout the next year as I fought my personal battle against this illness, with the help of the finest doctors, nurses and hospital staff you could wish for. This was the time when James and Fran had to look after me all of the time. I was barely surviving. The combination of the treatment plus the fatigue from the concerts where I never gave less than 100% meant I was constantly tired.

Joe Wildy, one of my fellow entertainers who has played in Blackpool and on tour with me, said at the time, 'I don't know how he does it (meaning me). It's been a terrible strain for him. How he's managed to get through it. It must be willpower.'

When I wasn't going straight back to Blackpool for treatment I would sleep in what became known as the 'Joemobile', the tour bus.

What particularly annoyed me when we got to Billingham Forum where we were to play two nights, and it is captured on film for all to see, were the swollen glands in my neck. On the *If I Never Sing Another Song* programme I show how bothered I was about them. I just came out with it like this:

'It's these bloody lumps, like bastard boiled eggs aren't they?' I wasn't happy about them at all – although I quite like eggs! Prefer mine poached or scrambled though. Little did I know that they were to end up the size of cricket balls.

I was still able to make jokes on stage about what I was going through.

I told one about a nurse who got my name wrong. She called me Mr Long Horn. 'Oh, I said, you've seen me without my clothes on then!'

The Friendship Club event which was held at the Hilton in Leeds saw the auctioning of three of my suits and with further contributions this total was swelled to just under £4,000 which again went between the hospitals in Leeds and Blackpool. This was where the key that I had been presented from the *Through The Keyhole* TV programme was also auctioned off.

The same evening as the Friendship Club party we performed at the world-famous City Varieties Music Hall in Leeds on my birthday, 31 May, and by then we had raised £7,000 for the Leeds General Infirmary. We presented the cheque to Professor Childs. We also raised a further £1,000 for the MacMillan Windmill Appeal at Blackpool Victoria Hospital.

I had got through the spring tour with only one or two cancellations, which were more due to the treatment not being completed in enough time for me to get to a venue than anything else. I really had tried my best to fulfil all of my engagements but the treatment had occasionally made life too difficult. I was reported as saying in May 2004:

'I have the steadfastness to go forward and give it a f***ing good fight. Going on stage is like therapy to me. I've now got to get through this summer's run. The last thing I want to do is let anyone down.'

Three weeks into the rehearsals for the *Summer Spectacular* it was time for Dr Kelsey to deliver the verdict.

I had been taking 35 steroids a day and had needed regular four-pint blood transfusions during the 12 week course of treatment, but it hadn't been successful.

Dr Paul Kelsey told me that my white blood count had stabilised and was just above the danger threshold.

That was the good news.

The bad news was that he decided that I should undergo six chemotherapy sessions over an 18 week period at Blackpool Victoria Hospital immediately after the close of the summer season's shows, and that a bone marrow replacement operation was not just my best way forward, it was now my only option if I wanted to live for anything like a decent time.

I put it this way at the time:

'The doctors choose what to do, it's a bit like chess. There are many possible moves but one wrong one and that could be it, checkmate.'

My family were first in line to see whether they could provide a suitable match, but none of them fitted the bill. My fans were next in line. They have never ceased to amaze me with their loyalty, tenderness, love and care they have shown me over the years. If it's money I'm short of they'll send me that. Bless them all. They've probably a lot less than I've had. If it's part of my body that needs replacing, they'll even offer me parts of theirs!

Sometimes it's not always possible to tell everyone just how much you think of them but every one of them has a special place in my heart. And one of them might have even had a special place actually inside my body too because hundreds of them registered with the Anthony Nolan Trust to see whether they were a match.

I had added my name to the Anthony Nolan Register as a possible recipient and my fans had followed suit as possible donors, of course not just for me but because of being made aware of the fabulous work the Anthony Nolan Trust carries out every day. How wonderful is that? I started working to raise funds for the Trust, which I had not heard of until then, immediately.

Due to the treatment I was going to have it was quickly decided that my next Australia tour, which had been scheduled for late 2004, would be rescheduled.

Around this time Dave Halford had to do so much rescheduling for me, cancelling tours and gigs, but he remained faithful to me throughout the time that followed and was there for me with tours as soon as I was back fit and able. His people at Artistes Direct are really very professional and ensure that I get to venues right across the UK.

Just before I started the summer season in 2004 I auctioned off most of my gold and platinum discs and special awards I had received over the years on eBay in aid of Cancer Research. There was the Best Newcomer Award of 1983 from the Variety Club of Great Britain and the Variety Club of Jersey Award I picked up in 1980. I really felt I ought to be doing something more and these awards were one way in which I could further contribute. We raised over £10,000. I really didn't think I needed them anymore and the money we raised was far more important. A number of my fans followed suit by also auctioning off their memorabilia of me for charity.

I was all set for the *Summer Spectacular* at the Opera House to be just that, and we had a fantastic line-up with the Stardust Dancers, singer Kiely Hampson, violinist Gary Lovini, the always wonderfully entertaining Johnnie Casson and Tony Jo as compere. It opened to fabulous reviews and a sell-out audience. I couldn't have wished for better.

It was scheduled for a nine week run (19 July – 19 September), five nights a week and negotiations were even under way to extend the season by a further two weeks. I fancied breaking my own box office record that year. But I was suffering. During August I struggled with severe back pains and those damned swollen glands. I was still giving it my very best shot every night but my body was rebelling. It was as though it was shouting at me that it had gone far enough. I just couldn't perform. It had got to the point where I was performing, then immediately being wrapped up in cotton wool and put to bed, sleeping until 7 o'clock the next evening and then coming to do the show. It was a little bit like being on the Pier again.

Normally I would have spent time with the fans after each show, but I was using up so much energy on stage that I had nothing left to give afterwards. I just went home straight after each concert, so I was only awake for the time I was performing.

I had performed 35 shows of the *Summer Spectacular* when it all caught up with me at last.

I couldn't stand throughout my performance, so I had an armchair brought on to the stage. My glands were also getting larger and larger and inevitably I was too weak to perform at all. I was so disappointed – not for me, but for the legions of fans. I knew this was a really serious time. It was the worst I'd ever been.

Dr Paul Kelsey and his team quickly decided that, although my blood count had remained stable during the *Summer Spectacular* concerts, the best course of action to deal with the swelling of my glands was to start my treatment earlier than he had originally planned. To be fair I don't think Dr Kelsey wanted to leave the treatment until after I'd finished the *Summer Spectacular* in the first place, but he knew how important the show was to me.

So there I was on 7 September 2004, admitted back into hospital for my first week of treatment. I was due to be in for seven days, with the *Summer Spectacular* still being performed, minus me. My intention was clear. I wanted to be back on that stage performing again before the season ended and preferably as soon as possible.

But it wasn't going to be that simple.

I had been told it would be like committing suicide to stay on stage. At that moment Blackpool Victoria Hospital was where I needed to be and James called it a real 'life or death' decision.

There was a story doing the rounds at the time when I was admitted that I had collapsed on stage during the last concert but that wasn't the case. I had collapsed several times off stage, but never on it.

I have always told my mam, 'There's always people worse off than me.' And I truly believe that. All of the affection I am constantly being shown by my fans is really wonderfully uplifting. They follow me throughout not just the UK tours but Australia, Cyprus, Spain and Vegas. How can I ever be worse off than others with that kind of support?

I was determined to get back in the action as soon as I could and on 18 September I returned – for one night only – the last night of the season.

Word quickly got around that I was to be back and once again we had a complete sell-out. Everyone turned up – of course the fans, but also many other stars from the world of show business. I was grateful to them all for showing their concern.

At the show we also managed to present cheques to Macmillan Cancer Relief and Cancer Research. The lady who received the cheque on behalf of Macmillan Cancer Relief said some beautiful words on the night that made me feel very humble. She said:

'Ladies and Gentlemen life is not measured by the number of breaths you take, but by the number of times your breath is taken away. Joe, you're truly inspirational. You're the finest ambassador for those living with cancer and you take our breath away a million times.'

It couldn't help but bring a tear to my eye. I'd never seen myself in that way – being an ambassador – I've just done what I feel is right.

Whilst my treatment continued there was at last some fresh hope on the bone marrow front. And it was really fantastic news.

Originally it had been thought that there would be even less of a chance of finding a suitable donor from outside of my family, but the reason why the Anthony Nolan Trust exists is to ensure that there is a big enough 'pool' of people that the chances of finding a suitable match are improved.

Let's hold on for that fantastic news just a bit, whilst I tell you why we should all be supportive of the work of the Anthony Nolan Trust.

I told you this wasn't a me-me-me book and this is what I meant by saying it earlier. It's important this, it's my bit where I get on my soapbox:

The important things in life are people, those who are your family, friends, fans and those who make sure you can carry on living.

Amazingly, given all of the monies our government puts into war efforts and paperwork, the Anthony Nolan Trust receives no direct government funding. The Air Ambulance is the same by the way. These amazingly vital, lifesaving bodies are simply registered charities that rely on the public and companies to fund their tremendous efforts. The Terrence Higgins Trust, the leading HIV and AIDS charity in the UK is another.

Personally I think it's criminal in this day and age that we spend so much of our time on other things when just a small proportion of what is spent elsewhere could improve so many people's lives, and allow them to live a normal life instead of living with the fear that every new day could be their last.

Maybe now you can understand what I mean when I say this is not a me-me-me book!

I was going to leave the next bit until the end but, in case you forget by the time you finish the book – and there is a lot more to come yet, quite a bit of heartache and then some of the best moments in my life – here is what you need to know if you feel inspired to register. And I hope most sincerely that you do.

To find out more about the:
ANTHONY NOLAN TRUST
Contact: 020 7284 1234
Or visit: www.anthonynolan.org.uk

The Terence Higgins Trust urgently needs your support too.

Whether you want to give money, time or both:
TERRENCE HIGGINS TRUST
Contact: 314-320 Gray's Inn Road, London WC1X 8DP

There are more details at the back of the book. Please do what you can, even if it is simply a donation. They are always looking for more bone marrow donors in order to help people, like they did with me.

Now let's turn to just how amazing the Trust turned out to be for me!

The Anthony Nolan Trust found seven donor hopefuls from its worldwide register of nine million people. That's why they need so many people on the register. It really is over a million-to-one shot that you find compatibility.

One of the seven was from South Africa, another from Germany and one was a girl from Wales. Professor Guy Lucas told me that the German one sounded probably the best bet because of their techniques over there. I think he might have been watching too many of those TV advertisements about German cars.

Vorsprung-Durch-Technic and all that! Anyhow he said that they were settling on this young lady from Wales. I'm told she was only 28. I've never met her, but of all the people I have said I am grateful to so far in this book she has to be right up there at the top – apart from my mam and dad of course! You saved my life, thank you, whoever you are, so much!

Of course finding a donor, a suitable match, is one thing. Going through the procedure is quite another, but we were on our way.

Have I mentioned gangsters yet? I mean THE gangsters? Which UK gangsters do you know? Yes, it's them, or at least one of the twins. Well it's about time I did then. Now this is a break that I bet you weren't expecting. And it's all true. You might need an even stiffer drink this time!

REGGIE KRAY

Well I've got to go now,
Well I guess I'll see you around.
I don't know when though,
'cause I don't know when I'll be back in town

Joe Longthorne *Funny How Time Slips Away* released 2008

On my grand piano, my cherished grand piano at home, which even came with me to the Grand Theatre in Blackpool last year, there stands a sheaf of papers. They are not the works of Don Black, who I admire greatly, nor are they any of the other great songwriters of the past century such as Sammy Cahn, Cole Porter, George Gershwin and Lennon & McCartney.

They are the works of a man who was better known for his partnership with his twin brother. I'm talking about Reggie Kray.

Back in the 1990s I received a call from a man called Frank Frazer who simply said, 'Reg wants to see you'.

I knew that the Krays liked my music because I'd heard that Ron had wanted me to sing at his wedding. It didn't happen but it was then that I knew they both liked my work. It turned out that Reg had been writing quite a bit in Maidstone Prison with another inmate and that when he was to be released he planned to have a recording studio in his new home. He had already written his own autobiography and a book of slang, but this was different. He had been collaborating with another inmate over song lyrics with a view to him and me turning them into songs. There is one called *Butterfly* that's on the top of the pile on my piano now.

When I went to see Reggie I was amazed at his appearance. He was wearing overly thick spectacles and he could hardly hear me. He couldn't do anything, probably couldn't even see anything whilst he was wearing them, and yet there were still extra guards on duty for my visit.

I spoke to the wardens about the spectacles he was wearing and the fact that he needed a hearing aid and apparently the week after my visit he had new specs and a new hearing aid.

I'm not getting involved in anything over why he was in prison, that's not my place. All I knew was the man I saw in front of me that day didn't look as though he was being treated properly. The next day I got a call from Frank Frazer again who said what I had done was a 'wonderful gesture'. To me it was just common decency.

I talked with Reg about his mother, of whom it is well documented he and Ron loved more dearly than anyone else in their lives. We talked about the film that the Kemp brothers had starred in, playing Ron and Reg. He liked the film, but the one thing he was bothered about was the way his mother had been portrayed.

'Our mother never swore as much as she did in the film,' he said. 'I'm still a bit upset about the way they did that.'

Then he said: 'I'm sending you some lyrics.' And that was it. One day I hope to release it as an album called *Inside Out* with all of the funds going to Reg and Ron Kray's charities.

CHAPTER THIRTY THREE

PRELUDE TO THE BONE MARROW

So deep is the night – no moon tonight
No friendly star – to guide me with its light
Be still my heart

Joe Longthorne *So Deep Is The Night* released 1993

I liked the idea of having my bone marrow coming from Wales after all it was the land of Dame Shirley. But there was plenty to go through before I even came close to receiving it.

Following that final appearance in the last night of the *Summer Spectacular 2004* my life for the next year would be one long round of chemotherapy, treatment, double pneumonia, a state of unconsciousness and hospitals. I honestly don't know how I came through.

There was just no way I could perform and everything in the diary was shifted so that I could concentrate on one thing only – finally beating this disease. We had to reschedule the charity concert I had been looking forward to in my home-city in December, where I had hoped to play what, for all I knew, could have been my last time, especially for my family, friends and fans in Hull.

DVDs were released along with further compilation CDs in late 2004 and the early part of 2005. It was the closest I would get to performing for some considerable time.

When I first met Professor Guy Lucas he explained to me that I had run out of options.

I only had one choice and that was the bone marrow transplant. He also told me that all he could offer me was a hard time. He said he had heard I was a bit of a character, although it could have been another word which I won't use here. I soon knew where I stood with him. He was in charge. He told me that I could either 'go forth and multiply' in as pleasant a way as possible, or I could do it his way.

It was in October 2004 that I had found out about the number of possible donors. By now I was under way with what turned out to be a further 24 weeks of chemotherapy taking me through until February 2005.

There had been a hope that the bone marrow transplant would take place following the course of chemotherapy, but the news I had been waiting for wasn't good – I still had to wait.

You can't keep me away from singing for that long.

Since I was waiting and I was feeling good again we announced that I would be performing three shows over Easter at the Paradise Rooms in Blackpool. They were scheduled for 26-28 March and I performed in them all.

Whilst I had been looking forward to performing again, and felt better than I had for a long time, I was also nervous. But I needn't have been because the audience was fantastic. All of my fans were there again over the three nights – some came to all three – and they really helped me through.

It was just after the Paradise concerts that I was very nearly in paradise myself! There were compatibility tests to undertake that were to last a further three months but it looked like we were getting close to the match I needed.

That was the time when I found out about the seven hopefuls, including my young lady from Wales.

I'd had the all-clear that my body was now clear of cancer cells, but I'd had that kind of promise before if you remember. The news was that the transplant looked odds-on for later in the year.

When the curtain fell at the Opera House for that last night of the *Summer Spectacular* in 2004 I had thought it might be the last concert I would ever play. But since that time I had managed to fit in a date at a club called the Willows, three sell-outs at the Paradise Rooms and had also been booked to appear at the same venue twice a week throughout the summer. I was feeling stronger again and actually I'd felt sharper in those three days at the Paradise Rooms than I had felt for a year or so.

In 2004 there had been some nights when I had only been on stage for 30-40 minutes and that isn't like me. When I'm out there I want to be out there for as long as I can. I didn't want anyone feeling short-changed. But now things were looking up again.

I was told, all along the way, that having the bone marrow transplant was not the end of it. There was far more to go through as my body might reject what had been administered. In short, my chances were not brilliant.

I could die just from the procedure itself. All I could do was put my trust in them and that's exactly what I did – up until that moment when I could hear those voices around me losing their faith, which is where we started this book.

How right they were. Not to lose their faith, but to warn me of what might happen.

I had also been told that I would need six to 12 months in order to recover.

But before all of that, and just a month or so of having come out of chemotherapy I was told it was time to start a new round of it, just so that when they undertook the procedure my body was completely free of cancer cells.

Professor Lucas had promised me a rough ride and this was only the start of it.

You might think that some rollercoasters you have been on have made you feel sick or dizzy. Let me tell you that although my life had been like living on a rollercoaster for many years, it was now time for the Big Dipper!

When you go down a dip you inevitably come to the lowest point – and I have come to that a few times in my life. The nervous breakdown was obviously one of those, but this illness has sent me down quite a few dips. I have suffered from depression regularly and there have been times when, because of what I have been going through, I have felt as though I just wanted it all to end.

The after-effects of chemotherapy, as anyone who has had to undergo it will verify, are like the worst hangover you can ever have – and believe you me I've had my fair share of those too.

When I am unable to perform I begin to wonder what my life is all about. It is what I was made to do. I know a lot of young people say that today when they are trying out for TV programmes but it really is what my life has been about.

I have often said this, but the people who suffer the most are those around you. When you're depressed you are feeling sorry for yourself, but that only makes things worse for your loved ones. In my case that's James, my family, my friends and all of my fans. They all look after me in whichever way they can and they are all the reason why I have come back from the brink each time over the years.

I've not made too many mentions of my faith up to now but I do believe in a higher authority. I'm not too religious, but I am a Catholic and I do believe in Jesus Christ. I'm not much of a good-doer, but what I do have is faith in the creator, whoever that is. I can't claim to know what he or she looks like, for all I know God, or whoever he or she is, but I do know God is all. I couldn't tell you any more apart from that I believe there is one. I do go to church, but not regularly. I take mass. I'm not a Bible-thumper but I do believe that the Bible makes sense of our lives.

James also makes a great deal of sense to my life.

As he will tell you that is often just common-sense too, but he has been wonderful for me and to me from the moment we got together. I owe this young man so much I couldn't possibly ever repay him. He knows everything about me; he understands everything that has happened in the past 12 years; and most of all he has been there for me every step of the way.

I don't think I could have come through all that I have without his constant support. Is this getting too mushy? Well I don't apologise for any of it.

James is a diamond. I do an impression of Neil Diamond, but James is the real gem. He calms me down when I'm overwrought and emotional, he won't let me do anything that he thinks will do me harm. If he thinks I'm doing too much he will tell me to stop, to rest. But most importantly of all, he is always there by my side. He doesn't make a big play of it; he doesn't want to be in the spotlight; all he is doing is looking after me in the best way he can and that's good enough for me.

How's all that for mush? Well it's not mush to me and I mean every word.

We were talking about being on a Big Dipper weren't we? Well, with no immediate prospect of a transplant in sight and buoyed by the success of my three nights in Paradise, the summer season was booked and Dave had even added dates at the Royal Concert Hall in Glasgow.

This particular Big Dipper of mine was starting to go up again.

My long-time show business friend Engelbert Humperdinck was keen to get me back to Vegas and if anyone had the contacts, he would have them. He was going to play a series of concerts in Paris and he talked about me joining him to play over there. It was all dependent on my next series of tests.

Typically for me, they didn't go my way, so the Paris idea was shelved. By now I must have had a pretty long shelf to keep all of what had been put on there.

My last performance before the ordeal that would see me on a hospital bed for nearly four months was once again at the Paradise Rooms on 30 May. We had it filmed and the DVD could have been my epitaph. The place was packed, it was a wonderful evening which included my sister Lizzie getting up to sing *Crazy* written by Willie Nelson but always associated with Patsy Cline. Lizzie sang it beautifully, like the professional I always thought she could have been. I did tell you that all of my family were great singers didn't I? It was another massively emotional night for me.

I told everyone that night: 'I am looking at the next few weeks as a journey. I have had a great and wonderful time. When I get through this next period of treatment and time in hospital undergoing the bone marrow replacement I'll be back in top form and top style – and I hope my hair will have come back again too!' My hair has gone five times over the years through all of the chemo I have had, but each time it has always come back.

Never was I to sing my final song so meaningfully. I think everyone felt what I was really feeling in the room when I sang *If I Never Sing Another Song*.

There were hankies out everywhere, tears running down people's faces. I think we all knew that this was it. This was the big one. My big dipper was about to go down – would it come back up again this time?

DEATH'S DOOR

And I shall hear, tho' soft you tread above me
And all my dreams will warm and sweeter be
If you'll not fail to tell me that you love me
I'll simply sleep in peace until you come to me

Joe Longthorne *Danny Boy* released 2006

Two weeks after the May concert we were finally under way. Would I ever come out of hospital alive?

Well yes I would actually. As it happens within a day! But that's because we hadn't reached the full-on procedure stage just yet. This was the preliminary. We were pretty much at base camp before taking on Everest – and I'm not talking about buying double-glazing.

On Wednesday 15 June 2005 I was admitted to the Manchester Royal Infirmary to have what is known as a Hickman line inserted into my chest. It was to be inserted to ease the administration of the treatment and I had been told that if there were no complications I would be discharged the following afternoon.

Step One was a success.

I went back on Monday 20 June after a lovely evening that had been laid on for myself and James at the Lowry Hotel in Manchester by one of Zeb's colleagues. We had been booked into the Presidential Suite and I remember the suite had a Yamaha grand piano. It was such another wonderful and lovely gesture. A Bentley had also been laid on for us, to and from the hotel.

When we arrived at Manchester Royal Infirmary the following morning at 8 o'clock I was ready. All I felt was that this was it. I'm here now, so let's get on with it. After all, I'd had long enough to think about this moment. It had been on the agenda for what seemed forever. At least, one way or the other, something was now going to be done.

At this point I have to thank Zeb again, because it was he who kept the fans in touch with what was happening to me during this time. We might have had our differences from time to time but he really did stick close by throughout this time.

At first I was receiving various chemotherapy treatments. I received two separate treatments in one day – ARA-C and Campath – and Lord did that hurt. I was also on morphine to counteract the back pain I had been suffering. I was, so I'm told, holding up well after the first seven days of treatment, but remember, this was only the chemotherapy. We were nowhere near the transplant just yet.

In fact I was in such good spirits at the time that I was already talking about when I would be performing again. I had felt that New Year's Eve would be as good a time as any, with a big 'Welcome Back' party. It's the only way I could really cope with what was going on, by constantly looking forward.

Professor Lucas told me I had been doing well and that the next step would be a smooth infusion of stem cells the next day 29 June. I had lost my appetite by now and had come down from 12st 7lbs to 11st 7lbs. I was reliably informed that would come down even further.

This was the real start of my countdown to the operation. Dr Paul Cahalin, who had been looking after me at Blackpool Victoria Hospital the previous year, was drafted in to the Manchester Royal Infirmary team. I was now receiving a powerful drug called Melphalan, along with others, which was intended to bring my immune system down to zero. The idea was to lessen the chance of infection when the bone marrow was infused.

Whilst all of this was going on I was receiving good luck messages from all around the world, from fans and all of my pals in showbiz. Amongst them was one from Andy Williams, and another from Engelbert.

On 29 June the bone marrow transplant was administered. It lasted around the length of one of my concerts, between an hour and a half and an hour and three-quarters.

There were more drugs to follow after the transplant including antibiotics, but I was doing well.

I should have known that things would get worse, just when I felt a little better. It's the way it has always been for me with this awful disease.

Five days after the transplant I contracted GVHD (Graft Versus Host Disease). I was now in the real danger zone. All of these months of preparation and my body looked like it could be rejecting what it had been given.

It wasn't all bad news. I was told I was making good progress regardless of the GVHD. We were now in mid-July, it was hot and portable air conditioning was needed. With the good progress I was making there was talk of moving me to Blackpool Victoria.

But that talk all turned out to be far too early. I wasn't out of the woods yet by a long way! In fact I'd only just entered the darkness of the woods. The worst time of all was to come pretty quickly now.

Just after receiving a report about how well I was doing I developed a chest infection and I understand my odds of surviving were halved at that stage. The bookies would have had a field day with me.

My whole body was starting to shut down and by the end of July I was deeply sedated and on a ventilator.

I was in no position to help anyone now. I couldn't do anything but lie there.

I now know just how much all of the dearest people in my life were going through, James, my close friends, my family and of course my fans. I know that everyone was praying for me. Candlelit vigils were being held in churches up and down the country.

James has told me that at one point he honestly thought that was it. He spoke to Pat in desperation and in floods of tears. He told her I was on a machine and that he finally thought I was dying. Of course he was still with me even then and he never left my side. There was nothing I could do, except somewhere deep inside me fight my way out of this. I believe I did it through my faith.

It was a really bad time for all of the people closest to me. All of my family were there now. My dear sweet mam was in bits, I think she'd nearly had enough herself. Pat had come and she couldn't believe it was me. There I was, this blown-up man. The drugs had done that to me. She knew all of the scrapes I'd been through over the years and had seen me bounce back from them all, but even she didn't think I could get out of this one.

The Three Fathers came including Father Geoff, a bit like 'We Three Kings..', except they didn't bring me any gold, frankincense or myrrh. Instead they gave me 'Last Orders!' Well, I knew I wasn't Jesus, but I had expected a little more hope than that! When I saw them something inside me told me that I wasn't dying.

Professor Lucas came back from his holidays and was apparently as surprised as anyone to see me still alive. When he had gone I don't think he thought I had any chance of survival. He knew that what had been done was all that he and his team could do the rest was up to me and my body. Fortunately for me, like I said, I had a bit more than that. I had faith plus the prayers of everyone around me; and those praying in churches or in their homes. It worked for me.

But even then that wasn't enough! It was time for my sister Anne to leap into action. Anne took over from the nurses one day when she saw that my blood pressure wasn't right. My temperature was 104. Anne dragged the pillow case from under my head and had it filled with ice. The more ice I got the more my blood pressure came right.

Of course I couldn't tell you about any of this at the time. I was unconscious for weeks so a lot of it is from what others have told me. What

I can tell you is that the thoughts going through my head were those that we started with at the beginning of the book.

I couldn't move, but there were times when I could hear things, or at least you think you can. I was sure that someone was talking to John-boy, telling him I would be going at 6 o'clock. 'We can't do any more,' was what I think I heard. At one point I really think they were going to switch me off.

By now, although I couldn't move, couldn't speak, couldn't communicate, I was fighting so much inside of me.

I had double pneumonia – bad news at the best of times, critical for me at this time. But still they were pumping me with drugs. Everything that could be done was being done to keep me going.

My fight was still going on even if they couldn't see it, but I was fast approaching the time when it was all becoming too much even for my faith.

That's when I felt I could hear them say the words, 'He's dead. He's dead. He's gone.' But I wasn't! I wanted to scream at them that I was still here. That's when I gave myself up. This is when I said to myself 'My Jesus this is it now. I'm f***ed.' He understands any language and I'm going through too much pain to care about being right. I'm dying. I've been on this slab for six hours, all of these people are trying to help but I'm now in too much pain. That's when I thought 'Dear Lord, if you've any decency about you take me now.' But then I heard a phone call. That's when I believe I heard the thing about not being touched with a barge pole – and that's when I changed my tune too. That gave me the extra spirit I needed.

I just thought Jesus, help me now. I didn't see his face. People say they do, but I didn't. It's just a feeling that he was there.

But we're still not even at the stage where I was back with my eyes opened just yet.

I remained unconscious for a fortnight. Two whole weeks taken out of my life! I suppose it was still better than been taken out completely.

A breathing tube had been inserted, but it was between my vocal chords. Now there was a concern amongst my nearest and dearest that even if I did recover I might never be able to talk again, let alone sing. Maybe the last song I had sung at the Paradise Rooms was going to become prophetic?

They moved the breathing tube from where it went through my vocal chords directly into my trachea. Apparently I was now also starting to produce healthy white blood cells, but the regular blood transfusions I needed were still taking place.

August had been almost non-existent for me in terms of doing anything. I had now regained consciousness and was through the worst of it. I tried to speak but couldn't. That was worrying. I had been told that I shouldn't attempt to speak straight away, but you do want to try. I couldn't help it. I didn't expect to be able to sing like Mario Lanza straightaway, but I so wanted to sing again or at least know that I could.

The very least I wanted to say was: 'Mine's half a lager!'

At one time I was using an alphabet chart to spell out what I was trying to say. James, Zeb, Anne and Pat all tried their best to lip-read too. James put his mobile phone to my ear so that I could hear mam's voice again. It was such a wonderful feeling. I had been through hell and was still in a lot of pain, but I had come through it all. Professor Lucas had told me only three out of every ten, who had endured what I had experienced, made it back to life.

Things started coming back to me slowly. When my hair first grew back I looked like Saddam Hussein. Not a good look!

The first thing I saw when the pipe was taken out of me was this beautiful nurse. I fell in love with her instantly and yet I never knew her name. I was too weak to ask, but she was around me all of the time. She really looked after me and was my very own personal Florence Nightingale.

By September I was well enough to be transferred from Manchester Royal Infirmary, where I had now spent 12 weeks, to Blackpool Victoria Hospital where I took up residency in the Macmillan Unit for three weeks before returning home for the first time in four months.

I recorded a message on my update telephone line promising all of my fans that I would be back on the road just as soon as I could. My voice wasn't brilliant at the time. It was weak and croaky, but I just wanted to let them know just how much I felt their prayers and good wishes had helped me.

Whilst I was in both hospitals I had kept thinking about when I might be back performing, but even at home I was still in the hands of the doctors.

By now I was bored. When all you have done for the past 35 years (at that time!) is to earn a wage singing for your living, constantly preparing for the next performance, it is hard to accept the fact that you need to just stay at home. But that's what I needed to do right then if I wanted to make a full recovery.

My first consultation following the operation was in November. I had been going in for weekly check-ups at Blackpool Victoria and was still having regular blood transfusions. As you might expect I was a bit apprehensive. In fact I'd had trouble sleeping the night before. If it had been bad news I wouldn't know how I would have felt. But it was good news. I was on the mend and my white blood cell count was now normal.

There was a charity show to be held in my honour in December, but the specialist advised me against going. I wasn't going to sing but I knew that, if I had gone I couldn't have resisted getting up. I didn't go, but I was there!

I had recorded a message on video.

It was a good job I hadn't either. In the first week of 2006 I was back in hospital again. Was there to be no end to this?

This time it was nothing to do with the bone marrow transplant. I was suffering from the effects of dehydration. It wasn't a relapse and the cancer hadn't come back. We were ready to roll. I was ready to get back on that stage at last. It was the best news I have ever had!

THE PALLADIUM

When you want to say 'I love you' say it with flowers
When you want to say 'I miss you' say it with flowers
For they have a language that is all their very own
And they can calm life's seas when stormy winds blow

Joe Longthorne *Say It With Flowers* released 1993

Nervous breakdown. Bankruptcy. Cancer. A bead up my nose. I'd come through it all. It was now 2006 and I was about to start making that journey once again in my singing career – the journey which is still on the up-turn.

Are you ready for the rollercoaster to start gathering pace once more? Well now is the time!

We were under way by April. It was Easter again, just a year on from all that had happened and I was back in the Grand Theatre in Blackpool. I was back doing what I was made to do.

Glasgow, Motherwell, Sheffield, Bradford, Whitley Bay, Darlington, Billingham, Telford, Worthing, Southend, Swansea and Purfleet were all on the tour schedule. It wasn't the biggest UK tour I'd ever done but it was a start. Dave Halford of Artistes Direct had been guarded not to give me too much too soon, and with James now having taken over managing me full-time we had a fantastic time. The tour finished back in my home city of Hull at the New Theatre and I was also back at the Paradise Rooms for a summer season, performing every Friday and Saturday.

It really was such a marvellous time for me. Everywhere I went the audiences, my fans, were on their feet giving me a standing ovation before I'd even started singing!

I've always received so many flowers at my concerts for so many years – but now I could have become Interflora. It's just another beautiful thing the fans have always brought me, and it confirmed to me what I had already thought - everyone coming to the concerts had been going through my pain and trauma with me.

But there was one extra special concert that really marked my comeback that year at The London Palladium.

Chris the Greek was the man who made it possible. I'd first met Chris way back in 1977 when I was appearing with Jim Davidson down in London at the Frog & Nightgown in the Old Kent Road. It's now a nightclub called

Virgo's. Chris told me then that I was going to hit the top. I remember saying, 'I'll see you again one day' to Chris. I didn't realise how long it would be. It was 28 years.

Chris and I had not been in touch since that time but he had contacted me whilst I was preparing to go in for the bone marrow transplant.

His track record in the music industry has included working for Harvey Goldsmith and putting on stadium gigs for world famous singers like Marvin Gaye, Stevie Wonder, Lionel Richie & The Commodores and Diana Ross.

How we got together to organise the Palladium concert was that Chris was putting together a charity night for a man called Joey Pyle (another gangster), known as 'Big Joey' in the London underworld in the 60s, who had Motor Neurone Disease. Joey had been best man at Ronnie Kray's wedding.

Apparently I was one of Joey Pyle's favourite performers. Why am I so popular with gangsters? Reggie Kray, Joey Pyle, the Richardsons, they have all been amongst my fans.

Joey had wanted me to perform at his charity night but I was dying at the time, so it was a little inconvenient! I sent one of my gold discs for the auction they were having.

James then rang Chris when I was making my recovery and, knowing how clever he is at arranging things, asked Chris whether he could sort the Palladium for us. He did a marvellous job. It was a sell-out.

I had appeared there many times during my TV career days, but usually as one of several stars on variety shows. This time it was my own night and I was even more determined to show not just my fans but the whole of the entertainment business that I was well and truly back. It was 10 September 2006 and once again it was another performance captured on DVD for posterity. It really was a remarkable and inspiring night.

The standing ovations I had received before I came on to the stage at every concert in the provincial venues were tremendous, but they were nothing compared to what happened at the Palladium. It felt as though for five minutes everyone just stood there applauding before I'd even opened my mouth! There was so much love in this historic theatre that night.

What was even more marvellous was that for the previous eight months the Palladium had been home to the multi-million pound production of *Sinatra*. What an honour. I was following the great man. It might not have been the great man himself but it felt good. Mr Sinatra and then me. It still brings a smile to my face thinking about it now.

Chris (the Greek) became part of the team after that concert. He came up to Blackpool, came on tour with me and for a long time he never went back to London. His lovely wife Marilyn had to come up and see him here!

Now I know what you're thinking by now. There's just bound to be some bad news along the way. Surely I couldn't go a full calendar year without something?

Unfortunately you're right – but it wasn't anything to do with my state of health, state of wealth, a nervous breakdown or fighting this time.

The touring was going well. All of my dates had been packed out – and then my dad died. It was early in December.

Dad, as I said at the start, was such an important part of my life. I know that might sound obvious, but it's really not the same for everyone. Some people in this life never get to see their father, let alone have someone as supportive as my dad was with me. Mam set me on the road with the advice she gave me, but it was dad who took me to all of those clubs throughout Yorkshire and the North East when I was younger. He looked after me, nurtured me and fought for me. He was everything a father could be.

Those were great days, the days when I was leading such a simple life really, performing wherever it was possible to sing. But it wasn't all about the singing. Dad was much more than that to me. When he died I didn't just think about the singing, I thought about those days when, even at the age of three, I would go out on the rag-and-bone cart. We would be singing songs together even then, as we travelled all around Hull.

Mam said some really nice things about dad too. She said that I had inherited my musical ability from both of them – him and her. She said that Fred could make a piano talk, which he could, and that when he was in the Royal Navy he used to entertain the rest of the crew in similar way to the way I do today.

Dad had been diagnosed with prostrate cancer four years earlier, but he never made a thing about it. He was always more concerned with my illness. Lizzie said at the time that it had broken his heart that he hadn't been able to come and see me in Manchester Royal Infirmary the year before but he was too ill himself. He died at the age of 84 in Hull Royal Infirmary.

It doesn't seem enough to leave it at that does it? So I won't.

My dad was a fantastic man. We had our moments along the way like dads and sons often do, but he was always there for me, always believed in me and, like I said earlier, he was the man I respected more than any other in the world – and he still is. There you are dad. I'm sure you heard that somewhere, I certainly hope so.

CHAPTER THIRTY SIX

LIFETIME ACHIEVEMENT AWARD

You to me are sweet as roses in the morning
You to me are soft as summer rain at dawn
In love we share that something rare ...
You'll see the mountains tumble ...

Joe Longthorne *Concrete & Clay* released 2008

If 2006 had seen a triumphant return to the stage then 2007 was about to see us move back to a massive tour schedule. I really was determined to show everyone that I was back to stay!

Everything was now in place, and properly, for the first time in my life. My voice was 100%. The absolutely stunning Joe Longthorne Orchestra now had such a terrific sound that we are a major force to be reckoned with against any other live performance band. I'd have backed the boys 'Stretch', Si, Paul, Alan, Andy and the rest against anyone!

But it wasn't just the on-stage side of things that was spot on, and has been now for the past four years, it was everything else.

James is the superb manager I always knew he would be. Since he took over managing me it is no surprise that my career has been on a continuous up-swing.

Even television appearances have started to come my way again, after a long time in the TV wilderness.

But it's not just all about me, Andy and James either.

What we have here and now is a real team effort. My family are all there too - my brother John; and my nephews Keith, John-Boy and Michael. They all have massively important roles to play. At this point I must also mention my niece Julie, who cut and styled my hair for many years. She's now involved in the film industry in London.

John-Boy has been with me since he was about 15. We're like glue and we stick together no matter what. One day, a long while ago, I smashed up what I thought was James' phone in frustration. Then I found out I'd smashed up the wrong one. It was John-Boy's! He just laughed because he found it so comical.

John-Boy's a bit like me. He will chat away with anyone and when he was in his teens he was with me on the Canberra as we were going to Australia. Even then he was able to have a proper conversation with an 80-

year-old judge on the ship! He's a great chess player as well. You need great concentration for that and he's got it.

There's the wonderful and lovely Fran, who has looked after and supported me all the way. And there's Dave Halford of Artistes Direct, whose management agency books all of the theatre dates, liaising closely with James.

Jean (Parkes) is still handling some bookings for me too, and we keep in close contact.

It took nearly 40 years, but I now have a team around me that not only understands me, they also care about me. We work together as a family. And in 2007 that meant we could shift up a gear, or three, heading on up for overdrive!

Following on from 2006's 20-date tour, we started a 46-date UK tour in Glenrothes in Scotland. Dave (Halford) said he'd only anticipated it being around 20 dates once again, but the tour just grew. We finished in July, but there was even more to come.

Paul Iacovou, who had made what had become by now a highly acclaimed documentary of me in 2004, through Vegas Films, was back again, this time following me on *The You & Me Tour* and putting together another DVD. Once again it was another quality production and it led to what was to be an extra-special time, with an extra-special award coming my way in June 2007. We'll get to that pretty soon.

Dave had promoted the tour and he spoke on camera that it was very rare to see a performer who is simply loved the way that I am by my fans.

I have always felt that love from all of the audiences at my shows, and I try to give that same love back with every song I sing. It is always nice to hear someone say it though, especially a tour promoter like Dave who has seen so many performers in his time.

The *You & Me* DVD is another of my personal favourites, mainly because it catches me in a very natural way. There are some wonderful moments captured on it too – and one of those involves 'Stretch'.

Just listen to his playing on *You'll Never Know* that Paul Iacovou and his team recorded when we were playing at a private function that year. As Frank Sinatra said about one of his songs on his own *A Man & His Music* album, 'The way it was being played even a myna bird could have had a hit with the song.'

Don Black gave me possibly the biggest compliment ever that year. He was even good enough to put it on to the DVD programme for posterity. This is what Don said, and it brings tears of gladness and humility to me every time I think of it:

'Instantly you realise his voice is from the Gods. It's a different kind of talent. It's so in-your-face. It's so obvious that he is special. When I first saw Joe, I got goosebumps. When I come across talent, to me that is the greatest aphrodisiac, just phenomenal and Joe is a remarkable talent. In this world of Pop Idol mediocrity he shines like a beacon. He is a great, great talent, but he should be in Vegas, he should be on Broadway. He should be lighting up the West End, but life isn't fair and he's had a lot of bad luck. When I have sat at a concert with Joe Longthorne singing those hours just fly by. He's very, very special and in today's world I can't compare him to anybody because all the great people have gone – the Sinatras and the Dean Martins and Sammy Davis'. They no longer exist and Joe is up there with those kinds of people.

'When I sit and watch Joe singing my songs it's obviously an extra special kind of thrill, particularly If I Never Sing Another Song. It has an extra meaning because of what he has been through with his health, so when he sings 'If I never sing another song, I'll get by, but I'm not sure how,' it really is quite heartbreaking. He's earned the right to sing that song. You have to have gone through a troubled life to sing that song.'

When you get sentiments like that from the great man himself, who has written so many fantastic lyrics, that is the kind of thing that makes me feel so humble. As a singer you are really only as good as the songs you sing and the people who perform with you. That's why Mr Sinatra always used to make a point of mentioning the songwriters in every song he ever sang, and always made sure his band was credited. I try to do the same.

In the past three years we have dramatically changed the show. There are new songs, new routines, new funny one-liners and sketches, and they culminated in the recording of my first studio album for nearly a decade when *You & Me* was released the following year in 2008 through Union Square Music.

I have felt so fresh and reinvigorated ever since the bone marrow transplant. It is as though all of those years of living under the fear of losing my life are now behind me.

My dad always taught me: 'Joe, don't take a backward step. Sometimes take a sideways step, but never a backward one.'

That's what we have been doing for the past three years, we have worked in such a way that we are always looking forward, and we're still doing that now.

Now, about that special moment!

June 2007 saw another wonderful experience for me. Whilst I've always looked forward this was one night when I was able to look back on my life a little, as the Variety Club of Great Britain honoured me once again this time with a Lifetime Achievement Award at the Palace Hotel in Manchester.

Lyn Staunton, the Development Director for the Variety Club told us of a problem they were having with putting on the event. They usually have around 350 people come to a 'do' like this, but within a very short space of time they had been inundated with requests and over 500 had been accepted, with a waiting list growing by the day! I understand the waiting list was up to 250! My heart was bursting with the knowledge that so many people wanted to come and see this lad from Hull pick up this special award. I also knew that the more people that wanted to come, the more would be made for the charity as well.

And it wasn't just my loyal fans from all over the world who wanted to come. There were many of my friends from the world of show business too. Ricky Tomlinson (from TV's *The Royle Family*) was there. I have even been mentioned twice in *Royle Family* scripts. Roy Walker, Lord Jeffrey Archer, Deputy Prime Minister John Prescott, Liz Dawn, Roy 'Chubby' Brown, Frank Carson, Don Black, Engelbert Humperdinck, Barbara Windsor, the late Mike Reid (*Eastenders*), Cannon and Ball, Johnnie (Casson) and the widow of Sammy Davis Jr, Altovise Davis, all gave their own personal tributes. The Lord Mayor of Hull at the time, Brenda Petch, was there to deliver some very kind words from my home city. They all meant so much to me.

Freddie Starr delivered a surreal tribute. In fact it was so surreal that 'Chubby' mentioned it in his very kind words to me! His actual words were, 'Is Freddie Starr a full f***ing shilling or what?' Now 'Chubby' sometimes gets a bad press because of his blue act, but he is one of the nicest, most considerate men in show business. He's from Middlesbrough originally and like I said earlier I was on the same bill as his pop group act when I was starting out in my career. We have been great pals ever since. After his first few gags, he turned really serious, probably the most serious many of his fans will ever have seen him. It's time to grab your hankies again. This is what he said:

'I'm not a religious man. I'm seeing is believing. I've probably prayed twice in my life. One was when Joe went in for his operation. We were sat in the car, me and my driver Keith. Joe had gone in for this bone marrow. You hear people saying only one in 10 survives you know, and I prayed for him, because I love him, everyone in this room loves him, that's why we're here. I went to his first show back and he sang If I Never Sing Another Song *and there wasn't a dry eye in the house, including me, we were all in tears. He is a fantastic entertainer, a giant in the entertainment world.'*

Professor Guy Lucas was there too. This was the man who had made sure I could get back on this Big Dipper of my life. He had taken time out from his vital work in saving other people's lives to be a part of this evening. Do you know there are some times when even humble isn't the right word. Surgeons, consultants, doctors, nurses – what I have learned is that they are the most important professions in life, not singing or writing, or performing or any of the other jobs we all have. These are the wonderful people in our lives, the people who help us carry on living and let us achieve whatever we want to achieve. Without them I would have been gone a long time ago.

It was that night that I also found out just how worried even the great man himself had been for my voice, although he hadn't shown it at the time. I suppose that's what they call a very good bedside manner.

Usually it is other people giving me a standing ovation but that night I didn't even care if it was only me who stood up and applauded this wonderful, wonderful man. I gave Professor Lucas my own personal standing ovation. James stood too. Then everyone in the room joined myself and James. We were both trying desperately to hold back the tears throughout his speech. We had been through so much together.

Ricky (Tomlinson) made sure that people knew that this really wasn't all about looking back though. He wanted to tell everyone, the way I am still trying to show everyone, that I am back, not just the way I was before but better and bigger than ever. He said this:

'Joe, I just want to say lad, it's easy when you're a star, you're right up there, money's rolling in, elation's rolling in and there's people surrounding you and giving you compliments. But when things go bad, both in health and in work-wise, it's only a superstar that can get up from the ashes and make it again, bigger and better, and become more loved, that's you!'

If I hadn't been filling up before I was overflowing now!

Barbara Windsor was next. She couldn't make it to the 'do' but she did send a really heartfelt message:

Dear Joe,
I am absolutely devastated I can't be at your tribute dinner. You know how much I love you. You know what a fan I am of yours. You are one of our greatest performers in this country - the consummate performer. When I did my album I said to my producer can you please, please get me Joe (Longthorne) to guest on it, and you did. You shot down and did it all in one take – and we had a ball.

All of the messages and speeches meant so much to me, especially the one from Altovise Davis who sent the following message. Now this was some compliment!

Dear Joe,

..... You are a true showman following in the steps of all who have been honoured with this accolade and I know speaking for the Sinatra and Martin families when I say you are singlehandedly keeping variety alive and well over there in the UK.

I only wish you had been around in Las Vegas in the 1960's at those legendary performances the boys gave at The Sands. Had they known about you, they all could have had a night off together and let you perform the entire show!

Enjoy the evening and I know Sammy would have been so proud of you.

God bless,
Altovise Davis

I was actually turned down by Frank Sinatra one time you know. Frank Warren was putting on the great man at the Excel Centre in London's Docklands and he had sounded me out about being his support act! But apparently, from what I heard, Mr Sinatra didn't want another singer on the bill. I came that close, but not close enough.

Engelbert went even further with his praise, but you're probably starting to think I'm going on a bit about all of this now, and I really don't want this to turn into that 'me-me-me' thing I was mentioning earlier. So let me finish this section off with what Lord Archer said. For me this was yet another example of how what I do on stage seems to reach all walks of life, from the normal, every-day folks like me and my family to great authors such as Jeffrey. He said this:

'Many years ago my wife and I were dining at the Café Royale in London when I heard this voice. I just simply got up, left the room, moved up one floor and listened to one of the greatest talents I have ever heard in my life. Many of your fellow professionals have stood on this stage tonight Joe, and they have talked of you with an affection and respect because they have worked with you.

'I represent the millions of people out there who are simply fans. We are the people who know how good you are. I tell you how you judge a fan – and I'll ask you in this room. How many of you have a Joe Longthorne recording in your car so that it's always with you? Hands up! (And Jeffrey

put his hand up immediately). I've got in my car Ella Fitzgerald, Frank Sinatra, Bobby Darin, Tony Bennett and Joe Longthorne. And the reason I have Joe Longthorne next to those four is because he's damned well as good as those four.

'When I listened to those who have come up on this stage it became clear that all of them have had their ups and downs to fight in this remarkable profession which you belong to Joe. But yours has been more extreme than any of us – debt, illness, you fight everything. And I think it's that persistence, that determination that is an inspiration to us all. 99 people out of 100 would simply have given up. Many of the reasons so many of your friends are here tonight, and the reason you have not only survived but come through your problems is because you don't give up.

'And in between, with all that happening, you've still continued your charity work. And that is why, and one of the many reasons why, the Variety Club honour you tonight. Joe, when all of us are gone and long forgotten, there will be a new generation that will still play your records, there can be no doubt about that.

'Have you noticed how the great stars, whatever profession they are in – Sinatra, Fitzgerald, Bassey, Olivier, Gielgud, Guinness. That is how you think of them. But the difference with you is that if you look at the sign up there Joe, the word JOE is bigger than the word Longthorne. And I'll tell you why. It's because all of us believe we know you, all of us believe you're a friend, and all of us want you to go on forever. Good luck!'

Right. Hankies away now, let's get on with what the Variety Club is all about and the good work that is done by people like Professor Lucas. I said the next bit on the night when I accepted the award. So let's have no more about me for a bit just at the moment. These are my words, but just don't think about me here, think about what I'm saying, please:

'In some way the Variety Club doesn't shout about what it does. It doesn't scream and bawl, it does it in a really fantastic way and it is first and foremost with charity in mind, looking after the children. What a terrific organisation it is. Then there's the great Professor Lucas, surely these are the people we have to admire, we have to look after, and make sure they get the right funds. Raising money is really what tonight is all about.'

I said I was 'goosed' for words, which brought a big laugh– and thanked everyone for the award. I told everyone this was one award that wouldn't get on eBay!

It was the most fantastic night. We raised a record figure of £40,000 through the auction that followed, with Lord Archer in charge. My big darts mate Phil 'The Power' Taylor, who I also speak with regularly, paid thousands for a very special diamond encrusted watch.

I just had to sing after all that didn't I? So I sang five songs at the end of the night, when I have to say I was a little the worse for wear.

Here's another little note, just so that you're getting the idea of where I am coming from with this book. It's another advertisement, but I'd like you to keep this in mind:

The Variety Club of Great Britain
Formed: 1949
Purpose: To make a real and lasting difference in children's lives
If you would like to make a difference or would like more information
please contact:
VARIETY CLUB OF GREAT BRITAIN
4th Floor
St James' Buildings
79 Oxford Street
Manchester M1 6FQ
Tel: 0161 236 0500
Email: varietyclubnw@btconnect.com
Web: www.varietyclub.org

CYPRUS & DON BLACK

Hold back the morning light
Don't end this magic night...

Joe Longthorne *You You You* recorded 1975

All of Blackpool's main entertainment venues have been wonderful for me – the record-breaking 1993 summer season at the Opera House in the Winter Gardens complex; the North Pier, where I have had some brilliant times as the 'Captain'; those emotionally-charged nights both just before and following the bone marrow procedure at the Paradise Rooms; and then there's the Grand Theatre.

The Grand Theatre, like the Palladium, is a Matchem's theatre. It may not have the size of stage, or the size of auditorium as the Opera House, but it has an amazing atmosphere and I have had some perfect nights there. I played there in 2007 through September with yet another full production show. It was a fantastic season and we had a great line-up. Maurice from the Grumbleweeds was compere; we had the lovely and brilliant Leanne Fury and comedian Carl Schofield who had even come up with a very funny 'rap' all about me!

Later that year we were back at sea.

We had been booked to play on the Royal Caribbean, but that's not where we were heading. And again we didn't start from the UK. That would have been too easy!

We had flown out to Norway – well it is quicker than walking you know! We were boarding the ship in Bergen, which was then sailing to Amsterdam and then back to Harwich. Simple, you'd think wouldn't you, but not if you're with the Joe Longthorne Touring Party.

Norway was good, but it's very expensive.

Eight quid a pint! I know that I'm not very good with money, but surely that was far too much! At that rate I'd be back in financial trouble before long. The food was great though. I ate fish. I love fish. I had crab and just about every form of seafood I could get, but I didn't eat the whale sandwiches. They do have them.

Now remember, this was me on a cruise again, in foreign parts again. It couldn't all go that easily could it? Well it was soon to get complicated.

We got off in Amsterdam – and that was our first mistake! Chris (the

Greek) and the lovely, adorable Marilyn, Chris' wife, decided to go off and do a bit of shopping. There was nothing wrong with that. Then they both ended up joining us in a café where *Don't Worry 'Bout A Thing* by Bob Marley was being played. That's because we were in the world-renowned Bob Marley Café.

To cut a long story rather short we all ended up a bit the worse-for-wear, if you understand where I'm coming from. If you don't understand then I think the phrase 'we were stoned' will do. We'd been on the 'happy cake' and on the way back to the boat we nearly knocked five bikes over and were close to being killed under four trams! I was then attacked by some dogs as we were going back to the ship, interfering bloody Beagles, and Marilyn nearly didn't get back on at all!

Once we'd got to Harwich we picked up the next set of passengers and sailed to Lithuania. It was hardly the Caribbean, but it was a tremendous time on board and the people we played to were fantastic.

2007 also saw the release of two more compilation double CDs - one titled *The Ultimate Entertainer*, which includes one CD of my live show material where I sing as me and another CD which features all of my 'special guests'. This is the only time in my career that one whole CD has been devoted to just that. The other double CD was released through Demon Music and is titled *Joe Longthorne – The Essential Collection*.

More CD releases, a Variety Club of Great Britain award, cruises, constant touring and summer seasons – who needs television! It would be nice though, so don't start getting any funny ideas that I don't want to be on – in fact I have been back on screen in the last few years and I'm hoping these pages might just help in leading to even more appearances. Remember that *An Audience With* ... idea, if any TV producers are reading this.

It's been a brilliant time for me in the recent past. I've been back in the studio recording new material, touring massively, hosting brilliant summer seasons with some great new performers, and there have been other notable highlights along the way.

Being invited to sing for Don Black's 70th Birthday Tribute at the London Palladium was right up there with the high achievements, a real honour; going back on TV for the really popular *Loose Women* and *Alan Titchmarsh* shows; and playing in Cyprus in my show *Joe Sings To The Gods* have brought me so much joy.

Writing this book has also been a major undertaking and I couldn't have done that without the man who is now another of my good friends Chris Berry, who has put together this book from all of what I have told him. He comes from Hull too, so he understands our home city, and he's a singer who works very hard at his craft too, so he understands some of what I have gone through as well. He is also a very talented writer and the way in which we have worked on this book together has been great therapy for me. Thanks Chris.

But we're not finished by a long way just yet – oh no! It's time for that rollercoaster to get under way again.

Two more releases were on their way– first there was yet another compilation double CD this time titled *The Joe Longthorne Collection 'All The Songs I Love'* on H&H Music.

Then there was that first all-new studio album in a decade *You & Me*. I cannot express to you just how much I enjoyed putting the album together and I need to thank both Andy Mudd and Colin Skinner here publicly for all of their help in arranging all of the tracks between them.

I love everything about the CD and have never felt happier in the studio. The title track *You & Me* is my favourite on the album and has been recorded by both Frank Sinatra and Peter Allen, who are both no longer with us. Everyone knows Mr Sinatra, but the passing of Australian-born Peter Allen, who I mentioned earlier during the 'FAVOURITES' section, and who wrote this song, was also a sad loss to the music world. He wrote some great songs, as well as being a fantastic singer.

Another of my favourites on *You & Me* is *If*. It was written by that brilliant singer/songwriter Bill Gates! Those of you who come to my concerts will understand why I've put it that way. I know it was really written by David Gates – the one who finished second in Pop Idol!

The 2008 tour was even bigger again than the previous year. This time we started out around Easter, as we have done each year since the bone marrow transplant, and continued right through until November. We played every weekend in Blackpool, Friday and Saturday from the beginning of August to the beginning of November.

I was particularly happy to be playing Blackpool in 2008 because I had heard that the North Pier's future was in serious doubt. This fantastic and historic period-piece pier is one of the oldest pier theatres in the country and it has seen some of the world's finest comedians and singers tread its boards.

Of course I also have a very strong emotional feeling for the place as it was here that James and I first got together. It was also here that I spent those evenings as 'Captain' of my own ship. This wonderful theatre sits at the end of an uninterrupted 500-yard long pier and it was here that I first came into contact with the beautiful Pat Mancini MBE. How could I not want to help this place after all it had done for me, after all it had given me?

It was also here that Johnnie (Casson) and I struck up such a terrific friendship. That's also why it was really good to appear with Johnnie again in 2008, along with a full production show involving the Joe Longthorne Orchestra, dancers and a variety of lovely female solo singers, including the lovely Leanne Fury, the charismatic Carol Kaye and the terrific Tracey Jordan.

It was nice to be able to play a small part in ensuring its future and I'm happy to say the North Pier is now back thriving again.

I hadn't known it at the time, but Don Black's very kind words the year previously were also to translate into an invitation from him for me to play at his special 70th birthday tribute show at the Palladium in August 2008.

Now when Don Black invites you to play you just do not turn that kind of thing down. Don has won an Oscar, several other Academy Award nominations, and been responsible for some of the most amazing lyrics ever written – *Born Free*; *Ben* (for Michael Jackson); *As If We Never Said Goodbye* (from *Sunset Boulevard*); *Diamonds are Forever*; and *If I Never Sing Another Song* – the list goes on and on.

It was an absolute honour to sing for him and of course I just had to sing *If I Never Sing Another Song*. We brought the house down with it and that's when Michael Parkinson, who was MC, said 'we cannot possibly follow that' and the show went into a break. It was a great feeling especially as on the same bill were people like Gary Barlow, Lee Mead, Lulu, Mica Paris, Elkie Brooks, Marti Webb and Craig David. The whole evening was recorded for BBC Radio 2's *Friday Night is Music Night*.

Don says that the first time he remembers seeing me was when I was in a cabaret show. With him at the time was Charles Strauss, who wrote the musical *Annie*. They were both, in Don's words 'blown away' by my vocal range. Apparently Charles still goes on about my 'machinery' today.

The Don Black Tribute was one of the two massive 'live' highlights for me in 2008.

The other was thousands of miles away on an island in the sun.

This time though, there was no Rupert the Drunkard Bear, no Pancho 'Overtime' Villa, no fog machine problems and no Demis Roussos costume – although we were nearer to his homeland than Jersey.

There have been those who have been so very kind over the years, telling me that I have a voice that must have been given to me by the Gods, and in September of 2008 I was to sing to them!

Now don't start thinking I'm getting ideas above my station at this point! It's just that I had been booked to play a quite extraordinary concert in Cyprus. And not just in Cyprus, but an open air, evening performance at the world-famous Kourion Amphitheatre that dates back to 500BC.

I have never played a place like it before in my life. I have played the Royal Albert Hall and the Sydney Opera House, as well as several other amazing venues but this was simply magical. It wasn't just the setting that did it for me though, with the amphitheatre looking out to the Mediterranean, it was the fans once again.

We had completely sold out the show weeks beforehand, families and parties of friends had planned their holidays around coming to see me and getting some sun of course. I just loved the evening and would play there again tomorrow. It was all organised by our 'Man in the Med', Paul Iacovou.

There were no support acts, just me and the Joe Longthorne Orchestra, and when I went into the audience part-way through what ended up being a two hour show there was just so much warmth there – and yes, I know we were in Cyprus which is a warm place anyway, but I think you know what I mean.

I knew then that the past three years since the bone marrow transplant had shown not just me, but many more, that I was now not just on a roll. I was fit and hungry for more and more, and more.

CHAPTER THIRTY EIGHT

BENIDORM PALACE

Look into these eyes my love and see
All the lovely things you are to me

Joe Longthorne *The Shadow of Your Smile* released 2008

In November 2008 we headed for the Costa Brava, for a very special one-off concert at the beautiful Benidorm Palace. This proved to be another spectacular night as we took out the whole band and put on yet another stunning show.

We had the three amigos back together for this trip – Pat was there with me and James.

And there was, of course, a problem or two along the way. Pat says that no matter where she has been with me there has always been some kind of laughable or 'iffy' moment. This one had all the hallmarks of those days when I used to 'pull a fast one' to get out of some scrape or other.

After a concert I do like to wind down.

Mr Sinatra called it 'boozing time' and I'm no different. I like a beer, or two, or three. I also like chatting with people and generally just having a good time. I guess it's a bit like I've finished my job for the day, now I can relax and enjoy. It's just that – for performers – that happens at a different time to others. What that means is that sometimes we might only get to bed by four or five in the morning, but I then won't get up until the afternoon.

It's a routine I find hard to shake off, so I stick with it quite a bit when I'm not performing as well. Unfortunately it was not a routine that went down too well with the hotel.

The day we were meant to be coming home I couldn't get out of bed as I was that tired. I knew we could always get another flight, so that wasn't the issue, but the manager of the hotel wanted my room. Patricia, who knows one or two things about hotels, knew they had 200 rooms so she felt they were being a little bit stroppy over it.

The other two amigos, as well as Chris, start telling the manager that I'm not well and so the hotel calls our bluff by saying, 'if he's not well you will have to get a doctor'. I really wasn't feeling very well. I had a hangover.

They get a doctor. He arrives a quarter of an hour later.

James comes up to the room with the doctor and wakes me up. I may have already opened my eyes on several occasions slightly before this, but who's to know! James can talk us out of any situation.

I tell the Spanish doctor that I just can't get up. James explains that I've been working the night before and that I'm totally exhausted. He tells him I need at least another five hours' kip.

The doctor then goes down to the manager and says, 'This man cannot be moved for five hours'.

We missed the plane, but at least I was fresh when we did leave. I don't know what convinced the doctor the most – my act, James' act or the 100 Euros we bunged him along with a copy of my DVD! It certainly made Pat laugh anyway.

When I'm at home I do tend to drink and smoke more. I also get more time to discuss things, to talk. James is around quite a bit of the time and looks after me, making meals for me and Fran is there. We chat about anything. It's also the time when I have chance to catch up with my really good friends, either by phone or with them coming to the house.

Bobby (Ball) lives not too far away and he pops by from time to time. Jean and Mal come for a cuppa. All of the family get over if they're not already here! And it's also a time when I get back over to Hull to visit them.

And of course I've got the piano in the front room so there is always time for playing that and working on new songs.

I'm happy being at home looking after Kennedy, my golden retriever, and just relaxing. When I'm at home it isn't long before I need the adrenalin rush of performing. If I've been at home for too long I feel as though I want to be off, and up in front of an audience once again. I have done drugs, yes, but performing has always been my biggest drug of the lot.

FORTY YEARS!

There've been so many things that have held us down
But now it finally looks like things are comin' around..
... Ain't no stoppin' us now, we're on the move ...

Joe Longthorne *Ain't No Stoppin' Us Now* released 1980-81

2009 was the year that saw me back on mainstream TV for the first time in many years; it was also the year when I was finally 'spotted' by the US, through Mr Sinatra's manager, Eliott Weisman; and it was also the year that saw me sing for three quite different but huge legends at their own Variety Club of Great Britain award evenings.

It was also the year I celebrated 40 years in show business with yet another massive tour of the UK, with dates also in Spain and the Emerald Isle and again a tremendous summer season once again at the wonderful Matcham-design Grand Theatre in Blackpool. Frank Matcham, who died in 1920 was responsible for the way many theatres were designed including the London Palladium, Victoria Palace, Hackney Empire and many more provincial theatres. The year also saw me performing on David Gest's special *Soul Spectacular* at the Opera House.

We started the year with a little holiday. We knew it was going to be a busy first six months otherwise and we'd had yet another long year prior to it so James and I needed a break. We'd originally thought of going to Morocco, then we changed our minds at the last minute and decided on Amsterdam. Not much of a difference there then! It was freezing. I was going to put a word in front of 'freezing' but I don't think you need me to tell you any more!

Our next destination was Thailand.

The world really is a small place these days, and as if to prove it Jimmy White was there too. Jimmy is a mate of Chris the Greek and when he found out we were in town, in Bangkok, he drove over. He'd just won a tournament over there. We had a great time together and it was a lot warmer than Holland.

The three Variety Club award functions I sang for included an award evening for Tommy & Bobby (Cannon and Ball) at the Reebok Stadium in Bolton; Engelbert Humperdinck's Lifetime Achievement award at the Palace Hotel, Manchester in March; and this was followed by the Bee Gees' Silver Heart award in April at the same venue.

Tommy and Bobby's night was full of fun and laughter as you might expect with anyone who is anyone from the world of comedy present.

Engelbert is one of the most consummate performers I know. The feeling between us is definitely one of mutual admiration. I brought the Joe Longthorne Orchestra with me and they played for him too. We also sang together.

Engelbert has always been so encouraging to me and it was a wonderful moment in my career when I was introduced to Mr Weisman, who had purely come over to see Engelbert collect his award.

I was back in Manchester just weeks later to sing for the Bee Gees, as part of their award too. Once again I took the band and they not only backed me but also played for Ronan Keating, Richard Fleeshman, the legendary PP Arnold and the amazing Bee Gees themselves! Ti Amore, a group of four sensational tenors from Hull was also involved. I sang the two songs I mentioned earlier *I Started A Joke* and *Morning Of My Life* which have since become a popular part of my show.

The 40th Anniversary Tour saw me perform nearly 100 dates from March until December taking in theatres, hotels and even a castle.

The castle itself deserves a special mention. It is Craig Y Nos Castle in the Swansea Valley in Wales. It's a magical place with a wonderful little theatre. We have performed there a number of times in recent years.

There was another double CD compilation out in 2009, but this time with a big difference! It included a double DVD package and the whole thing was called *Joe's 40th Anniversary Collection*. It included *Wonderful Tonight*, the first time I had ever recorded the song, and it features many songs from throughout my career including the duets with both Barbara Windsor and Liz Dawn.

CHAPTER FORTY

BEST SELLER & A SILVER HEART

Dear Sir or Madam, will you read my book,
it took me years to write will you take a look…

The Beatles *Paperback Writer* Joe Longthorne becomes an author 2010

After years of thinking about it I finally found the man who could write my life story with me. I could never have written it on my own and hadn't felt comfortable with others who had approached me. The difference with Chris is that he is also a singer; he comes from Hull too, so understands where I have come from; we share a faith; and he's a great writer. Together we spent hundreds of hours trying to get everything into the book that I'd been asked to write so many times.

We worked on it throughout 2009 and again this year (2012) to bring it bang up to date with this paperback edition. As you will see that old rollercoaster just carries on going up and down, but I have to say it has been more up than down in recent years.

James gave our 2010 dates the title of 'The Official Book Tour' and once again we set off on a massive run of performances throughout the UK with Chris also singing on tour.

Just 10 days before the official book launch I was to be honoured once again by the Variety Club of Great Britain at The Hilton in Blackpool when I received their Silver Heart award. It was another tremendous evening with Cannon & Ball on top form as they took over the stage. Bernie Nolan looked fantastic and said some very kind words; Johnnie Casson had us all in stitches; and Frank Carson, who has since become another sad loss, was also on top form. Jimmy White arrived on cue, but said he needed a rest! Snooker lovers eat your hearts out. Special thanks must go to Marj Boyer, chairman of the Variety Club for the North West and all of her team. We even managed to get hold of the very first copy of the hardback version of the book in a special case for the night. It raised £3,000 for charity.

Fittingly the very first event where the books were on display was back in my home city. I was one of two special guests at the Hull and East Riding Literary Luncheon with the other being Pauline Prescott, wife of John, who had just released her book. She's a really wonderful charming woman and it was a delightful event.

Book launch week was set for Monday 29 March and in the coming fortnight I saw so many fans at Waterstones and WHSmith bookstores in

Hull, Manchester, Blackpool, York, Sunderland, Glasgow, Stockport and anywhere else we could fit in with the tour. It was disappointing not to be able to include everywhere in the UK as I know many fans were asking whether I would be able to conduct signings but I'm afraid I can't split myself into two or three.

We were booked on to several TV and radio shows including a breakfast TV interview with the lovely Lorraine Kelly and a great live show with Sir Terry Wogan on BBC Radio 2. It was just like old times and I think Terry was a little taken aback by the noise made by the fans. You know who you are and thank you from the top and bottom of my heart. Terry even said that he felt it was as though it wasn't his show that day and that the Joe Longthorne Friendship Club had taken over the studio.

I also made a number of other appearances on TV stations including *Calendar* on ITV, at the TV studio in Leeds where my broadcasting career kicked off with *Junior Showtime*. Presenters Duncan Wood, Gaynor Barnes and Christine Talbot are a great team and I hear that Christine has recently been conducting her own personal battle after finding out she has breast cancer. My thoughts are with her and her family.

The book launch went so well that after just two weeks of its release we found out it was a best seller! It topped two of the Amazon charts for biographies under Entertainment and Cabaret. It also remained top of the Cabaret chart for 10 weeks. Whilst we felt that my life story may have all the hallmarks of being a best seller it was nice to see it for real. We're hoping to make it back to the top with this book too!

Having promoted the book and received the Variety Club award it was time for the tour to get under way in April and we took in nearly every venue you could think of from Hastings to Hayes; Truro to Torquay; Dartford to Dundee; and South Shields to Southsea. It was exhausting and there were times, I will freely admit, that I just wanted to go home. Let's just say I had my moments when it would have been easier to walk away from it all than be cooped up in a car for hours on end.

There are also many times when I wonder about our booking agent's sense of geography. Our tour schedule can see us in the North East one night but in Kent the next. It's crazy. We were seriously considering using Sherpas for much of the tour! Playing the New Theatre in Wimbledon during Wimbledon fortnight is also either a masterpiece of planning or a nightmare coincidence dependent on your view. I know which mine is.

Summer Season was at The Grand Theatre in Blackpool, a beautiful auditorium where I always feel at home. We had a great run and that led to my first appearance at the Indigo Room at the O2 Arena in London.

In October 2010 I was back working on behalf of the Variety Club once again as Neil Sedaka was honoured with his Silver Heart Award at The Palace Hotel in Manchester. But still we weren't finished. There were concerts right up until Christmas and yet another New Year's Eve Special in Blackpool. And the book sales kept on coming.

After such another busy year I was all set for a break. Not a lucky one, just a holiday break this time and some quieter moments for myself and with James. It really was a brilliant year though and one I will never forget including my own book and a silver heart; a long tour, plus an O2 appearance. It seemed as though everything was looking good. But you know me by now and how my life goes, surely there had to be something that wouldn't quite work out and would go against me. You're not wrong. Now where's that drink gone? You might well need it again here. Oh and grab another box of Kleenex whilst you're at it.

CHAPTER FORTY ONE

CRASH & LOSING PAT

So here comes the night, the darkness descending
The story's not right and there's no happy ending

Joe Longthorne *I Wish You Love* released 1993

You know just when you think you're on a roll again there's always something to bring you back down to earth. For some people that happens with little things, but it's never been that way with me. In my case they've always got to be great big problems, something mega-dramatic.

I suppose with the amount of travelling I've done over the years there has always been a greater chance that I could have been involved in traffic accidents along the way, but mercifully I'd got away with very few until 2011.

Way back in 1995 we'd had a close shave in a helicopter. The *Daily Mirror* reported it at the time: 'Comic Joe in Copter Crash – Entertainer Joe Longthorne cheated death last night when his helicopter crash-landed in a field.'

Hilarious!

That wasn't anything like what happened to me, James and John Boy in June 2011. The helicopter in 1995 was flying myself and Big Mick Johnson from Turpin's to a concert in Birmingham when all sorts of lights had started flashing and I told the pilot he would have to land in a farmer's field. We landed amongst a herd of bemused cattle and a few red-faced country gents, or 'joskins' as we call them in cant, armed with what looked like trumpets. It was like a scene from The Beano! These 'trumpets' were what others would call blunderbusses.

It was as though we had to prove to the local gentry that we weren't aliens, but we were only in a ruddy helicopter. It wasn't some kind of spaceship!

As we had been coming down to land in the field I wasn't sure we would be able to make it, so it certainly shook me up but we weren't hurt and we made for the nearest public house, nerves still jangling.

That was the worst incident I'd had since my driving indiscretion I mentioned much earlier. But what happened in 2011 was very different. This wasn't any kind of scene that you could laugh about later. It was the near-death real thing.

I was in the back of the Mercedes, with John Boy driving and James sat alongside him in the passenger's seat. It had been a long drive in awful conditions; a five-hour haul from Portsmouth up to Alvaston Hall in Cheshire. Another planning masterpiece from our booking agents! Keith was following in the car behind. It was a customary night-time drive, just another in our regular touring season before settling in Blackpool for the Summer.

I always sit in the back of the car - unless I'm driving because otherwise that would look a bit daft wouldn't it! I had my earphones on listening to some music and was having a can of lager. I couldn't have told you where we were. I never can. I just try to relax. We could have been heading for Fife or Forfar for all I know but I found out later we were only fifteen minutes from the venue when our world very nearly came to an end.

So far as I was concerned we were doing our normal thing, travelling from where I had just performed to a hotel either close to the next venue or at the venue itself.

No-one can be exactly sure about what happened next but what I can tell you is that this time I really did think my time had come, as well as James' and John Boy's. What we now know is that the car turned over three times as we continued travelling up the road.

I now understand what some people say when they tell you that your life turns into slow motion at the time. That was certainly true for me. Amazingly though, even in those split seconds you do get time to think and they play back in your mind.

I was bracing myself for the impact as our car became a ten-pin bowling ball and I was holding on for dear life. Fortunately I was wearing my seat belt and the air bags worked too, otherwise that would have been the end of all of us.

The first thing I was fully aware of when the car came to a standstill was that we were upside down. It's quite a sobering experience when you realise you've come that close to losing your life and I was now thinking very clearly. The car wheels were spinning and the car hadn't half taken a hammering. It was unbelievable. There was creaking of metal, the smell of fuel and for the briefest of seconds everything went quiet as though we had frozen in time. Then I remember hearing screaming from James and not without very good reason as it turned out, but I couldn't hear anything from John Boy. At least by hearing James I knew he was alive, but what about John? Fortunately it wasn't long before he came round too.

Sat there, in what was now not just a mess but a possible tomb, I remember thinking to myself there's steam all around us and this thing could blow. Get out! You're not going to die here. Get out now! But I couldn't because of the air bag. It had pinned me in place as it had been designed.

Thank God for German engineering! I could still hear James screaming and wanted to help him as he was hurt badly.

I'm sure Keith had expected to find three dead bodies when he pulled over with his son Michael, but we were all still very much alive even though James, particularly, was in excruciating pain.

Ambulances and fire engines arrived at the scene very soon and the paramedics took over. As ever they were excellent and we were soon despatched to the local infirmary. We all ended up in Leighton Hospital, Crewe where we were looked after very well.

I managed to come out of the evening's drama with just whiplash, a broken rib and a broken nose; some other facial abrasions and my neck in a brace. It was a lucky escape. James wasn't quite so lucky. He suffered a shattered ankle and even now, just over a year later it's still not right and may never be. His golf, the sport he loves, has suffered and I feel so bad about that. I know the accident wasn't anything more than just that, but for James to lose out on playing the sport he not just enjoys but was also very good at makes me feel guilty. He was kept in hospital for a fortnight and he's still going for physio over a year later. John Boy was also injured but not too badly.

Once I'd rested up for a while I was soon back on stage at The Grand in Blackpool for another Summer season; but very real tragedy was about to strike again and this time there was loss of life.

My dear friend Patricia Mancini MBE passed away on 21 July 2011 aged 72. I cannot begin to tell you how much more this hurt me inside than the physical pain I'd had from our car crash the month previously.

This lady had been our rock. James and I both loved her dearly and we still do, but we had known her time was near. A year earlier she had been diagnosed as having a malignant brain tumour and it had been just a matter of time. In November 2010 I had asked the Variety Club if they would consider honouring the work she had done in looking after entertainers through her hotel. She had been responsible for helping many others not just me. It was my way of trying to give Pat something back for all she had done for me and James. She had a heart of gold and worked hard for lots of charities. If anyone ever wanted anything Pat would be first in the queue to help.

The Variety Club thankfully agreed and were delighted to honour her with a special Show Business award, something that is normally only given to those who perform. I know she was suitably thrilled and enjoyed a wonderful night.

But I also saw tragedy in her eyes in her final months. She certainly didn't want to go. She loved life and she put up a real fight. I know not a lot of people want to die, but for Pat it was really annoying. She had enjoyed everything she had achieved and she'd come up from nothing over in Manchester to be 'Queen of Blackpool'. She wasn't going to let go in a hurry. She knew she was going, but she was mad about it.

Her funeral took place at Our Lady of the Assumption Church and we all attended – myself, James, Johnnie Casson, Bobby Ball, Roy Walker, Chubby Brown and countless others whose lives had all been touched by this marvellous woman who will forever remain one of the loves of my life. I shall always be in her debt for what she did for me and James.

If it hadn't been for Pat I certainly wouldn't have been able to rebuild my life the way I have since I met James. And I certainly wouldn't have been back on the ocean wave, cruising and singing once again as I was in 2011. And I wouldn't have been appearing back in London's West End for the first time in a while in September of that year. Patricia you will always remain in our hearts. We love you very much.

Appearing at Leicester Square Theatre was the first of a number of high spots that have followed since the crash and Pat's passing. I'll play anywhere, but playing the West End is always special and my good friend Jeffrey Archer even managed to get along. This is how he very kindly reviewed my show on his personal blog. I don't even know what one of those is, but I'm assured it's all above board!

'I dashed back into London last night to attend Joe Longthorne's concert at the Leicester Square Theatre, with my old friend Patti Boulaye. Joe was on top form, and the audience clearly loved every moment, giving him a standing ovation three times during the performance. Joe has one of the most loyal fan bases of any artist I've ever known, and if it were not for so many sadnesses during his life, I suspect he would still be filling the Palladium night after night.'

I think a thank you is called for there. Thank you so much Jeffrey.

2012 - 2013

In the daytime, I will meet you as before
You will find me, waiting by the ocean floor

Joe Longthorne *The Morning of My Life* released 2010

We're nearly up to date now. At the time of writing this book it is nearly the end of Summer 2012 and I have to tell you life is looking good. There are one or two things that could be better but I'm thankful for what I have and this year has already been particularly kind to me.

At the end of 2011 James and I were both exhausted. We had managed another whole year of touring, summer season, cruise ships and the West End. It was a very pleasing version of exhausted. We had played everywhere and the audiences had been marvellous.

James had arranged a break for us and on 3 January 2012 we flew out to the United States. We went to Fort Lauderdale, which is known as the 'Venice of America'. We've a great friend Len Rawcliffe who lives there as well as owning property back in Cleveleys, Blackpool and we spent a lot of time with him.

The idea was to get away from it all for 3 months. I liked the idea. We enjoyed ourselves immensely but after about 3 minutes I wanted to be up and singing again, that's one withdrawal I can't do with. There's only so much champagne and lobster – and mushy peas – that you can eat you know!

We were invited to a charity show at a theatre in the town and you can pretty much guess the rest. I'd listened to a few of the others but was itching to be up there myself. The next thing I know there is a microphone being passed to me and I'm there on stage. I decided to give them my impression of Barry Manilow singing 'Can't Smile Without You'. It wasn't the way I perform it back in the UK, it was the full-on impression without making too much of a joke about it all. At the end of the song the place went up in the air. What a feeling!

That performance led to a meeting with Billie Wells of Wells Entertainment based at Lighthouse Point in Florida. Billie is a wonderful woman who is an agent and promoter for Jack Jones, Gloria Gaynor, KC & The Sunshine Band and Kool & The Gang to name but a few. I'm now on her roster of artistes and Billie is booking me dates for 2013 and already 2014 throughout the States. I've still not cracked the big venues on The

Strip in Vegas, but this appears to be my best chance yet since Chicago and Philadelphia way back in the day, as they say in the States. And I'm looking forward to touring wherever I'm booked. Vegas is still on my agenda. I haven't lost my ambition, but I'm always prepared to work to get there.

We also invited Andy (Mudd) and Leye D. Johns, who had supported me fabulously on tour during 2011, to join us in Fort Lauderdale and it was great to have them come over.

When we returned to the UK three months later I was refreshed and ready to swing right back into action. Andy and I had been working on putting together a new album of all my own songs and we released it just before the new tour started in April. It's album title 'Lady Blue' was taken from one of the songs I wrote a number of years ago and we've been playing them throughout this year's concerts.

I'm getting such a thrill out of singing these once again. It's very personal for me. These are all my own work, along with Ernie Dunstall, Lewis Osborne and Barry Mason. I've been singing 'Lady Blue' and 'Joanna' regularly in concert and by the end of the year I hope to have introduced some of the others. They've all been locked away for a while, but now I've let them fly again and it's a really pleasing feeling, old friends that have come back to me.

And the 2012 tour couldn't have started in a better setting – Grimsby! Now there's nothing wrong with Grimsby at all, but when your second night of the tour is a return to a sell-out Leicester Square Theatre, just six months after you've appeared there, then that is something else. It set the tone for what was an amazing first half of the year.

New album of all my own songs; a new US tour in prospect for 2013; an Australia tour for November this year; another great West End appearance; what else could possibly happen?

You're probably thinking it's time for that rollercoaster to head downwards again, but not a bit of it.

As we were travelling back from a concert in April I received a call from James. He doesn't come along to the concerts too much these days, preferring to stay at home because he believes he can get more done that way and to save his ankle from any more duress. He told me we had received a letter addressed to me from Buckingham Palace. My first thought was what have I done now?

I couldn't believe it when he told me that I was to receive the MBE.

What a wonderful thing. It is in honour of my charity work, raising funds for the various charities we have supported and continue to support. I've been in show business for a long time and I am so honoured and humbled by this award. I see it as a kind of ambassadorship. I've always enjoyed not just raising funds but also making people aware of the needs of others. I've done it all my life, giving to others who are in need where I can. I should also mention at this point all of those who have come along to my concerts over the years as they have also contributed to my work in raising funds and awareness. Well done everybody. The Friendship Club has done a fantastic job over many years and continues to do so.

When the announcement of the Queen's Birthday Honours was finally made I was due to perform that night at the Wyvern Theatre, Swindon. As soon as I put my foot on the stage the roof went off! There was a standing ovation without having to do anything.

I try to be a guy who just goes about his business, but it would be wrong to say that receiving the news of the MBE hasn't given me a real sense of pride and joyfulness. The most important thing though is that this award is a tool that can be used to raise even more funds for charity and give greater awareness to the plight of others.

I'm looking forward to visiting Buckingham Palace later this year to pick up the MBE.

One of the most recent charity fundraising events we have been proud to be involved with has been the Joe Longthorne Celebrity Invitational Golf Day. This all came about through my good friend and tremendous comedian George King, who has been with me on tour this year. George worked so hard on pulling this event together and we will hopefully have raised enough monies to help various local charities including Bryan House, which is a care centre for special children.

November 2012 will also see me back in Australia for the first time in over a decade. Of course you may only be reading this after I've been, but I've had a number of invitations to tour in recent times where the timing hasn't been right. This time we're going for four weeks and we have quite an itinerary stretching right across the country. I'm also hoping to see a little more of the cities than I've seen in the past. With me on tour is the gorgeous, Grammy award-winning Melissa Manchester. She's had some big hits over there and we're due to be singing at least one song together. The plan is then for us to work together in the US too.

The other part of the plan is another little break again at the start of 2013. It's meant to be another relaxing time in Fort Lauderdale but you know, it could yet turn from a little relaxing break into my biggest break yet!

CHAPTER FORTY THREE

JAMES

It may have appeared to go unnoticed
But I have got it all here in my heart
I want you to know I know the truth
Of course I know it
I would be nothing without you

Joe Longthorne *The Wind Beneath My Wings* released 1989

I've said enough times that this is not a 'me-me-me' book, but of course it is my life story so it is obviously going to appear a bit that way. But fittingly I'd like to draw this book to a conclusion with the man who I have always been proud to have as my partner.

James is a wonderful man with a big heart. We're actually quite opposite but respect each other immensely. He likes his golf and is very good at organising everything. He's not a show businessperson, even though he does love the finer things in entertainment like musicals and opera.

Living with someone like me or any singer or performer can be difficult but our relationship has grown through the years. He's a great man and together we have shared an amazing rollercoaster ride since we first met in the 90s.

I have a photograph of James and me when we first met and I look as pleased as Punch. It says to me 'here we go'. Well we've come a long way since then and James has been with me every inch of it. We've lost old friends during that time, no more so than Pat Mancini last year, and we've had our share of life's ups and downs but I still love him dearly. And he loves me. He's a great calming influence on me too and I always feel more settled when he's around.

There are many old sayings and the one I would use for James and myself would be that I knew we were right for each other when we first met. We are well suited and regardless of whatever happens in this amazingly dramatic life of mine I don't want to imagine life without him.

So what happens next for James and myself? Could it be Vegas? Who knows! What I can tell you is that my life has been nothing short of dramatic so far and somehow I don't think that will ever stop being the case. Come with me in the coming years. The London Olympics and Paralympics have shown us just what can be achieved if you set your mind on it. My mind is fixed. I want to entertain you. See you soon … or if we're going American,

'See y'all real soon'!

Take care, may Jesus be with you, and may you keep in good health and happiness.

All my love,

JOE'S CHARITIES

JOE LONGTHORNE works tirelessly to raise funds on behalf of a number of charities. If you feel inspired by this book to either donate monies or go on to the Anthony Nolan Register here are some useful contacts:

THE ANTHONY NOLAN TRUST

To become a donor you need to be 18-40 years old and in good health. The Anthony Nolan Trust specifically needs to recruit more young males donors and those from ethnically diverse backgrounds.

The Anthony Nolan Trust is a registered charity. It is dependent on the public and companies to fund its lifesaving work as it receives no government funding.

To find out more about how to join the bone marrow register and what is involved, or simply make a donation, please call:

020 7284 1234
www.anthonynolan.org.uk
Email: newdonor@anthonynolan.org.uk

TERRENCE HIGGINS TRUST

The Terrence Higgins Trust is the leading HIV and AIDS charity in the UK and the largest in Europe.

To make a donation, please contact:

Terrence Higgins Trust, 314-320 Gray's Inn Road,
London WC1X 8DP

DISCOGRAPHY

THE ORIGINAL RECORDINGS

JOE : HIS FIRST RECORDINGS
(CD ALBUM)

Never previously released until now. These were all recorded in sessions at Fairview Studios in Hull during 1974-1975.

Track Listing:
1. My Life Is Just Like A Symphony
2. Hurt
3. Crying In The Rain
4. You You You
5. I Can't Get Enough
6. Until It's Time For You To Go
7. Get Down
8. The Way We Were

FEELINGS   (45 rpm SINGLE)

Released 1977. Recorded at Arny's Shack recording studio in Blandford, Bournemouth.

Track Listing:

1. Feelings
2. This Ol' Heart Of Mine
3. The Way We Were

LIDO DE FRANCE   (45 rpm EP)

Released 1977. Recorded at Arny's Shack recording studio in Blandford, Bournemouth.

Track Listing:
1. Lido de France
2. Thank You For The Music
3. Joe's Song
4. Misty
5. It's Not Unusual
6. Till
7. Forever & Ever
8. The Wonder Of You
9. My Way

ONLY ONCE (FIRST LP RELEASE)

Released on the ROXON label in 1980-81. Recorded at Arny's Shack recording studio in Blandford, Bournemouth.

Track Listing:
1. She Believes In Me
2. You To Me Are Everything
3. I Know I'll Never Love This Way Again
4. To Live Without You
5. Fame
6. Only Once
7. What Do You Wanna Make Those Eyes At Me For?
8. Ain't No Stoppin' Us Now
9. Imagine/Woman
10. Mandy/Could It Be Magic?/I Write The Songs
11. Love On The Rocks
12. 2001/CC Rider/American Trilogy
13. I Never Dreamed You'd Leave In Summer

THE SINGER (SECOND LP RELEASE)

Released on the GREAT BRITAIN RECORDS label in 1986. Recorded at The Shambles recording studio in Marlow.

Track Listing:
1. When Your Old Wedding Ring Was New
2. Don't Laugh At Me

3. Hurt
4. Danny Boy
5. Just Loving You
6. You're My World
7. My Mother's Eyes
8. My Prayer
9. Answer Me
10. It's Only Make Believe
11. To All The Girls I've Loved Before
12. I'd Be A Legend In My Time
13. Love Is All
14. The End Of The World

THE JOE LONGTHORNE SONGBOOK
(FIRST MAJOR LP RELEASE ON MAINSTREAM LABEL)

Released on TELSTAR RECORDS label in 1988. Recorded at CBS Studios, London; The Cottage, Cheshire; PRT Studios, London; and The Shambles studio in Marlow.

Platinum Seller. Reached No. 16 in the UK charts. Stayed on the UK chart for 12 weeks.

Track Listing:
1. You're My World
2. My Prayer
3. Always On My Mind
4. My Mother's Eyes
5. Just Loving You
6. It's Only Make Believe
7. To All The Girls I've Loved Before
8. End Of The World
9. It Was Almost Like A Song
10. Hurt
11. Answer Me
12. Danny Boy
13. I'd Be A Legend In My Time
14. Don't Laugh At Me
15. Love Is All
16. When Your Old Wedding Ring Was New

ESPECIALLY FOR YOU

Released on TELSTAR RECORDS label in 1989. Platinum Seller.
Reached No. 22 in the UK charts. Stayed on the UK chart for 10 weeks.

Track Listing:
1. I Wanna Be Where You Are
2. You're The Best Thing That Ever Happened To Me
3. Let's Not Lose It
4. Crying In The Rain
5. Joanna
6. Wind Beneath My Wings
7. I've Waited So Long
8. What's Going On
9. One Love In A Million
10. Seven Wonders of the World
11. Let The Heartaches Begin
12. Everybody Loves Me

THE WIND BENEATH MY WINGS
(JOE'S FIRST MAINSTREAM LABEL RELEASE 45RPM SINGLE)

Released on TELSTAR RECORDS label in 1989.

Track Listing:
1. Wind Beneath My Wings
2. Let's Not Lose It

THE JOE LONGTHORNE CHRISTMAS ALBUM

Released on TELSTAR RECORDS label in 1989. Gold Seller.
Reached No. 44 in the UK charts. Stayed on the chart for four weeks.

Track Listing:
1. Wonderful World
2. Morning Has Broken
3. My Love For You

4. Bridge Over Troubled Water
5. Christmas Song
6. Silent Night
7. Somewhere
8. Winter Wonderland
9. Christmas Time is Here
10. I Still Love You
11. If I Never Sing Another Song
12. Mary's Boy Child
13. White Christmas
14. Auld Lang Syne

I WISH YOU LOVE
(FIRST RELEASE ON EMI)

Released on EMI RECORDS label in 1993.
Reached No. 47 in the UK charts. Stayed on the chart for four weeks.

Track Listing:
1. Young Girl
2. Lady Blue
3. So Deep Is The Night
4. If I Only Had Time
5. Mary In The Morning
6. Say It With Flowers
7. Where Are You Now
8. Runaway
9. Over & Over
10. True Love
11. My Funny Valentine
12. Never Say Never
13. Walk In The Room
14. I Wish You Love

LADY BLUE
(45 RPM SINGLE)

Released on EMI RECORDS label in 1993.

Track Listing:
1. Lady Blue
2. Say It With Flowers

YOUNG GIRL
(JOE'S FIRST EVER CHART 45RPM SINGLE)

Released on EMI RECORDS label in 1994.
Reached No. 61 in the UK charts. Stayed on the chart for two weeks.

Track Listing:
1. Young Girl
2. I Wish You Love
3. Do I Care?

PASSING STRANGERS
(45 RPM SINGLE, WITH LIZ DAWN)
Released on EMI RECORDS label in 1994.
Reahed No. 34 in the UK charts. Stayed on the chart for four weeks.

Track Listing:
1. Passing Strangers
2. Midnight In Paris

LIVE AT THE ROYAL ALBERT HALL

Released on EMI RECORDS label in 1994.
Reached No. 57 in the UK charts. Stayed on the chart for two weeks.

Track Listing:
1. Mary In The Morning
2. If I Only Had Time
3. What's Going On
4. Unchained Melody
5. It's Not Unusual
6. To All The Girls I've Loved Before
7. Pop Star Medley (Daniel, I Just Called To Say I Love You, Stand By Me)
8. This Is My Life

9. I Believe I'm Gonna Lose You
10. Rock Medley (Whole Lotta Shakin', Great Balls of Fire)
11. Life On Mars
12. The Lady Is A Tramp
13. Perfect Love
14. You're The First The Last My Everything
15. The Wind Beneath My Wings
16. Matt Monro Trilogy (Born Free, Portrait of My Love, Born Free)
17. If I Never Sing Another Song
18. Somewhere (Instrumental)

REFLECTIONS

Released on TELSTAR RECORDS label in 1999.

Track Listing:
1. Mack The Knife
2. We Don't Cry Out Loud
3. How Do You Keep The Music Playing?
4. Always Something ThereTo Remind Me
5. I Will Drink The Wine
6. Midnight In Paris
7. Perfect Love
8. On The Sunny Side Of The Street
9. I Believe I'm Gonna Love You
10. The Long & Winding Road
11. Love Letters
12. One For My Baby
13. You Will Be My Music

JOE LONGTHORNE LIVE IN CONCERT

Released on RITZ MUSIC GROUP label in 2001. Concert recorded in Aberdeen.

Track Listing:
1. MacArthur Park
2. As If We Never Said Goodbye
3. Mary In The Morning
4. River Stay Away From My Door

5. He Ain't Heavy, He's My Brother
6. To All The Girls I've Loved Before
7. Something
8. Big Spender
9. I (Who Have Nothing)
10. Delilah
11. Sweet Caroline
12. Mack The Knife
13. Love Is All
14. You're The First The Last My Everything
15. When A Child is Born
16. Crazy
17. The Man That Got Away
18. I've Got You Under My Skin
19. Midnight in Paris
20. Great Balls of Fire
21. American Trilogy

YOU AND ME
(JOE'S FIRST ALL-NEW STUDIO ALBUM FOR A DECADE!)

Released by UNION SQUARE MUSIC in 2008.

Track Listing:
1. Let Me Try Again
2. On Days Like These
3. September In The Rain
4. Welcome To My World
5. Concrete & Clay
6. The Shadow of Your Smile
7. Help Me Make It Through The Night
8. It's Impossible
9. Smile
10. Les Bicyclettes Des Belsize
11. Love Is In The Air
12. If
13. Jean
14. Rose Garden
15. Cycles
16. You & Me

17. When You Were Sweet 16
18. You'll Never Find
19. Funny How Time Slips Away

LADY BLUE

(featuring a whole album of Joe's own songs)

Released by Joe Longthorne in 2012

Track Listing:
1. Lady Blue (Longthorne, Dunstall)
2. Joanna (Longthorne, Mason)
3. Wave Breaking Over Me (Longthorne, Dunstall)
4. I Wish You Love (Longthorne, Dunstall, Osborne)
5. Do I Care (Longthorne, Dunstall)
6. I Still Love You (Longthorne, Dunstall)
7. Seven Wonders In The World (Longthorne, Dunstall)
8. Never Say Never (Longthorne, Dunstall)
9. Where Are You Now (Longthorne, Dunstall)
10. Over And Over (Longthorne, Dunstall)
11. True Love (Longthorne, Dunstall)
12. I've Waited So Long (Longthorne, Mason)
LIVE Bonus Track. Midnight In Paris (Longthorne, Winters, Holiday)

There have been many compilation releases, as well as several limited edition 'live' recordings, but here we have tried to keep to the main studio or general release 'live' recordings.

More details of these and Joe's video and DVD releases are available on *www.joelongthorne.com* and *www.tmpromotions.co.uk*

VIDEOGRAPHY / DVD-OGRAPHY

THE SINGER

Year: 1989
Released by: TELSTAR

1. Just Like Magic
2. Joanna
3. All By Myself
4. One Love In A Million
5. You'll Never Walk Alone
6. I'm So Excited
7. Wind Beneath My Wings
8. Everybody Loves Me
9. Don't Give Up
10. He Ain't Heavy, He's My Brother
11. Heartache Tonight
12. If I Never Sing Another Song
13. My Love For You
14. Bridge Over Troubled Water
15. You're The Best Thing That Ever Happened To Me
16. Dancing in the Street
17. Almost Like A Song
18. Somewhere

THE VERY BEST OF JOE LONGTHORNE

Year: 1991
Released by: TELSTAR

1. My Girl
2. I Who Have Nothing
3. Forever Man
4. April Showers
5. California, Here I Come
6. American Trilogy
7. I Love You Because

8.   Reach Out I'll Be There
9.   Somewhere Over The Rainbow
10. I Can't Stop Loving You
11. Try a Little Tenderness
12. Let The Heartaches Begin
13. Unforgettable
14. The Best Of Times
15. 1-2-3
16. If I Loved You
17. Dancing In The Street
18. I Get Around
19. I've Waited So Long
20. Rock 'n' Roll Medley
21. I Get The Sweetest Feeling
22. Say It With Flowers
23. The Heat Is On
24. The Impossible Dream

LIVE IN CONCERT

Year: 1994
Released by: EMI
Recorded at: Opera House, Blackpool

1.   Somewhere
2.   Crazy
3.   If I Only Had Time
4.   It's Not Unusual
5.   Till
6.   To All The Girls I've Loved Before
7.   Whole Lotta Shakin'
8.   Great Balls of Fire
9.   Daniel
10. I Just Called To Say I Love You
11. Stand By Me
12. Say It With Flowers
13. If I Never Sing Another Song
14. Falling in Love Again
15. This Is My Life
16. The Man That Got Away

17. Sweet Caroline
18. It's Now or Never
19. Nessun Dorma
20. When You're Smiling
21. Hello Dolly
22. You're The Best Thing That Ever Happened To Me
23. Could It Be Magic
24. Wind Beneath My Wings
25. Unchained Melody
26. If I Loved You
27. Somewhere (instrumental)
28. I Wish You Love

THIS RECORDING HAS NOW BEEN SUPPLEMENTED BY
'93 DIRECTOR'S CUT
Released by: CLEARVIEW

In addition to the original footage this now includes two other songs:

You're The First, The Last, My Everything
You'll Never Walk Alone

It also includes an additional 30 minutes of footage.

LIVE AT THE ROYAL ALBERT HALL

Year: 1995
Released by: PMI

1. Mary in the Morning
2. If I Only Had Time
3. Whole Lotta Shakin'
4. Great Balls of Fire
5. Unchained Melody
6. It's Not Unusual
7. Till
8. Daniel
9. I Just Called To Say I Love You
10. Stand By Me
11. Say It With Flowers

12. This Is My Life
13. Sweet Caroline
14. Life On Mars
15. I Believe I'm Gonna Love You
16. It's Now Or Never
17. The Lady Is A Tramp
18. Perfect Love
19. Wind Beneath My Wings
20. Born Free
21. If I Never Sing Another Song
22. Somewhere
23. You'll Never Walk Alone

A MAN & HIS MUSIC

Year: 1996
Released by: POLYGRAM

1. Somewhere
2. Stormy Weather
3. The Long & Winding Road
4. Midnight In Paris
5. All The Way
6. Delilah
7. Big Spender
8. I've Got You Under My Skin
9. You Will Be My Music
10. One for my Baby, and One More For The Road
11. Don't Cry Out Loud
12. So Deep Is The Night
13. American Trilogy
14. How Do You Keep The Music Playing?
15. For All We Know
16. You Belong To Me
17. Release Me
18. What Kind of Fool Am I?
19. You're The First, The Last, My Everything
20. When Your Old Wedding Ring Was New
21. Somewhere
22. Turtle Nights

THE ULTIMATE COLLECTION

Year: 1997
Released by: TELSTAR

1. Somewhere
2. I Saw Her Standing There
3. He Ain't Heavy, He's My Brother
4. I Who Have Nothing
5. I Get A Kick Out of You
6. Joanna
7. Dancing In The Street
8. Put The Weight On My Shoulders
9. Say It With Flowers
10. You're The Best Thing That Ever Happened To Me
11. I'm Gonna Make You Love Me
12. The Impossible Dream
13. Bridge Over Troubled Water
14. Let The Heartaches Begin
15. Wind Beneath My Wings
16. American Trilogy
17. One Love In A Million
18. I'll Never Love This Way Again
19. Try A Little Kindness
20. You'll Never Walk Alone
21. Till
22. My Girl
23. Don't Cry Out Loud
24. Somewhere Over The Rainbow
25. 1-2-3
26. Runaround Sue
27. Great Balls Of Fire
28. Oh Boy
29. That's Alright

THE GENIUS OF JOE LONGTHORNE

Year: 2002
Released by: VCI
Recorded at: Southport

1. Introduction
2. As If We Never Said Goodbye
3. Mary In The Morning
4. If I Only Had Time
5. Perfect Love
6. I've Got You Under My Skin
7. When A Child Is Born
8. You're The First, The Last, My Everything
9. Delilah
10. Till
11. Big Spender
12. I Am What I Am
13. Love Is In The Air
14. Don't Cry Out Loud
15. Copacabana
16. Life On Mars
17. I Left My Heart In San Francisco
18. Love Is All
19. Great Balls Of Fire
20. Unchained Melody
21. I Will Drink The Wine
22. You'll Never Know
23. American Trilogy

JOE LONGTHORNE … With Love

Year: 2004
Released by: Clearview
Recorded at: Sheffield City Hall

1. Macarthur Park
2. As If We Never Said Goodbye
3. Mary In The Morning
4. River Stay Away From My Door
5. As I Love You
6. I Wanna Be Where You Are
7. Don't Cry Out Loud
8. Big Spender/Something
9. Delilah
10. Is This The Way To Amarillo

11. Hello
12. Sweet Caroline
13. To All The Girls I've Loved Before
14. You're The First, The Last, My Everything
15. I Believe I'm Gonna Love You
16. What Kind Of Fool Am I?
17. For The Good Times
18. Life On Mars
19. The Man That Got Away
20. It's Now Or Never
21. 24 Hours From Tulsa
22. Nessun Dorma
23. American Trilogy
24. Once Upon A Song

JOE'S BACK

Year: 2005
Released by: CLEARVIEW

1. Play On
2. People
3. If I Loved You
4. Mack The Knife
5. As I Love You
6. Where Are You Now?
7. Too Much Too Little Too Late
8. Amarillo
9. Mary In The Morning
10. Big Spender
11. Delilah
12. I Who Have Nothing
13. Quando Quando Quando/The Last Waltz
14. It's Now Or Never
15. You're The First, The Last, My Everything
16. Just The Way You Are
17. Born Free
18. Love Is In The Air
19. Hello Again
20. Sweet Caroline

21. I Believe I'm Gonna Love You
22. You'll Never Know
23. One Man Woman
24. The Lady Is A Tramp
25. My Way
26. Woman
27. Music
28. Always Stop To Cry
29. Can You Feel The Love Tonight?
30. Roll Over Beethoven
31. Great Balls Of Fire
32. Unchained Melody
33. American Trilogy

LIVE IN PARADISE

Year: 2005
Released by: CLEARVIEW
Recorded at: THE PARADISE ROOMS, BLACKPOOL

1. Overture
2. People
3. If You Love Me
4. Mary In The Morning
5. As I Love You
6. Mack The Knife
7. What I Did For Love
8. For Once In My Life
9. You'll Never Know
10. Where Or When
11. I Left My Heart In San Francisco
12. The Lady Is A Tramp
13. My Way
14. So Deep Is The Night
15. Crazy (Performed By Joe's Sister Lizzie)
16. I Wanna Be Where You Are
17. If I Loved You
18. Quando Quando Quando/The Last Waltz
19. Born Free/Portrait Of My Love
20. You're The Best Thing That Ever Happened To Me

21. If I Never Sing Another Song

LIVE FROM THE LONDON PALLADIUM

Year: 2006
Released by: CLEARVIEW

1. When Your Old Wedding Ring Was New
2. Somewhere
3. People
4. For Once In My Life
5. If You Love Me
6. Mary In The Morning
7. Mack The Knife
8. As I Love You
9. Big Spender
10. Till
11. Love Is In The Air
12. Hello Again/Sweet Caroline
13. The Lady Is A Tramp/My Way
14. You'll Never Know
15. When A Child Is Born
16. You're The First, The Last, My Everything
17. Just The Way You Are
18. The Impossible Dream
19. For The Good Times
20. If I Never Sing Another Song

IF I NEVER SING ANOTHER SONG

Year: 2008
Released by: VEGAS
DOCUMENTARY FILM featuring Joe On Tour

Performances include:
1. As If We Never Said Goodbye
2. I've Got You Under My Skin
3. American Trilogy
4. Hello Again

5. As I Love You
6. My Way
7. My Mother's Eyes
8. Somewhere
9. I Believe I'm Gonna Love You
10. You're The Best Thing That Ever Happened To Me
11. Mary In The Morning
12. Woman
13. Sir Duke
14. Lately
15. Can You Feel The Love Tonight?
16. That's What Friends Are For
17. If I Never Sing Another Song

THE YOU & ME TOUR

Year: 2008
Released by: VEGAS
DOCUMENTARY FILM featuring Joe On Tour

Performances include:
1. Somewhere
2. Mack The Knife
3. My Way
4. Something
5. If You Love Me
6. The Impossible Dream
7. If I Never Sing Another Song
8. Don't Cry Out Loud
9. Mary In The Morning
10. Can't Smile Without You
11. The Lady Is A Tramp
12. As I Love You
13. Just The Way You Are
14. Love Is In The Air

Also includes Joe's VARIETY CLUB OF GREAT BRITAIN AWARD
CEREMONY for his Lifetime Achievement Award

JOE LONGTHORNE SINGS TO THE GODS

Year: 2008
Released by: VEGAS
Recorded at: KOURION AMPHITHEATRE, CYPRUS

1. Overture
2. Somewhere
3. For Once In My Life
4. Let Me Try Again
5. Love Is In The Air
6. September In The Rain
7. If
8. To All The Girls I've Loved Before
9. Delilah
10. Big Spender
11. Something
12. Hello
13. Sweet Caroline
14. Born Free
15. Can't Smile Without You
16. You're The First, The Last, My Everything/Just The Way You Are
17. I Left My Heart In San Francisco
18. When A Child Is Born
19. Piano Medley: Georgia On My Mind/Imagine/Whole Lotta Shakin'/ Great Balls Of Fire
20. Wind Beneath My Wings
21. If I Loved You
22. So Deep Is The Night
23. You're The Best Thing That Ever Happened To Me
24. What Kind Of Fool Am I?
25. The Lady Is A Tramp
26. My Way
27. In The Ghetto/The Wonder Of You/American Trilogy
28. If I Never Sing Another Song

THERE HAVE BEEN 3 DVDs of 'A YEAR IN HIS LIFE' produced in 2004
These contain footage of BBC/ITV interviews and concert footage